SCIPIO AFRICANUS

SCIPIO AFRICANUS
THE FIRST IMPERATOR

DEXTER HOYOS

REAKTION BOOKS

I dedicate this book to

Jann, Camilla, Anthony, Scarlett and Henry

Published by
REAKTION BOOKS LTD
2–4 Sebastian Street
London, EC1V 0HE, UK

www.reaktionbooks.co.uk

First published 2025

EU GPSR Authorised Representative
Logos Europe, 9 rue Nicolas Poussin, 17000, La Rochelle, France
email: contact@logoseurope.eu

Printed and bound in Great Britain by Bell & Bain, Glasgow

A catalogue record for this book is available from the British Library

ISBN 978 1 83639 099 2

CONTENTS

ROMAN FIRST NAMES

Most Roman men used only one of fifteen or twenty *praenomina*. For convenience, those appearing in this book are given in their usual abbreviated form, for example, P. Cornelius Scipio.

A.	Aulus
Ap.	Appius
C.	Gaius
Cn.	Gnaeus
L.	Lucius
M.	Marcus
M'.	Manius
P.	Publius
Q.	Quintus
Sex.	Sextus
T.	Titus
Ti.	Tiberius

Bust of Scipio from the Tomb of the Scipios, Rome, end of the 2nd century BC. Previously thought to be a bust of the later dictator Cornelius Sulla, it likely depicts Africanus, according to Filippo Coarelli.

Preface: Scipio and His Narrators

Publius Cornelius Scipio defeated Hannibal. This is today the best known, or only known, feat by the man who was the greatest general in Roman history. Scipio's full career was astonishing: appointed to a critical overseas command in his mid-twenties, victorious over four Carthaginian generals and masterful in diplomacy, a gifted strategist and tactician, a charismatic commander and a personality complexly winning enough to captivate foreign kings and maybe even his foe Hannibal. Throughout his life he blended his charm with calculation, humaneness with harshness, popular appeal with aristocratic arrogance and opportunist ruthlessness, with a strong strain of religion.

In war – by contrast with Hannibal, Julius Caesar, Pompey the Great and Trajan, generals of matching or greater fame – Scipio never lost a battle or a campaign. Like these later Roman leaders he expanded Rome's power and possessions; he defeated Carthage and its allies in the western Mediterranean and organized peace on Rome's terms across the Hellenistic East a dozen years later. By then he was a household name not only at home but among Greeks, Carthaginians and Spaniards. He gained the novel sobriquet Africanus and was, it seems, the first Roman to be called *Imperator*, victorious commander – a title with a long and versatile future.

At the same time, Scipio's career and fortunes were stamped with paradox. He was brilliantly successful by the age of thirty – driving Carthage from Spain, being offered (but declining) a royal title by the entranced Spaniards, becoming consul at Rome – but success itself, coupled with his unshakeable self-confidence, drew suspicion and hostility from other leaders like Fabius Maximus, the celebrated 'Delayer', and the long-lived

Cato the Censor. In civil life, especially once the great war with Carthage was over, he found it hard to achieve the eminent role in the state that admirers expected and critics feared. More than once his efforts were blocked by political opponents and his achievements and motives were denigrated. Later he became a target of partisan inquisitions. Finally, the man who had conquered Spain and Hannibal, and imposed a victorious Roman peace on the eastern Mediterranean, exiled himself from his homeland to die in a distant countryside retreat and be buried there.

We do not know Scipio Africanus in his own words. Speeches and writings have not survived, except two letters in Greek that he and his brother wrote in 190 BC to Heracleia and Colophon, small cities in Asia Minor, and they are only official diplomatic messages. So the closest we can come to him is through his much younger contemporary Polybius, the Greek historian of Rome's rise to empire. Polybius became a friend of the family nearly twenty years after Africanus' death, and admired both him and his grandson Scipio Aemilianus immensely. In the 140s–120s he wrote the *Histories*, forty books (that is, scrolls) covering Roman, Greek and other Mediterranean events from 264 to 146. The Scipios figure extensively in many of them.

Later ages' politics, wars and neglect have left only Books 1 to 5 of the *Histories* complete, along with Byzantine-era extracts, some small, some substantial, from most of the rest. In these ways about a third of Polybius survives. This is a blow for more than one reason. Even if wrong or obscure in places – and emphatically sure of the rightness of his own views on everything from military tactics to world geography – he is a well-informed researcher, experienced in politics, diplomacy and warfare, presenting a powerful central theme: how the Romans, in less than 53 years, were able to bring the whole Mediterranean world under their power. It was the start of the Roman Empire. Scipio Africanus was one of its chief creators.

Polybius demanded high standards of research and objectivity from historians, aimed to apply them himself, yet had his limitations. He insisted on a historian's duty to be balanced and accurate but let this ideal wobble on subjects where he had strong feelings. Admiration for both Rome and Scipio – admittedly with qualifications – colours much of what he wrote. On Africanus his character portrayal, when the young leader first appears as a general, in 210, is a roster of praises ('virtually the most outstanding man in history'); much later on he does much the same for the grandson Aemilianus. Overall there is lighter criticism and greater esteem in how he records both men, not to mention that he lets in some plain mistakes, for instance having Africanus elected curule aedile, a middle-level office, side by side with his younger brother Lucius. In reality, Lucius Scipio became aedile eighteen years after his brother. Yet Polybius' generally sober narrative, though it survives only in part, is not often to be corrected like this through other sources or documents. It remains one of our two chief sources for the career of the man who defeated Hannibal.[1]

The other chief narrator is the Roman historian Livy (Titus Livius), who spent nearly half a century, from around 30 BC on, researching and writing his history *From the Foundation of the City* (*Ab urbe condita*). Again like Polybius, and too many other ancient historians, what we have of it is less than even half of the whole. When complete it told the story from Romulus to the middle of Augustus' reign in 142 books. A quarter remains: its first ten books, then 21 (the preliminaries in 220–219 to the Second Punic War) to 45, reaching the year 167 (but with parts of the last five books missing from damaged manuscripts). Fortunately this includes the fullest narrative we still have of Scipio's career and the wars he fought, not to mention the troubles of his last years. What survives of Polybius shows that Livy sensibly used him as a major informant, even though the Roman writer chose to name him as a source only six times over the period they both narrated, in *From the Foundation*'s books 21 to 45.

From the Foundation is not an impartial narrative. Livy makes this clear in its preface. Rome was a power guided to greatness by fate and marked by the moral strength of its people and their leaders – although more recently the moral strength had slipped, he mournfully comments. One of the high points of Roman valour and virtue, for him as for others, was the Second Punic War, in which Rome fought and broke the might of Carthage and its leader Hannibal. This he narrates in books 21 to 30, and one of the war's heroes – its greatest, in fact – is Scipio.

Livy's stories of his courage, patriotism and judgement have fixed Scipio's reputation for later ages: saving his father's life in battle as a teenager, rallying faint-hearted fellow officers after the disaster of Cannae, destroying Carthaginian power in Spain and Africa, yet preferring peace and moderation to vengefulness. A range of carefully crafted speeches given to him brings his character and charisma to life in Livy's finest rhetorical style.

Even so, the historian allows nuances. Scipio's habit of communing with Jupiter in the god's Capitoline temple before making important decisions was – our historian hints – as much for public consumption as it was from real piety. Nor does Livy take seriously the fable, carefully undenied by Scipio himself, that he had been conceived thanks to a god masquerading, myth-like, as a visiting bedroom snake. That Scipio condoned his officer Pleminius' criminal actions at Locri in southern Italy, late in the war, comes out clearly in Livy's telling. In the legal and political strife that beset Scipio's final years, Livy's account is generally sympathetic yet does not hide that the hero brought much of the trouble on himself. Paradoxically, the historian's handling of Hannibal (again the fullest we have) follows an opposite trajectory: it grows kindlier post-war under Rome's persecution of him, until Hannibal is driven to a pathos-imbued suicide.[2]

Another sizeable historical work, in several books, is by Appian of Alexandria, a retired Greek imperial official in the late second century AD. He wrote narratives of Rome's wars region by region, with Scipio naturally prominent in his various Second Punic War accounts. Appian's compositional method, typical of Greek and Roman historians dealing with distant times, relied on previous larger works; of course these varied in reliability, as Appian's own methodology did. The ones he chose for Second Punic War campaigns can hardly be guessed, but they were not the finest and they led him into sometimes fanciful mistakes. Confusing the Spanish city of Saguntum (Sagunto) with New Carthage (Cartagena), and yet putting it north of the river Ebro, was one of many. Ravines packed with Punic troops in ambush in his version of Cannae is another (they should have been at the Battle of the Trebia). Scipio's Spanish victories at Baecula in 208 and Ilipa in 206 are somehow run together; by contrast, the battle of the Great Plains, one of his three North African wins, is not mentioned at all. Later it comes as no surprise to find Scipio and Hannibal fighting hand-to-hand during the Battle of Zama, quite unhistorically (as they do in Silius Italicus' imaginative epic poem *Punica*). Appian is useful and important but has to be used with caution.

Scipio's life supplied plentiful grist for anecdotes relayed by Roman and Greek writers. Cicero tells of his friendship with the poet Ennius, one of the founders of Latin literature. Compilations that mention Scipio include Valerius Maximus' nine books of *Memorable Deeds and Sayings* of Romans and non-Romans, as does Julius Frontinus' collection of historical Greek and Roman war stratagems. An antiquarian and philological essayist of the second century AD, Aulus Gellius, includes some important anecdotes about Scipio in his collection *Noctes Atticae* (Attic Nights). Livy's history and other large-scale works – most now lost – supplied many or most of these compilers' snippets, but need not have been the only ones. We do not know which writer supplied Valerius Maximus' cheerful picture of Scipio and his best friend Laelius when on holidays, leisurely wandering along the seashore south of Rome to gather cockles and mussels.

The philosopher-biographer Plutarch around AD 100 borrowed from Livy to narrate Scipio's supposed post-war conversation with Hannibal, with the Carthaginian's subtle blend of praise and put-down for his one-time opponent; Plutarch also included a short collection of Scipio's sayings in an essay on noteworthy sayings of Roman leaders. Given his sensible use of sources and his interest in his subjects' personalities, the non-survival of his life of the general is a loss much to be deplored.

Some other historical works that included Scipio's era have survived in a sadly tattered state. The Sicilian Greek author Diodorus, contemporary with Julius Caesar, put together a Mediterranean world history down to his own day in forty books, as usual based on copious predecessors; but its second half is represented only by Byzantine-era excerpts, a few of them on the Punic Wars and after. Similarly, Cassius Dio (twice consul in the early third century AD and a model example of aristocratic Greeks' synthesis of Hellenistic and Roman culture) researched and wrote an eighty-book *Roman History*, only for the first 35 books, down to 69 BC, to be lost save for some Byzantine excerpts, plus a drastically shortened epitome of books 1 to 21 by the eleventh-century Byzantine scholar John Zonaras.

Ancient writers always have to be used with care. The total quantity of historical materials, literary and otherwise, available for Scipio's times is far more limited than those available (for instance) for the life and times of Cicero and Caesar. Every source that survives must be consulted for materials detailed or brief. But with most composed long after, the care and intermittent scepticism needed for the consultations often lead to plentiful debate and lively disagreements among moderns.

Plentiful writings do not survive at all. Plutarch's life of Scipio is just one such. Hannibal's career was told by two Greek friends, Silenus of Sicily and Sosylus of Sparta: Polybius knew (and despised) their works, Livy cites Silenus once, and a sole papyrus fragment of a page from Sosylus' book survives, telling not of Hannibal but of a naval battle in Spain. In Scipio's own day, his family's most dogged opponent was M. Porcius Cato, called the Censor, who then wrote Latin literature's first history of Rome, with much prominence given to his own part in it and probably as little praise for Scipio's as he could decently allow. A senator called L. Cincius Alimentus, for a time a prisoner of Hannibal's – with whom he had amiable conversations – later wrote a history of Rome in Greek, which Livy consulted once at least. So did a kinsman of the famed general Fabius Maximus 'the Delayer', named Q. Fabius Pictor, and Livy mentions his work too (once). A plentiful stream of Latin historian-compilers followed Cato, only a few of whom earn like mentions. Most notable were two in the generation before Livy, Valerius Antias and Claudius Quadrigarius. With these, when Livy names them for a detail or event, his citation often includes a pained aside on their fondness for exaggeration or fiction.

Another loss is the seven-book account of the Second Punic War – the first military monograph in Latin – by one Coelius Antipater, who composed it about sixty years after Scipio and Hannibal died. According to Cicero, Livy and others, Coelius wrote with rhetorical flair but also took care with issues. Not always successfully: he argued for the Little St Bernard as Hannibal's pass, a thesis rejected as early as Livy, and he also implausibly tried to sink Scipio's fleet invading Africa later.[3]

None of these Latin works remains outside the not too frequent citations in Livy or other extant writers. Two other, later books on Scipio would have made interesting reading, by Julius Caesar's intimate friend C. Oppius and the emperor Augustus' cultured freedman Julius Hyginus. Their biographies seem to have combined facts with sensationalism – like the story of their hero's snake-conception, transmitted by Aulus Gellius a couple of centuries later.

Scipio did not escape poets' attention. His friend Ennius wrote a poem about him (it failed to reach us); and *The Annals*, an ambitious epic history of Rome from Romulus to his own time in adapted Greek hexameter verse, must have given Scipio attention too, though the plentiful short excerpts surviving from it include very few on him. By contrast we have the full seventeen books of ex-consul Silius Italicus' epic poem *Punica* on the Hannibalic War, written late in the first century AD and, disconcertingly, Latin literature's longest though not finest extant epic. Scipio's role in it is naturally second only to his rival's. Composed (in Pliny the Younger's opinion) 'with greater diligence than talent', *Punica*'s reputation among literary critics has much improved in recent times – but not much of it is history apart from its broad outlines. Instead the full pageantry of epic convention, drawn largely from Homer and Vergil, is in play – digressions telling past myths and legends, heroic soldiers achieving valorous feats, the Olympian gods involving themselves at every point. Scipio arrives early on the scene, later has to descend into the Underworld to meet Roman ghosts (and learn that Jupiter really is his father) and in the final book fights the obligatory duel at Zama with Hannibal (whom Juno rescues before Scipio can kill him).

Material evidence, such as inscriptions and coins, is thin on Scipio even though a notable quantity exists from the later third and early second centuries BC. The letters that he and Lucius Scipio sent to cities in the Greek East have been mentioned. A few years before, in 193 BC, the community of the isle of Delos had voted to honour him with a laurel crown, as another inscription shows. A cameo portrait in profile, found at Capua in Italy with the artist's signature Dioscorides, has been thought to show him, with thin cheeks and plentiful hair. More recently, a bust found near the Scipio family's vaulted tomb in the city's southeast, half a kilometre beyond the old Porta Capena, has also been claimed as his portrait, after long being thought to show a much later Roman. Welcome as these pieces of material are, they are only tantalizing hints of the range of pictures, effigies, statues and perhaps paintings that once existed to commemorate the conqueror of Hannibal and Carthage.[4]

GAUL
Rhône
Durance
Massilia
SPAIN
Ebro
ILERGETES
Ilergetes
Emporiae
Tarraco
Balearic Is.
EDETANI
Saguntum
Tagus
Sucro
Ebusus
Anas
Castulo
Baecula
Italica
Baetis
Aurgi
Ilipa
Hispalis
New Carthage
Gades
Carteia
NUMIDIA
MAURI
Siga
N
0
200
km

Scipio's Punic War.

1

The Cornelii and Rome

Scipio's family went back a long way. It was one of the families of the *gens Cornelia*, meaning its sons all bore the *nomen* Cornelius and every Cornelius' daughter was named Cornelia. A *gens* was a group of families who shared an early (often legendary) ancestor, though in historical times the links between them were not invariably close. For centuries only patrician family groups counted as *gentes*; when prominent plebeian families then tried using the term, it caused annoyance.

Cornelii were among the most prominent members of Rome's elite from almost the beginning of the republic. One Servius Cornelius was listed as one of the consuls of 485 BC, alongside an aristocrat of the equally potent *gens Fabia* (a clan that would one day loom large in Scipio's own life). Later records gave Servius Cornelius the added name (*cognomen*) Maluginensis, maybe from a village or estate – Maluginum? – that his family owned. Such third names started as nicknames or epithets, became standard but not compulsory later on and might vary from father to son. The Scipios may have stemmed from the Maluginensis family, with a subsequent change of *cognomen*.

The Cornelii overall were a busily prolific family group, with *cognomina* plentiful down the centuries – Maluginensis and Cossus early on; Blasio, Cethegus, Lentulus and others later. So was the name Scipio, first given – it was said – to a dutiful Cornelius who supported his infirm father's steps like a staff (a *scipio*). This, the first Scipio on record, was a Publius who became a military tribune with consular power in 395. (This early office was quite different from Rome's civilian plebeian tribunes and Roman legions' military tribunes.) The *cognomen*, though, may have been bestowed on him only in later tradition, as there was no further Scipio until the solidly historical L. Cornelius Scipio Barbatus, consul more or less a century later, in 298.

Barbatus was the first of the family to have a tomb – the Scipios did not cremate – in the vault outside Rome, and both his sarcophagus and epitaph survive. His extra name, 'the Bearded', was a nickname not handed on by later Scipios, but Barbatus was obviously content with it. Nor did Roman aristocrats hide their achievements. The epitaph lists his public offices – consul, censor, aedile – and exploits as a wartime commander ('he took Taurasia and Cisauna in Samnium, subdued all Lucania and bore away hostages'). In a style that Romans of later eras would rarely repeat, Barbatus also recorded his personal qualities: 'a brave man and wise, whose fine looks matched his valour'. Pride and self-confidence, verging on arrogance, was already a Scipionic characteristic.[1]

The Cornelii and five other patrician *gentes* – the Aemilii, Claudii, Fabii, Manlii and Valerii – were the *gentes maiores*, the 'greater clans'. A much larger number of patrician clans counted as the *gentes minores*, so called in later ages at least, although in the early republic many were hardly less prominent (for example the *gens Iulia*, which one day would come again to greatness). Over the centuries many of the *minores* dwindled or disappeared, but the *maiores* lost none of their status, influence and political success, even though growing numbers of non-patricians (the Roman term for whom was 'plebeians') joined the ranks of the elite, held consulships and excelled in warfare and politics.

The proper métier of the high-status Roman male was to practise these callings. A young aristocrat served not as a foot soldier but in the cavalry; then, after gaining experience in war, he might be chosen as one of a legion's senior officers, its military tribunes. Distinction in war was a necessity for election to office; terms of office could then alternate with further periods of military service. Not every young Roman of status could, or wanted to, compete for office, but the politically minded ones would look to the censors to enrol them in the Senate, and this was a lifetime appointment. Of course, to be a simple senator, not holding public office, was hardly enough for any purposeful young Roman. Magistracies multiplied *dignitas* and *gloria* – eminence and renown – in the successful aristocrat's public career and added to familial lustre. Not every senator did make it to even one office, but it was those who did who counted in politics and government. And the higher the office, the better.

The political system that allowed the elite to flourish was uniquely Roman. Evolving over centuries, it embodied two essentials. Every Roman male was entitled to vote on legislation and at elections; and all voting took place in assemblies consisting of grouped units and at Rome. In practice, this meant a polity hedged around with restrictions.

A political career was vigorously competitive. The republic had several colleges of magistrates. To become a senator of real consequence, office beyond the lesser colleges (quaestorship or aedileship) was essential. For ambitious plebeians, the tribunate of the *plebs* was the first higher stage. A tribune even had the power to curb action by any other office-holder, even a consul (it was not often used, for sensible reasons). Energetic, industrious and well-connected aspirants – and, from time to time, high-born aristocrats without the first two qualities – could aim for a praetorship, and then a few of them for one of the two consulships a year. At the apex of the republic's politics and society stood the ex-consuls (the *consulares*), the Roman men who had attained the most *dignitas*, *gloria* and the moral weight that these qualities brought, *auctoritas*. These were the state's leading men, Rome's *principes viri*.

The republic also had several electoral and legislative assemblies. The assemblies were each formed of units: *centuriae* organized in *classes* – voting levels – based on property ownership; or 'tribes', *tribus*, representing the Roman state's constituent territorial districts (from the verb to 'assign', *tribuere*). The assembly of the centuries, the *comitia centuriata*, voted on laws and elected the senior magistrates: consuls, praetors, censors. The plebeian assembly of tribes, the *concilium plebis*, elected the ten plebeian tribunes (a quite separate office from the military tribunes, as just noted) and could legislate for all citizens – even though patricians did not belong to it. Another 'tribal' assembly, the *comitia tributa*, consisted of patricians and plebeians together, elected lesser magistrates like the quaestors and aediles, and it too could vote to pass or reject laws.

Universal male suffrage did not make Rome a democracy. The principle of voting by units was crucial, with every male Roman enrolled in a *centuria* and a *tribus* by the five-yearly censors. In the *comitia centuriata* more than half of its 193 centuries were for affluent property owners only, while most citizens were enrolled in the fewer centuries of the 'classes' below. All Romans owning little or no property – up to half the voting population – were registered in one single century. When the *centuriata* met just outside the city, on the then-open Campus Martius near the Tiber, each century cast one vote that was decided by the members attending. Well-off Romans, a minority of the population, enjoyed an unsurprisingly permanent dominance. The *centuriae* of poorer Romans rarely voted, the *centuria* of the propertyless perhaps never: the voting and the vote-counting started with the upper-level centuries and stopped as soon as a majority of units was reached for the proposal or the candidate.

The city itself was the venue for the tribal assemblies, with voting based on the 35 territorial *tribus* – again with a single vote per tribe. The city population was parcelled into four tribes; of the rest, those more recently created through territorial expansion were naturally more distant from Rome. Predictably, attendance was limited to men who could afford to take time off from their normal tasks: another advantage for the more affluent, especially from the rural parts of Rome's increasingly far-flung territory.

So although the census of 225, when the future Africanus was a boy, recorded 273,000 adult Roman citizens, the citizens who gathered in any assembly for an election or to vote on laws were always a small minority – a few thousand at best. The unit votes, by centuries or tribes, were decided by the better-off men who attended. This was no surprise, nor an accident.

The system worked all the same, for many reasons. Despite its restrictions, ordinary Romans did have a say in affairs, even if the say was unequal. Nearly all magistrates held office for one year. Only a dictator, appointed for short emergency or ritual needs, and the five-yearly censors (with an eighteen-month term) did not. Re-election for the year following was banned by convention, and by law for the consulship. Thus a misbehaving magistrate could afterwards face prosecution for misconduct, an ordeal that even Scipio would face one day. Moreover, competitive politics, changing family fortunes and constant wars prevented the aristocracy from becoming a frozen, inaccessible caste, even if newcomers to its higher levels – the consulship above all – needed to work hard for success.

Elite citizens' status and careers were supported by strong social links between them and many of lesser status. Some were their personal friends (*amici*), like Africanus' lifelong confidant Laelius. Others, not so close, could be called *clientes*, and *principes viri* might count these in the hundreds or even more. Links were formed in many ways – family friendships, ancestral tradition, economic dependence, old soldiers' loyalty to their old commanders and ties both legal and sentimental between freed slaves and their former masters. Links might wax and wane over generations, but in his lifetime a Roman aristocrat like a Cornelius could count on many fellow citizens for devoted support. Predictably, the opposite was common as well: personal enmities, *inimicitiae* – sometimes continued over more than one generation – could play on political relationships as powerfully as *amicitiae*.

Voters at election time almost always favoured candidates with distinguished names and eminent *amici*. The Cornelii and the other *gentes maiores* enjoyed – and took for granted – *dignitas* and *gloria* at levels other Romans found hard to equal. Patricians, of families both major and minor, continued to win magistracies well out of proportion to their numbers in the citizen population. It did not block every vigorous candidate of less grand position from reaching office, but one consul every year was a patrician, and often enough he belonged to one of the *maiores gentes*. The *fasti* of the republic, its year-by-year lists of consuls, repeat over generations the names of a few dozen grandee houses, not least the Cornelii.

The many-branched Cornelii were the most lastingly prominent of all. Of the third century's two hundred or so consuls, nineteen were Cornelii – more than double the century's ten Fabii and eight Valerii combined. Three patrician *gentes* thus accounted for nearly a fifth of the century's consuls. Second consulships were less common, but again the Cornelii shone. Besides Africanus himself in 205 and 194, four Cornelii held the office twice: P. Arvina's second was in 288 (his first had been eighteen years earlier), P. Rufinus won it in 290 and 277, then Cn. Blasio in 270 and 257, and Cn. Scipio (Africanus' great-uncle) in 260 and, unusually soon, again in 254, both during Rome's first war with Carthage.

Voters clearly liked Cornelii. Rufinus won his consulships despite a reputation for greed, though this caught up with him later – he would be expelled from the Senate for owning too much (10 pounds' weight, or 4.5 kg) silver plate. In 260 great-uncle Scipio's rash naval attack on the Carthaginian-held island of Lipara made him their prisoner, but after ransom and return he was elected again only six years later. It helped that his brother Lucius, consul in 259, had won sterling victories over the enemy in Corsica and Sardinia. Cn. Scipio earned the mocking nickname Asina ('she-ass', no doubt especially mocking in this feminine form), but his own sense of humour allowed him to pass it on to his son. This son and his two cousins, the sons of L. Scipio, all became consuls too between 221 and 218, a remarkable quadrennium of Cornelian lustre. One of these cousins, Publius, consul in 218, was the father of Africanus.

By their day, Rome's senatorial elite included patricians and plebeians at every level. Plebeian meant, in effect, not patrician (its disdainful sense is modern). Patricians had never monopolized magistracies and government even in the early republic (though they liked to think they had). There were plenty of ambitious and popular plebeians in every era seeking electoral office. They came from a much wider range of families than patricians did, but all politically prominent plebeian families were of marked social and economic status. No cobbler or butcher or small farmer is ever recorded in a magistracy of the Roman People.

For most offices, plebeians had to compete with patricians, but the ten annual tribunes of the *plebs* had to be plebeians, and an energetic tribunate could be a stepping stone to greater things. In Africanus' boyhood a controversial tribunate in 232 propelled a progressive firebrand, C. Flaminius, to become consul nine years later and then censor in 220 (as censor he built the Via Flaminia, which still runs from the centre of Rome to the northern Adriatic coast). But though such advances by a new plebeian leader could happen, they were not common by the third century. For greater chances of success it was better for a non-patrician to be a Licinius, Caecilius or Sempronius, or to come from one of the other plebeian families of note – preferably a consular one, or else one with many past praetors.

Plebeian leaders had always played important roles in the republic (and, in legend at least, even under the ancient kings). Scipio's mother, Pomponia, was a plebeian aristocrat, kin to two brothers, M'. and M. Pomponius Matho, who were consuls in 233 and 231 respectively. Quite likely she was their sister. These brothers were to be the only consuls in their family, long-established though it was and though other kinsmen did make it to praetorships. More lastingly consular were the plebeian families of two of Scipio's close friends, P. Licinius Crassus and Q. Caecilius Metellus. Just like the Cornelii, the Licinii and Caecilii would produce consuls down to the end of the republic and then beyond. Africanus' heirs would have his daughter Cornelia marry Ti. Sempronius Gracchus, son of a Hannibalic War hero, and they would be parents of the famous and tragic reformer brothers Tiberius and Gaius Gracchus.

Attaining the consulship was the apex of a man's political career. A family, patrician or plebeian, with consuls in its lineage enjoyed grander *dignitas* and *auctoritas* than others who progressed no further than even the praetorship. And within Scipio's lifetime men of consular ancestry were being called, unofficially but tellingly, *nobiles* – 'notables'. A plebeian who succeeded in the arduous career trek to a consulship was a 'new man' (*novus homo*). A condescending epithet, yet his obvious energy and capacity would make him, like Flaminius or, not much later, Cato the Censor, a political force to reckon with. A 'new man' could make as much impact on affairs of state as the most patrician of patrician leaders, even though, like every Roman in politics, he needed to fashion alliances and weather fervid opposition – sometimes even from kinsmen. Flaminius' own father, it was claimed, opposed him bitterly.[2]

Scipio Africanus was born into this elite in an age when the republic had begun to put its stamp on the world outside Italy. It was no longer an ordinary city-state, even though all the republic's institutions and functions remained centred on the physical city. Most Romans lived outside Rome, in the countryside or in smaller cities and towns. Roman territory, the *ager Romanus*, in Scipio's boyhood covered about a fifth of Italy, with about one-third of the peninsula's population. Its other towns, cities and rural communities were very varied – some of them annexed and incorporated in earlier times, like Tusculum in the nearby Alban mountains and Antium on the coast, some founded by Rome as *coloniae* (Alba Fucens in central Italy's mountains, for instance, and Luceria in Apulia) and still others – the wealthy Campanian city of Capua and its dependent neighbours – bound to Rome since 340 in a nexus of half-citizenship which the Campanians were now beginning to chafe against.

Across the Italian peninsula outside the *ager Romanus*, Rome was the hegemon. Two and a half centuries of wars with its many neighbours had made it, by the year 272, master of them all. The other Italian peoples were a broad variety of large and small city-states and cantons from Etruria and Umbria in the north to Greek colonies like Tarentum, Rhegium and Locri in the toe. The most privileged were the Latins, called simply the *nomen Latinum*: they lived in cities of Latium east of Rome (roughly today's Lazio) or in *coloniae Latinae* further afield, places settled with Roman and other colonists as regional strongpoints. They and the rest of Italy, the 'allies' (*socii*), governed themselves locally, with their own aristocrats and 'new men', but had to obey Rome's foreign policies and its military needs. Without the Latins and Italian *socii*, the Romans' new wars, naval as well as military, would have been impossible.

The Romans were a society attuned to war. Every adult male citizen could be called up for military service. Not only were there 273,000 male Romans over sixteen registered in 224, but with them (Polybius records) were another half a million Latins and Italian allies. Whether Rome was under threat or not, almost every year Roman consuls would levy legions of farmer-soldiers and allied contingents to march out for combat elsewhere in Italy or, after 264, further afield. They seldom lost, even if they had to fight hard.

Roman power was being projected further afield. The first war with Carthage (the war in which Scipio Asina failed to shine) gave the republic a world-class navy headed by quinqueremes, the prime battleships of the era, crewed chiefly by coastal Italian *socii*. A 23-year fluctuating struggle on sea and land, it ended in 241 with Rome controlling most of the populous cities and communities of Sicily – the first example of what would come to be called a territorial *provincia*. Sardinia not long after became the second. Then, during Scipio's boyhood, the broad plains north of the Apennines, called Cisalpine Gaul after their chief inhabitants – some of whose forebears had once captured and burned Rome itself – were brought under Roman hegemony (though not yet as a taxed province) by C. Flaminius, Scipio's uncle Gnaeus and others.

Rome had long been an important mercantile state (not the inward-looking bastion of rude rustics that later Romans liked to imagine). Roman merchants, like other Italians, traded across the Adriatic and

Mediterranean, as far as Spain and Carthage. Now the republic was a leading naval power too, thanks to its victory over Carthage. This enabled the Roman state to start extending its influence eastward as well. A short Adriatic war in 229–228 turned some of the piratical Illyrian peoples across that sea into allies or protégés, making business safer for Roman and Italian merchants – though at the same time worrying the adjoining great power, Macedon.[3]

To Macedon and the other great kingdoms in the Hellenistic East the republic was still an undervalued or even unknown quantity, in spite of the First Punic War. To Carthage it was now a suspect and resented equal. In Scipio's lifetime these perceptions would be forced to change dramatically. One of the principal agents of change would be Scipio.

2
Boyhood, Youth and War

Publius Cornelius Scipio, one day to be Africanus, was born probably in 235 BC, at Rome or on a family estate in the country. Aristocratic families generally chose from only a few first names, *praenomina*, for sons; the Cornelii kept largely to five – Publius, Gaius, Gnaeus, Lucius and, less often, Marcus. Young Scipio's father was also Publius, and his paternal uncle was Gnaeus (by contrast, his mother Pomponia's brothers were Marcus and Manius, *praenomina* common in that family). Both Gnaeus Scipio and the elder Publius were elected consuls when young Scipio was a teenager, and so too their cousin, the son and namesake of Cn. Scipio Asina of Punic War notoriety. The future Africanus and his younger brother Lucius were more or less marked out from the start as future consuls too.

After he became Rome's most renowned and – by some – revered general, Africanus endured, enjoyed and perhaps encouraged a rumour that he was actually a supernatural product. A serpent had slid into Pomponia's bedroom and bed, she then became pregnant (whether thanks to the serpent or her husband) and Publius was the result. While he was a baby it was supposedly common, too, for people to see a huge snake slithering through Pomponia's bedroom yet doing no harm. It all pointed to involvement by a disguised god.

Polybius, who knew the family and describes Publius' early years, makes no mention of the tale. The commonsensical Livy treats it as absurd, but notes that Scipio always avoided denying it. Divine procreation was an accolade drawn from mythology, with Rome's twin founders Romulus and Remus the most obvious examples. The notion was conferred by admirers on men of rare charisma – specifically, by Greek admirers on charismatic Greeks and, even more specifically, on Alexander the Great. Much the same snake-conception tale had been told of him.

It was not a Roman religious notion, despite Romulus and Remus. Scipio's snake story likely was developed in the Greek East during his time there in 190 and 189, by Greeks keen to flatter a conquering Roman. That any Roman then or later took it seriously is more than improbable, least of all Scipio himself (even though it was later claimed as a fact by Julius Caesar's literary friends Oppius and Hyginus). But if he found it a conceit both flattering and perhaps useful, that need not surprise. He would put religion to good use more than once in his career.[1]

As boys and teenagers Publius and his brother Lucius would have had the education and training typical of members of the Roman male elite. Literacy, horsemanship and training in weaponry were necessary skills. So too, for a growing number of Roman aristocrats, was learning Greek. This was the international language of government and diplomacy as well as the vehicle of Greek culture. During the third century Romans were intensifying their interest in Greek literature, art and also religion. Asclepius, the god of healing, had been given his own temple on the Tiber island in 293. In April 205 the sacred stone (a meteorite) of the Great Mother goddess would be brought from Asia Minor to her new temple, escorted by the citizen judged Rome's most virtuous: none other than Publius' own cousin and namesake P. Scipio, nicknamed Nasica.

A Greek from Tarentum in southern Italy, Livius Andronicus came to Rome some years before Publius' birth, taught Greek and staged a series of Latin adaptations of Greek tragedies as well as composing a translation of the *Odyssey*. A contemporary Roman writer, Cn. Naevius, had begun to write Latin comedies adapted from Greek originals and would also present his own versions of tragedies. Later he was to compose Latin literature's first historical epic poem, a telling of the first war against Carthage (he had fought in it).

Young Scipio was likely enough aware of these literary events. Rome in the third century was still a compact city, the aristocracy a small part of its population and educated aristocrats an even smaller part. Livius Andronicus apparently had the Livius family, of plebeian consular status, as patrons, and one of them was consul in 219 along with the patrician L. Aemilius Paullus, whose daughter Scipio would marry. Naevius was associated with the Claudii Marcelli, a great plebeian and consular house (distinct from the patrician *gens Claudia*). Its leading figure at the time was M. Marcellus, consul in 222 with Publius' uncle Cn. Scipio; the two completed Flaminius' military subjection of Cisalpine Gaul. With these family connections, Publius as a young man may well have seen performances of some of these innovators' plays. Certainly as an adult he was strongly attracted to Greek culture – too much so for some other Romans (like M. Cato the Censor). The attraction surely developed early.

Another attraction, from early on again, was girlfriends. Naevius the poet, who in later years had a penchant for satirizing important aristocrats, made Africanus the target of one gibe that looked back on a youthful indiscretion: 'Even he whose great deeds have often garnered glory, whose feats now flourish, who stands out sole among nations – him, in just a cloak, his father dragged home from his dearie.'

Not only must Publius' 'dearie' (so *amica* means in this context) have been a sex worker, but Naevius implied that father Scipio had caught them in the act. It might be just a piece of scurrilous libel. Still, the anecdotalist Valerius Maximus claims that he 'is said to have spent his early youth in loose living' (primly adding that he stayed 'still far from extravagance').

Polybius himself affirms that Africanus was 'fond of women', and his army in Spain soon became aware of it. After they captured New Carthage within a year of his taking command, some soldiers brought him a particularly beautiful girl prisoner as a gift. Scipio famously restored her to her Spanish family instead, a propaganda coup that became the subject of many a Renaissance and Enlightenment painting – but he assured his men that had he been merely a private citizen, no gift would have been more welcome. How faithful he was to his wife both on campaign and in peacetime we may wonder.[2]

By the time he reached adulthood, Scipio was practising other habits that his fellow citizens found odder. He regularly claimed to be visited in dreams by divine visions that guided him. Polybius' inaccurate anecdote of him winning the curule aedileship beside his brother Lucius includes just such a dream. In the anecdote Publius is younger than the ambitious Lucius but, aware that he himself enjoys much greater popularity, joins his brother in standing for election so as to ensure Lucius' success, after assuring Pomponia that he has twice had a dream of this. The story is spurious: Publius was older and held the aedileship in 213; Lucius reached it only in 195, no doubt much aided by his brother, by then the most famous Roman in the world.

If not totally invented (Polybius implies the tale came from Africanus' close friend Laelius), the tale may have arisen from an elderly Laelius' distorted recollection of Lucius, a not over-attractive personality, standing for aedile in the 190s and Publius not only backing him but telling their anxious mother (Polybius stresses how anxious Pomponia was) of a repeated dream that her son would succeed. Whether he did so dream, and whether he was truthful during his life about dreams of divine guidance, there is no way of telling. Livy, at least, was suspicious of them.[3]

In his late teens or, rather likelier, his early twenties Publius was co-opted as a member of an ancient body of priests called the *sodales Salii*, the 'leaping comrades' (*salire* means to leap or dance). There were two *sodalitates*: the Salii Collini, devoted to Rome's city-god Quirinus (later identified with founder Romulus), and the war-god Mars' Salii Palatini. Tradition dated them to the era of Rome's kings, with ceremonial dress and rites suitably archaic. A Salian *sodalis* wore a bronze breastplate and pointed helmet, carried a spear and a sacred shield (called an *ancile*) shaped like our figure 8 and draped a blood-red cloak over his shoulders. At their ceremonies in March and October (traditionally the start and end of campaigning) the Salii paraded through the city, not marching but leaping in rhythmic patterns, clashing their spears on their *ancilia* and chanting a hymn so ancient that its meaning was no longer understood. They then enjoyed a proverbially fine banquet.

As guardians of the sacred shields – only one was a genuine gift from the god, the rest were exact replicas – the Salii were seen as the links between their patron gods and Rome's citizens, ensuring divine favour for the fighting in a given year. In practice, at Rome that meant more or less every year. Only patricians could be co-opted, and a new member's father and mother must both be living. As his father was killed in battle in 211, Publius' induction into the priesthood had to pre-date that year. Like other Roman priests, a Salius was not barred from taking part in public life. Usually (it seems) he would step down from the role once he was elected to office, partly at least because official duties could get in the way of performing the rites. Scipio, though, would be different: he was still a Salian priest, we happen to know, when he was in his late forties and on campaign in the eastern Mediterranean.

Young Scipio developed another religious habit that drew, and was meant to draw, notice. Once officially an adult, from his mid-teens, he would rise before dawn, leave home (his family lived near the Forum) and walk up to the Capitoline Hill and the imposing temple of Rome's chief deity, Jupiter Optimus Maximus ('Best and Greatest'). Supposedly the temple's fierce guard dogs always fell silent on Scipio's approach, amazing the sacristans. In its inner sanctum he would sit alone for long periods to meditate on whatever task or plan he was undertaking. He was to keep up this practice all his life when at Rome.

Was it true *pietas*, pious devotion, or carefully constructed self-promotion? 'Perhaps he genuinely had a superstitious bent,' comments Livy guardedly, 'or perhaps he sought unhesitating acceptance of his orders and plans by vesting them with some oracular authority.' Romans even in later ages held strong religious beliefs (a few philosophers excepted). Nothing suggests that Scipio, in youth or maturity, was a sceptic or a freethinker, any more than that he was surrounded by religious fanatics. He may well have united a genuine devotion to the gods – Jupiter and Neptune are mentioned in various contexts in his life – with realistically calculating the benefit of parading this. From early on, in other words, he knew how best to burnish his undoubted charisma, via intimations of otherworldly mystery.[4]

Something is known of the friends he made and kept probably from boyhood. Two were mentioned earlier: P. Crassus and Q. Metellus. Crassus (who earned the extra *cognomen* Dives, 'Rich', for solid pecuniary reasons) held an aedileship in 212, the year after Scipio, and became his fellow consul seven years later. Athletic and eloquent, he may have had a more outgoing personality than his solemn friend. In 212 too, he was chosen as the new *pontifex maximus*, chief priest of the republic, in spite of much more senior competitors – one of them a consul that year and both of them eminent generals. Metellus, like Crassus, was about the same age as Scipio but held two aedileships some years after they did, in 209 and 208. Nonetheless, he would be consul the year before them and then, as a leading ex-consul, would back Scipio solidly in the Senate against trenchant critics.

While young, Scipio became a friend too of quite a different person, not a high-ranking aristocrat but a young man of comfortable means, perhaps from a Latin city, C. Laelius. Laelius was the ideal friend for a young and ambitious member of the Roman elite: a trustworthy confidant, a model of support in every situation, able but not brilliant, upper-class but not Scipio's social equal. They were close enough friends by 210 for the newly appointed proconsul to take Laelius with him for the perilous war in Spain, and were still friends when Scipio died almost thirty years later. A generation later, Laelius' son would be the no less dear and trusted friend of the next Africanus, Publius' grandson and namesake.

Also when still a young man, Scipio became a husband. His bride was Aemilia, the youngest daughter of the patrician grandee L. Aemilius Paullus. The marriage likely took place in or before 216, given that their younger son, Lucius, was a praetor in 174 and by then praetors had to be at least 39. Young Lucius was already old enough in 190 to accompany his father and uncle to war in the eastern Mediterranean. In turn, his elder brother (inevitably, a Publius) must have been forty or older by 174. Two daughters would follow much later, after Africanus returned from war in 201: one of them the future mother of the controversial reformers Ti. and C. Gracchus.

Marriages linking powerful families would entail more than romantic love. Scipio's father and Aemilia's must both have had a say. Scipio's father-in-law was one of the consuls of 219, his own father likewise in 218. Each had been preceded in the office by kinsmen, close or distant, in recent years – three Aemilii between 232 and 225 (ending a fifty-year gap since their ancestor); young Scipio's uncle Gnaeus and Gnaeus' cousin the younger Asina still more recently. Perhaps the two fathers initiated arrangements before the elder P. Scipio sailed for Spain as proconsul in spring 217. If the marriage itself followed that year or next, Publius had become son-in-law to L. Paullus by the time the Battle of Cannae was fought in August 216. Paullus, consul again, became one of its thousands of dead.

Polybius admired Africanus but took a more caustic view of Aemilia. She loved stylish and expensive clothes, goods and carriages, loved showing them off at festivals and ceremonies and was always accompanied to these by a retinue of equally presentable servants. An anecdote by Valerius Maximus (to be mentioned later) could suggest she was a generous mistress. Even so, when she died about twenty years after her husband she was able to leave a large fortune to their grandson Scipio Aemilianus. Though Polybius describes her in old age (he was in Rome by then and was friends with her grandson), she must have been lively and self-assured in earlier times too – and needed to be, with a husband who was away at war for half of their first fifteen years of marriage, had left her with two small boys to raise and was not always faithful.[5]

Well before becoming a husband, Publius became a soldier. A new war with Carthage began in 218, requiring the two consuls – his father and Ti. Sempronius Longus – to levy and lead military operations. Aged seventeen, Publius accompanied the elder Scipio for what would be the teenager's first campaign. He was assigned to his father's cavalry escort as the consul's army boarded a fleet to invade Carthaginian Spain.

The Carthaginian republic had recovered spectacularly from its shattering defeat by Rome two decades before. Although it had lost its provinces in Sicily and Sardinia, it had more than made up for them by mastering a growing dominion in the southern Iberian peninsula, exploiting the region's gold, silver, produce and human resources. Carthage also continued to be overlord of the wealthy and populous peoples of its own hinterland, the region Greeks called Libya – more or less today's northern Tunisia. From early in the 230s, the state came under the effective rule of an aristocratic faction headed first by its ablest general, Hamilcar, nicknamed Barca (which may mean Thunderbolt); then by his son-in-law Hasdrubal and – after an aggrieved Spaniard assassinated Hasdrubal late in 221 – by Hamilcar's eldest son, Hannibal, the sole Carthaginian whose name still enjoys instant recognition.

Hannibal was a dozen or so years older than young Publius Scipio. Like his predecessor he was based at the city of New Carthage, today Cartagena in Spain, founded in 228 by his brother-in-law. Hasdrubal had called it simply Carthage, like his home city (*Qart-hadasht* in Punic, 'new city'); the Romans probably from the start clarified it as Carthago Nova. Political foes at Carthage accused Hasdrubal of aiming to set up an independent Spanish lordship, but most Carthaginians ignored them.

As with Hamilcar and Hasdrubal, the family's dominance at Carthage and the backing of the army in Spain guaranteed Hannibal's control of Carthage's affairs both in peace and in war.

The Barcids, as they can be called, like various other families in Carthage kept close links with princes of the small but energetic kingdoms of neighbouring Numidia. One of Hannibal's older sisters – he seems to have had three – was betrothed, and maybe then married, to Naravas, prince of the Massyli, a powerful people in the region of Cirta (modern Constantine in Algeria). Numidian military allies, above all their tirelessly agile horsemen, were crucial to every army Carthage fielded in its wars. Young Scipio would find this out for himself one day.[6]

As Rome's overseas trade included Spain and Carthage itself, the Romans were aware of the Carthaginians' doings at home and abroad. They mostly ignored these. They made direct contact with Hannibal's brother-in-law Hasdrubal only when Italy was menaced by a massive Gallic invasion from Cisalpine Gaul, backed by warriors from southern Gaul proper. An embassy sent to him in 225, at his city of New Carthage, gained his promise not to extend Carthaginian power beyond the river Ebro in northeast Spain; thus – implicitly – not into Gaul, where an intrusion could have caused further upheaval.

Only when Hasdrubal's new and assertive successor pushed nominal Carthaginian control of Spain up to the Ebro in 220 did the Romans pay fresh attention. Hannibal now received a new Roman embassy's demand to respect Hasdrubal's compact and, incidentally, leave alone the Rome-friendly trading city of Saguntum beside Spain's Levant coast. This démarche was most likely meant to remind him, and Carthage, that the new Barcid imperialism had limits in Roman eyes. That Saguntum, far south of the Ebro, was to be respected too sharpened the point, for legally speaking the agreement with Hasdrubal left it open to Barcid dominance. Not surprisingly, Hannibal took the new demand as a challenge and a threat. In 219 he attacked Saguntum, spent most of the year besieging it and at last sacked it.

Rome did nothing, not even diplomatically, to help the besieged friend. Instead both consuls – one being L. Aemilius Paullus, young Scipio's future father-in-law – went off eastward with powerful naval and military forces to reimpose Rome's challenged hegemony across the Adriatic in Illyria. They were back before summer ended, but no intervention in Spain followed. Senators did, it seems, discuss what line to take over the siege of Saguntum, with a distant kinsman of the Scipios (the then *pontifex maximus* L. Cornelius Lentulus) calling for military action and a Fabius, probably the soon-to-be-famous Q. Fabius Maximus 'the Delayer', urging caution. But it was only on the news of Saguntum's fall, late in 219, that opinion swung to Lentulus' side. By the start of the new year, the consuls for 218 were elected: young Scipio's father and Ti. Sempronius Longus. Quite likely these added extra weight, as consuls-designate, to demands for a strong response to Hannibal's defiance. Then on 15 March they entered office.[7]

War was now unavoidable. In the new sailing season an embassy, including the previous year's consuls Aemilius and Livius, sailed to Carthage and called on its ruling senate to hand over the disobedient Barcid for punishment. Then they declared war on the spot when the Carthaginians refused as the envoys knew they would. At home, the new consuls started levying troops and ships: P. Scipio to invade Spain via southern Gaul, Ti. Longus Africa from Sicily. This was when P. Scipio selected his son to accompany him. He also took his own brother Gnaeus as his deputy.

Young Publius was attached to a cavalry force guarding his father. A consul's personal escort, *delecti extraordinarii*, were cavalry and infantry specially selected from an army's Italian allied contingents. Publius took command of one troop of horse. It turned out to be vital for the lives of both him and his father.[8]

Hannibal threw Rome's strategy into confusion by marching from Spain across the western Alps, to debouch around 1 November in Cisalpine Gaul. The consul with his army and fleet had reached the mouth of the Rhône river when he learned what was happening. He made the portentous decision to send his forces on with Cn. Scipio as their new commander, while he himself sailed back to Italy with his *extraordinarii* to take over a praetor's two legions in Cisalpine Gaul. These had been sent there because the newly subdued Gallic Insubres and Boii, on the plains of Lombardy, were back in arms and expecting Hannibal.

When the invader arrived he had only 26,000 horse and foot left – it had been a difficult, though forever famous, journey – and the consul not many fewer. As the two armies moved cautiously towards each other across the countryside, north of the river Po and just west of its tributary the Ticinus, their commanders rode out on reconnaissance. The consul led his cavalry, including his *extraordinarii* and a large contingent of Gallic riders, plus a force of light-footed javelineers. Hannibal had almost all his cavalry with him, 6,000 or so, facing roughly equal Roman opposition.

The first battle of the Second Punic War began unheroically for Rome, with the javelin men fleeing from the enemy riders through their own side's ranks. A vigorous fight developed between the mounted forces, some of them dismounting to fight on foot. P. Scipio, young Publius and the guard escort were in the midst of the action. Hannibal now activated one of his trademark manoeuvres – one that would repeatedly cost Rome dearly (until young Scipio adopted it). His light cavalry, Numidians on their small and infinitely agile horses, swung out around the flanks of the main battle and struck the Romans from the rear. As the Roman cavalry began to break up and scatter, young Publius' father and two or three guards became separated from the others and the consul was seriously wounded.

Polybius tells how Publius with his own troop of horse saw it happen, called on his men to follow him, then while they hung back charged alone against the attackers, scattered them and brought his father to safety. Once the battered Roman forces regrouped away from the battlefield, the elder Scipio saluted his son publicly as his saviour. If the encyclopedist Pliny the Elder is right, some while later the consul offered his teenager the *corona civica*, the chaplet of oak leaves awarded to a Roman who saved a fellow Roman's life, but Publius modestly declined the offer.

This was the version of the incident that was generally accepted. But not the only version: Livy found another in Coelius Antipater's monograph on the war, which made the rescuer a slave from Liguria (the mountain region between the gulf of Genoa and the Po valley, regularly at war with Rome). For a Roman's slave to be on a battlefield near a commander, he must have been the commander's servitor or batman, and to extricate him from a press of mounted attackers he must have been armed and probably horsed. It looks unlikely, though not impossible.

Scipio Africanus was to incur plentiful critics and denigrators in the decades to come, Naevius the poet and Cato among them – notable writers both. Claiming that the feat had been done by a slave, only to be appropriated by a fame-hungry son, might well be a sneer too spicy for a critic to resist. Livy is right that probability favours young Publius.

His father, shaken by the defeat and badly hurt, avoided any fresh combat until his colleague Sempronius Longus arrived from the south with his own legions and took over operations. Disaster followed. Longus (people said later) was too combative, his colleague too weakened to prevent him. Drawn into battle beside the river Trebia in freezing late December rain and snow, the Romans were shatteringly defeated. Hannibal sprang a surprise ambush behind them, led by his youngest brother, Mago, then his elephants, skirmishers and cavalry enveloped them. Of about 40,000 troops, only the garrison holding their camp, some cavalry and 10,000 infantrymen escaped to Placentia on the Po. The wounded consul could not fight, so had remained in the camp, as must his son. A vicious winter prevented further operations.

Neither the elder P. Scipio nor the younger were involved in the following year's campaign in Italy. The elder Scipio recovered from his injury and was authorized to take over command of the forces in Spain. He now became a proconsul with continuing *imperium*, the legal power to command, and with his brother becoming in practice his deputy again. The two would wage war against the Carthaginians with varied success and without fresh reinforcements for the next six years. Young Publius, his brother Lucius and Pomponia would never see them again.

Publius is not recorded as fighting in 217, when Hannibal marched into Etruria and on 21 June annihilated the new consul C. Flaminius' army on the northern shore of Lake Trasimene. The invaders and their Gallic allies were now free to penetrate into the heart of the peninsula, while the Romans struggled to regroup. Hannibal chose not to march directly on Rome but far south into Apulia, expecting that his presence would win over southern cities and peoples dissatisfied with Rome's hegemony. A series of marches, counter-marches, thrusts and parries across central and southern Italy took up the rest of the fighting year. Hannibal reached Apulia, then moved across the central Apennines into the wealthy region of Campania along the west coast, still seeking to win over restive or fearful Roman allies. He was shadowed, but not attacked, by a new army under the newly elected dictator Q. Fabius Maximus, head of the oldest of all patrician *gentes* and already twice consul.

Hannibal won no new supporters in Italy but Fabius failed to damage him. At Rome, angry criticisms of the dictator's delay tactics multiplied, especially after Hannibal tricked his way back to Apulia out of a trap that Fabius had laid for him in northern Campania's hills. Fabius' energetic deputy, the master of horse M. Minucius Rufus, was elevated to be his codictator – a total innovation – by vote of the *comitia centuriata*, but he too failed to win a victory and nearly suffered another Hannibalic entrapment. The only solution, the Senate and public opinion agreed by autumn 217, was to levy a massive army that would overwhelm the invaders by plain weight of numbers.[9]

The consuls for 216, after a strong electoral tussle, were Publius' father-in-law L. Aemilius Paullus once more and a plebeian 'new man', C. Terentius Varro. Greek and Roman writers were to damn Varro as a boastful parvenu who reprised Sempronius Longus' rash role of insisting on an unwise battle, and laud Paullus as a new version of Longus' reluctant colleague. In reality, the Senate instructed Paullus and Varro to bring Hannibal to battle. It was only a question of when and where. They levied an army four times the size of a regular consular army, eight legions of citizens with about as many Latin and Italian allies. Each enlarged legion was officered by its military tribunes, young men elected by the *comitia centuriata* or appointed by the consuls. One of these was nineteen-year-old Scipio, chosen for the second legion.

To be appointed a military tribune, a young man normally had to have served for five years in armies. Scipio obviously had not. But he had shown mettle at the Ticinus, even if he then went back to civilian life and marriage. He was becoming well known in Rome, and of course he had the support of influential kinsmen. The emergency gripping the republic, with an apparently unstoppable invader loose in Italy and Rome itself potentially threatened, was a powerful impulse for Scipio to put his name forward and for the authorities to accept it.

In the discussions with their senior officers that followed, the consuls disagreed only on the time and place. In practice they had little choice: to avoid an ambush or some other Hannibalic trick they had to fight on flat open ground, preferably with at least one flank protected by a river. Apulia offered much flat ground and below the hilltop town of Cannae the plain was bisected by the river Aufidus, flowing to the Adriatic. There was no more suitable terrain for a massive battle. Paullus perhaps hesitated even so. The Battle of Cannae, on 2 August 216, was Varro's decision.

What Scipio did in the battle is not recorded. As a military tribune, his role was as one of the leaders of the mail-clad legionary infantry who were the core of a Roman army. But nearly all the infantry, Roman and Italian allied, who fought in the battle were killed when Hannibal's envelopment manoeuvre, executed in plain sight, closed them in a trap of steel. Many fewer – but still many – became his prisoners. By contrast, Scipio and some other military tribunes fought their way out to reach Canusium, a town 16 kilometres (10 mi.) southwest, before nightfall, unpursued by their exhausted enemies.

The first mention of him since 218 is at Canusium. According to Livy, he and three other military tribunes learned that a group of well-born young men, in despair of the situation, were planning to flee abroad. Scipio led his fellow tribunes to the lodging where the men were discussing their plan, then with drawn sword made them swear not to desert the republic and put them under guard. He and a colleague, Ap. Claudius Pulcher, then took charge of the troops in the town until they were joined by their commander Varro with the rest of the surviving army. Scipio's father-in-law was dead.

The Canusium story is not universally believed. Sceptics (there are many) see it as only another piece of later Scipionic hagiography: Scipio boldly assuming leadership, making a histrionic speech and gesture and striking terror into the cowards. It was the first recorded act of leadership by the young man Livy solemnly calls 'the fate-ordained commander in this war'. Yet Livy's basic account is credible even if over-theatrical. The other tribunes with him are plausibly named (the son of the recent dictator Fabius, Ap. Claudius of that patrician *gens* and a Publicius Bibulus of a prominent family of plebeian praetors). So too the absconders' ringleader, L. Caecilius Metellus – probably brother to Scipio's own friend Q. Metellus – who two years later when quaestor was disgraced by the censors for cowardice. Though the story is not told in the relative section of Polybius' history (this breaks off right after Cannae), that hardly counts as disproof.[10]

After Cannae and between 216 and 210 the only event recorded in Scipio's life is that he was one of the curule aediles for 213. He may have served in the continuing war against Hannibal during 215 and 214, but this is not known. There were two curule aediles each year, as well as a less prestigious pair of plebeian aediles, all responsible for the upkeep of the city of Rome. When Scipio put his name forward as a candidate, the tribunes of the *plebs* objected: he had not reached the legal age, so Livy writes. But Livy probably misunderstood the point, for legislated minimum ages for office were yet to come. The tribunes probably meant he had not done enough years of military service, as convention demanded. He had not even been a quaestor, against convention again.

Scipio, all of 22 years old, challenged them. 'If all the citizens wish to make me aedile, I am old enough,' Livy makes him say. His candidacy aroused so much popular enthusiasm that the tribunes stopped objecting. No doubt he had strong family backing. Though his father and uncle were both in Spain (they could of course write home), his older kinsman Scipio Asina, son of the Carthaginians' one-time captive and consul in 221, was at Rome. The other candidate for aedile was M. Cornelius Cethegus, another member of their *gens* and impressive in his own right – a gifted orator who that same year was created a *pontifex*, a member of that prime priestly college. Also at hand were his mother's consular brothers the Pomponii and their sons, one a recent praetor and the other an augur, another very senior priest. Just as voters recognized the promising qualities in young Scipio, so could his kinsmen. He and Cethegus were elected.

As curule aediles, they spent a sizeable sum on the great religious games the Ludi Romani, held every September in honour of Jupiter Optimus Maximus (especially significant to Scipio). This was obviously with an eye to future political progress. *Pietas* plus *liberalitas* always went down well with the Roman voter. Both the candidacy and his aedileship illustrate Scipio's developing career. First, his self-confidence – not far off arrogance – and impatience with inconvenient convention. Second, his access while still so young to plentiful funds. The amount spent is not recorded, but this was in the midst of a ferocious war, with much of Italy in enemy occupation or under attack. And third, his successful candidacy, showing the favourable attention that people – the voting public anyway – were now paying him.

An even stricter convention required ex-magistrates to pass at least one year, and often longer, before standing for another office. What Scipio did after his aedileship, from 212 to the first part of 210, is unknown, whether more military service or civilian business at Rome. He was waiting to be appointed a senator, as his aedileship made him eligible, but for that he had to await the decision of the next censors. They were due to take office in 210. Meanwhile, in 212 his friend P. Crassus was elected the new *pontifex maximus*, prevailing over two much older and more senior candidates (one of them a consul that year, Q. Fulvius Flaccus, a leading general). Some Cornelii as well as Licinii no doubt were among Crassus' strongest supporters, one of them probably enough his friend the popular ex-aedile.

The war with the Carthaginians was approaching a crucial point. Hannibal's invasion, which at the start had seemed to promise Carthage so much, had effectively stalled. Many of south and central Italy's states had deserted Rome for him – but not enough of them, and no Latins. Philip v, king of Macedon and long suspicious of Rome, and then the once great Sicilian city-state Syracuse, eager to recover its old dominance, both took Carthage's side too; yet neither brought Hannibal profit. By unprecedented efforts the Romans multiplied armies and fleets. By 211, 23 legions and equal contingents of loyal allies were campaigning in theatres across Italy, Cisalpine Gaul, Sicily, Spain and the Adriatic. At sea, Roman fleets repeatedly raided coastal Libya and intimidated the hapless Carthaginian navy into impotence.

In Italy, Hannibal won a few more victories after Cannae and from time to time enticed a few more defectors to his side, notably the rich and powerful Greek city of Tarentum as late as 212. Yet he could not force the Romans to ask for terms, or chase away the Roman armies shadowing him. Philip v gave up fighting Rome after 214 to focus on the troublesome Greeks to his south. In the year after young Scipio was aedile, Rome's most aggressive general, M. Claudius Marcellus, took and sacked Syracuse (fatalities included the scientific genius Archimedes). In Spain the elder Scipio brothers held at bay Carthaginian forces that might otherwise march to Italy, and they made friends in North Africa with the western Numidian king Syphax as a useful thorn in the enemy's side.

In Italy the Carthaginians' most important ally, Capua, came under relentless siege. Desperate to save it, Hannibal in 211 tried to draw away the besiegers by launching a famous lightning march on Rome from Campania, even camping outside the city walls. But by now the Romans knew how to frustrate, even if not yet to defeat, the invader. At Capua the siege went on. At Rome its garrison legions came out to offer battle. Instead Hannibal retreated deep into the south of Italy, leaving Capua to capitulate and be punished. Young Scipio may well have stood on Rome's walls to watch him march away.

Yet not all that happened in 211 was beneficial to Rome, or to Scipio's family. His father and uncle overreached their resources in Spain, underestimated the capacities of their Carthaginian adversaries and marched too far south from their bridgehead on the river Ebro. The three Carthaginian generals – Hannibal's brothers Hasdrubal and Mago and their colleague Hasdrubal, son of Gisco – helped by their able eastern Numidian ally, a young Massylian prince named Masinissa, and by the timely defection of the Romans' Celtiberian mercenaries, picked off first P. Scipio and then, four weeks later, his brother.

Most of the Roman forces were destroyed with their commanders. Only the remnants, rallied by two officers, L. Marcius Septimus and Ti. Fonteius, made it back to the Ebro and the Roman base at Tarraco (Tarragona). The gains made in the Iberian peninsula over seven years were nearly all lost. And once news of the double catastrophe reached Rome, fresh fears had to arise that Hannibal's brother Hasdrubal would finally obey his brother's call and bring over a new army to tip the balance in Carthage's favour in Italy too.[11]

Instead, Hasdrubal and his colleagues followed up their victory with a complacency that was typical of rather many Carthaginian generals. They took their time about pursuing their retreating foes to the Ebro. Afterwards, if Hasdrubal did launch an attack on the Romans' fortified position near the Ebro or Tarraco, it was beaten off. In Livy and other writers this becomes Marcius attacking them to win a smashing and no doubt invented victory. The Carthaginian generals' military misfire in 211 recalls Hannibal's own failure to move on Rome after either Trasimene or Cannae. The failure in Spain would have results no less baleful for Carthage.

The Roman reaction was a contrast. C. Claudius Nero, a propraetor with the armies at Capua, was given troops and ships and sent to Spain. Livy's report that he moved against the Barcid Hasdrubal and trapped his army in a defile called Black Stones (Lapides Atri) need not be a fiction, as is sometimes supposed. Claudius Nero's fresh forces brought the Roman army at the Ebro up to about 19,000, and Hasdrubal, it seems, had been left on his own by his fellow-generals – the three did not always get on well together. His troops would not be much more numerous. The trapped Carthaginian tricked his way out by pretending to negotiate a surrender and then absconding – not an obvious ending for a Roman-invented fiction.

But after that, Claudius Nero held his fire, even when the new year 210 came. It was too risky to move south without reinforcements. By guarding the Ebro line, at least he blocked any enemy effort to march from Spain in Hannibal's direction, and meanwhile he chose to wait for further instructions from Rome. He was in for a surprise.

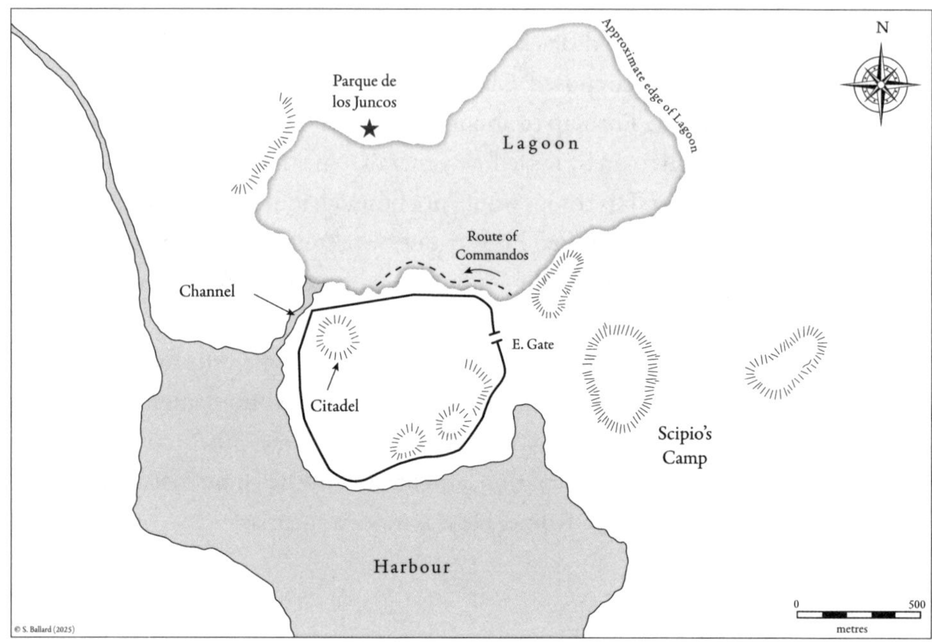

The Capture of New Carthage.

3

The Capture of New Carthage

The new consuls for 210 were seasoned commanders: Marcellus, the captor of Syracuse, and M. Valerius Laevinus, who had chased Macedonian forces out of the Adriatic theatre. Marcellus took over the operations against Hannibal in southern Italy, while Laevinus replaced him in Sicily to clear out Carthaginian troops there. They and the Senate realized that the army and fleet holding northeastern Spain must be strengthened. Not only that, but attracting Spanish military allies – ones who would remain loyal – was essential.

Soldiers were available, along with transports, warships and funds. After nine years of war there was no shortage of experienced men who could take command: for instance Q. Fulvius Flaccus, who had just captured Capua, or P. Sulpicius Galba (both recent consuls), or of course Claudius Nero, who was already in Spain. But none offered himself. Instead the Spanish command went to Publius Scipio, now 25 years old.

Livy offers a vivid imagining of the morning when the *comitia centuriata* met on the Campus Martius to appoint a new commander for Spain. Citizens were depressed about the situation and, worse, were perplexed because no candidate had come forward. 'Then, suddenly, Publius Cornelius – son of the Publius Cornelius who had fallen in Spain, and then about 24 [in fact, 25] years of age – declared his candidacy and stood on higher ground so he could be seen.' He was at once and unanimously chosen, even though the voters then wondered if they had done the right thing. Scipio soon held a public gathering to make an eloquent speech that allayed all their fears and reignited their enthusiasm.[1]

The drama of these events is no doubt over-coloured by the historian, a lover of meaningful scenes. Likely enough Scipio's candidacy was less unforeseen, and less universally acclaimed, than Livy's literary recreation (this perhaps came ultimately from Laelius, via Polybius or some other predecessor). Scipio's own kinsmen on both sides must have encouraged him to step forward, and so too friends like P. Crassus, the *pontifex maximus*. Crassus in this same year was one of the new censors and, further, was appointed deputy (*magister equitum*) to his recent rival Fulvius Flaccus when Fulvius briefly became dictator for holding elections.

The consuls, Crassus and some of the other *principes viri* in 210 may have known of Scipio's intention and accepted it – hence the lack of other candidates – but it probably came as a surprise to the voters, even if a welcome one. Less welcome maybe to a different leader, Fabius Maximus, the former dictator, whose dislike (and suspicion) of young Scipio was hardly new when it blazed up in the Senate five years later. The superseded Claudius Nero was surely not happy either. Opponents, though, kept their feelings largely to themselves.

For a young man who had reached only a junior magistracy, was still not a senator and had never commanded an army to receive *imperium* at a consul's level was unprecedented even in a war that was repeatedly casting old conventions aside. Commanders were holding multiple consulships – Fabius was consul four times during the war, two of them in successive years; Marcellus and Fulvius Flaccus three times each – and between consulships they and others could have their *imperium* prolonged over and over as proconsuls to ensure continuity in the field. Armies were being levied on a vast scale and kept on campaign for years, not disbanded and replaced by new ones as in past wars. Warfare was being carried on across virtually the whole of the western Mediterranean for the first time in history. But in appointing a middle-ranking man in his twenties, with no serious command experience, to a crucial theatre of operations where fresh defeat could overturn Rome's fortunes in the entire war, the republic took its most monumental gamble yet. It proved historic, for reasons both good and less good.

One reason for appointing Scipio, some have suggested, was that his father and uncle had built up good relations with many of eastern Spain's peoples in their eight campaigning years there. Sending over another Scipio would build on this. If so, it was not a secure calculation:

so his father's and uncle's desertion by their own Spanish friends had just shown. The gamble was tempered by having Scipio take a colleague with him. M. Junius Silanus had been a praetor in 212 and was an older man with military experience. In practice he would work as Scipio's deputy, though officially it seems both held *imperium pro consule*. Probably the two were already friends and Silanus was Scipio's choice.

Equally important (it turned out) was that Scipio's closest friend, Laelius, accompanied him to Spain too, more or less as another deputy – in his case, as Scipio's direct lieutenant in operations. Silanus would be sent on independent missions. A few other officers are known: a quaestor, C. Flaminius, son and namesake of the unlucky consul of 217, was assigned to the expedition as in effect its finance officer, while M. Sempronius Tuditanus and P. Cornelius Caudinus (one of the Lentuli) were probably among the military tribunes of Scipio's legions.[2]

It was probably now that Scipio took personal vows to pay honours to his elders' memory, should he succeed where they had failed. These honours he would pay four years later at New Carthage in Spain, but the likeliest moment for taking them was when he became the elder Scipios' military successor and potential avenger. That he was serious about the vows cannot be doubted, and they bring further colour to what can be seen of his character, firmly devout as well as sharply practical.

The new proconsul, as he can be called, was given a small army: 10,000 infantry and 1,000 cavalry – more or less a Roman legion and accompanying allied contingents – with a small fleet and a sizeable money chest of 400 talents. He would also, of course, have the troops already in Spain. When he sailed from Italy and when he arrived in Spain is not clear, partly because Livy impossibly puts these events in 211, the same year that his father and uncle were slain and Claudius Nero took charge. He then dates all the Spanish campaigns a year earlier than they should be. Polybius' account shows that the first campaign came in 209, so it is likely that late summer or early autumn of 210 saw the new expedition reach Emporiae, Rome's small Greek ally on Spain's northeastern coast, and then Tarraco 230 kilometres (nearly 145 mi.) further south.[3]

The situation in Spain was not quite as dire as feared at Rome. L. Marcius and Claudius Nero had kept their forces disciplined and ready for action. Nero went back to Rome (he would be a momentous consul in 207) but Scipio sensibly kept Marcius as an officer. Strategically, although the most powerful Spanish canton inland, the Ilergetes around Ilerda (now Lleida), were Carthaginian vassals with princely Ilergetan hostages lodged at New Carthage, Rome's coastal friends north of the Ebro, like Emporiae, Tarraco and a number of small cantons, were still on side. Better still, Scipio discovered how thoroughly the enemy generals in the south had shirked their opportunities.

Though two of the three were Hannibal's brothers, and all three had collaborated strategically to bring down the elder Scipios only the year before, they had now fallen out, for reasons unknown – each with the others. Nor had Hasdrubal obeyed the repeated summons from his elder brother in Italy to join him with reinforcements (it may have been one reason for the others' irritation). Instead, and most conveniently for Scipio, all three had taken their armies off to widely different locations in Spain's west and centre. Supply problems may have contributed to this, for Scipio was told that they were mistreating the local Spaniards too.

By the start of 209 the Barcid brother Mago was in the peninsula's far southwest, today's Algarve in Portugal. His sibling Hasdrubal, north of the river Tagus in central Spain, was trying to capture a town of the Carpetani (name not given). Meanwhile their colleague Hasdrubal, son of Gisco, sat by the mouth of the Tagus, close to where modern Lisbon stands. Each of them lay ten – or more – days' march from the capital of Carthaginian Spain. These details in Polybius came from Scipio himself, in a letter to the Macedonian king twenty or so years later; Polybius read it in the 160s or 150s. Livy assigns the generals to other places, but those had probably been where they wintered after their victories in 211.

If word had reached the Carthaginian generals about a youthful and inexperienced Roman leader arriving at Tarraco, they likely felt he would threaten little trouble. Scipio chose not to startle them right away. He passed the rest of 210 and the following winter gathering intelligence, making himself known and welcome to the remaining Spanish allies and planning his first campaign. This would be fast-moving and unorthodox.

Orthodoxy would have meant advancing steadily from the Ebro like his father and uncle between 218 and 211, to win allies, take strongholds and defeat enemy forces in battle. His subordinates, says Livy, expected this. Scipio chose to strike straight at New Carthage. It was the key to Carthage's Spanish dominion, a distant 530 kilometres (330 mi.) south of Tarraco. Founded around 228 by Hannibal's brother-in-law, it was already an imposing and prosperous city, close to rich silver mines, packed with workers, munitions and treasure, full of aristocratic young Spanish hostages – three hundred of them – keeping their parents and peoples loyal to Carthage, and the best natural port on Spain's Mediterranean coast. Scipio may have hoped too (though wrongly) that taking it would kill any further plan to send troops to Hannibal.

Secrecy was so vital that the only other person in the army to be told the plan was Laelius. Not Silanus, whose junior status to Scipio was now clear. Early in spring 209 he was left at the mouth of the Ebro with only 3,000 infantry and 500 cavalry – a calculated risk, but Scipio plainly had a sense of how apathetic the Carthaginian commanders were – while Laelius, in charge of 35 quinqueremes, and Scipio leading the army set out southwards. He had 25,000 infantry and 2,500 cavalry, all of them Roman and Italian.

Supposedly they covered the distance to New Carthage in seven days, the fleet keeping to the army's pace. This advance averaged 67 kilometres (42 mi.) a day – extraordinary for men marching and then fighting. Scholars generally judge it a Polybian or manuscript mistake (or a myth). Livy repeats it, but that shows only that he found it when he used Polybius. Worth notice all the same is that in 319 (at least according to Livy's older contemporary Diodorus Siculus, using good sources) Antigonus, one of Alexander the Great's ablest successors, in the same time had led an army twice the size of Scipio's over much the same distance in rugged central Asia Minor, to surprise an enemy. And in 49 BC Julius Caesar would march the 465 kilometres (290 mi.) from Corfinium, in central Italy, down to Brundisium in seventeen days, two of them probably rest days – a slower rate at 31 kilometres (19 mi.) a day than Scipio's, but Scipio had a fleet, and it very likely carried most of his army's equipment.

Or, just possibly, he put his infantrymen aboard ship transports – the ones that had brought Claudius Nero's and his forces from Italy, or other craft acquired in northern Spain – while he and the cavalry moved overland. At some point, infantry and cavalry would then have reunited, because the entire army reached New Carthage on land before his fleet entered its harbour. The fleet could have made a landfall, for instance, on the beaches at Cape Palos, 30 kilometres (18½ mi.) to the east, to disembark its military passengers. There was level countryside between that district and the city, and no enemy installations. If so, Polybius – and his echo Livy – expressed the arrangements poorly; or Scipio's own original account fudged the detail.[4]

New Carthage occupied a strong position, on and around a group of small coastal hills forming a short peninsula between the harbour on its southern side and, on the northern, a shallow 2-square-kilometre lagoon, in medieval times called the Almarjal. This was finally drained off in more recent centuries, to cause one more problem in analysing Polybius' and Livy's accounts. Lagoon and harbour were linked by a man-made canal alongside the city's western wall, cut as a passage for fishermen and the like. Towards evening, Polybius writes, water usually rushed out of the lagoon through this canal into the harbour, enough to lower the lagoon's already shallow level. Scipio knew of this phenomenon from helpful fishermen he interviewed at Tarraco.[5]

The Romans' appearance outside the walls totally surprised the city. The garrison commandant, another Mago, had just 1,000 trained soldiers, though he could arm a couple of thousand able-bodied civilians to help. Scipio encamped on the narrow neck of land just outside New Carthage's eastern walls, with the harbour by his southern flank and the lagoon on his northern. At the same time, Laelius' ships arrived at the harbour shore.

The proconsul now made a rousing speech to his troops, not only promising rewards once the city was taken but, significantly, assuring them that the plan of campaign had been revealed to him in a dream by Neptune, the god of the sea. Neptune would show his support in the attack. This speech, Polybius insists, hugely encouraged the men; not least because Scipio also promised a gold crown to those who first mounted the walls and rewards to the rest. The troops may already have known of Scipio's claims to divine communication and his ostentatious piety (besides his fondness for women). Now his charisma and promises powerfully enthused them. How genuine his dream was, of course, is a different question with an unknowable answer.[6]

Next morning, around the third hour – about nine o'clock – Mago sent out his scratch militia in a sortie as Roman troops formed up outside their camp. The Romans repelled their few opponents so forcefully that they nearly broke through the eastern gate into the city. Foiled in this, Scipio then launched 2,000 men with scaling ladders in a furious assault against the towering walls. Polybius adds a note: rather than join directly in the fighting, Scipio himself moved about with a trio of protective shield bearers, keeping his eye on developments and staying in sight of his men. This all 'contributed greatly to the success of the day'. It was certainly a sensible tactic for a general, though at the same time (as the historian no doubt knew, and perhaps wanted to hint), prudence like this was quite a contrast to how battle-loving warriors like Alexander the Great fought.

Laelius' fleet played a part too. The ships, 'furnished with all kinds of missiles', lined up outside the sea walls – not to launch an assault, clearly, but to keep the defenders under pressure and keep them from moving away to help the troops at the eastern gate. There Scipio's morning assault failed against bitter resistance. Recalling his men to camp, Scipio gave the Carthaginians a misleading respite. After a few hours, in the late afternoon he reopened the attack on the eastern walls and gate with more men and more ladders. The defenders now had to be distracted on every side, so the fleet under Laelius must have joined in again, though it is not mentioned. Then, as Polybius tells it, the level of water in the lagoon began to fall. Livy puts this around midday, not towards evening, and adds that a strong wind had sprung up too. These details must come from some other informant and have contributed to controversy, as we shall see.

Scipio had five hundred picked men ready at the lagoon's edge. He bade them follow Neptune as their guide. They waded along the edge of the swiftly shallowing lagoon, beneath the now nearly unmanned northern wall – defenders there had gone to the sectors under attack – and set their ladders to climb to the top without opposition. Livy describes Scipio as going with them, but this must be one of his imaginative touches. Polybius implies, sensibly, that Scipio's station was with the main body outside the eastern gate.[7]

It took little time for the task force to race along the top of the northern wall to that gate. They drove off the enemy there, cut the gate's fastenings and opened it. Resistance collapsed. Under orders from Scipio, his troops slaughtered everyone they met in the streets – civilians included – 'as is the Romans' custom', Polybius coldly comments. Scipio himself took a thousand or so troops to corner Mago and his remaining men in the citadel, on the steep Cerro del Molinete near the western gate. As soon as he received their surrender, he bugled a halt to the killing. Again according to standard Roman custom, Carthaginian Spain's capital was thoroughly looted, with the booty methodically stacked in the marketplace to await official distribution next morning. Mago himself and his staff, two senior Carthaginian senators and fifteen ordinary ones, were kept in honourable confinement to be sent to Rome.

This is largely the canonical account of the fall of New Carthage. Dramatic and renowned though it is, the first of Scipio Africanus' long roster of victories, more than one problem has been seen in it. Contested above all is its crucial feature, the triumphant surprise attack via the receding lagoon.

Polybius and Livy state that Scipio had been told of the outflow by fishermen, for whom it was a regular event. These must have been coastal entrepreneurs, able to ply their trade along the entire east coast. Their information, then, would explain why Scipio assured his soldiers that Neptune would guide their attack. Yet it is not clear how the phenomenon could happen predictably, or why Mago took no precautions even though he and every townsman, like the fishermen, must have seen it every day. Hence suspicion that the 'outflow' was misunderstood or grossly exaggerated by our sources, or even made up.

Today's tidal changes are shallow at Cartagena: between 0.2 and 0.8 metres (8 in. to 2½ ft) twice a day. Arguably these would have been too shallow, in the ancient city's harbour, to enable lagoon water to flow outwards through the connecting canal at low tide. One modern suggestion has the canal opened and closed daily by sluice gates to regulate salt flats around the lagoon; Scipio supposedly seized these gates to let the lagoon water out. But this is a guess with no support from any source. No salt flats are mentioned at New Carthage in ancient times, and the canal was on the city's western side while Scipio was assailing it on the eastern. A more sceptical interpretation is that the lagoon was shallow enough anyway for Scipio's task force to wade through: no outflow was involved, and it was shamelessly invented, perhaps by Scipio and Laelius, to enhance the proconsul's image of divinely rewarded *pietas*.[8] On the other hand, there is reason to believe Polybius' account in essentials, and Livy's, which largely (though not totally) draws on his.

During its existence, the now extinct Almarjal must have been fed by various inflows: streams from the surrounding country, periods of rain, even occasionally by storm-driven harbour water. If it had no outlet, then as its level rose it would eventually have flooded New Carthage's environs, undermined the walls and in the end joined up with the sea on the eastern side to turn the city into an island. This had not happened. The canal, made (Polybius implies) by the Carthaginians, who probably had improved an existing runoff, would have helped against such danger. So would hot summers and droughts, thinning inflows from landward streams and causing evaporation. But Scipio arrived not in summer but in spring – March or April 209.

No doubt the small daily tidal rises and falls in Cartagena's harbour occurred in Scipio's day too, around dawn and towards sunset. Even these small fluctuations could produce inflows and outflows via the canal. Polybius and Livy needed to refer only to the second outflow, the one in the late afternoon or evening. If Livy is right from some other source (not Polybius) about a strong north wind springing up to push the water out, that was an added bonus – it could not have been factored into Scipio's original plan. It might, of course, be just a fresh touch of Livian literary imagination.

Scipio's commandos, it is usually assumed, crossed the lagoon from its northern edge, over 700 metres (2,300 ft) from the city's northern walls. He had stationed them 'on the shore of the lagoon', Polybius writes. If their starting point was really that edge – a good 2.5 kilometres' tramp from the Roman camp, via the lagoon's eastern edge – the men would have needed an hour or longer to cover the distance, carrying their scaling ladders and weapons. They would have had to set out during the lull between the assaults, too, because their attack had to coincide with the second big assault on the walls. That is, they would have had to move in daylight, in clear view of the defenders at the east gate and along the walls.

Polybius and Livy make clear that Scipio gave the task force the order to move only after the fresh assault began. Almost certainly, therefore, his five hundred men did not cross from the Almarjal's north side. They raced along its shoreline beside the city's northern wall until they found a suitable place for the climb. Polybius in fact hints at this: Scipio gave the order 'when the water gradually receded from the edges of the lake'.[9]

Mago the commandant would obviously have known about any lagoon rises and falls. But it is not to be assumed that he had left the northern wall without defenders, and that this undermines the outflow report. Mago did not know what information the proconsul had and, with only a small garrison, was forced to decide on priorities. The northern walls overlooking the Almarjal, Polybius implies, did at first have some civilian defenders (as did the others). These then moved over to the eastern gates when holding that sector became crucial. Very likely Scipio kept up the furious assaults there, first in the morning and then later in the day, probably again with Laelius and the fleet putting pressure on the harbour fortifications with missiles and feints, to focus Mago's and the defenders' attention firmly on the city's east and south. It was at hard cost to Scipio's own soldiers, but he was clearly willing to pay their price.

Once taken, New Carthage was too valuable a prize to undergo a total massacre or enslavement like Syracuse three years before. Next morning, with the pillaging over and dead bodies cleared away, Scipio set about organizing results from his victory. Gathering the surviving male population of the city – nearly 10,000 in all – in the market square, first he told its almost 8,000 citizens to take their families home, 'think well of the Romans and remember their kindness' (this prompted tears of joy and relief, says Polybius). Then the city's 2,000 slave artisans were promised eventual freedom if they worked hard for Rome. The Romans had taken still other prisoners of war, probably some of them resident Spanish natives, others the crews of Mago's eighteen warships (which had done very little against Laelius' fleet the previous day) and of the 63 merchantmen in the harbour. Scipio conscripted them all for his now enlarged fleet.

The amount of plunder, including money, captured in the city was vast. Its treasury contained 600 talents, equivalent to more than 3.5 million *denarii*, Rome's newly launched silver coinage, or 36 million bronze *asses*. This more than doubled Scipio's funds. Polybius' other details are missing because the relevant extract ends, but Livy may draw on him for a portentous catalogue: 276 heavy gold bowls, silver utensils in quantity, raw and coined silver weighing 8,300 kilograms (18,300 lb); hundreds of artillery pieces large and small (catapults, *ballistae*, scorpions), piles of armour and weaponry and 74 military standards. On the seized merchant ships were 400,000 bushels of wheat and 270,000 of barley. Such lavish and varied booty meant new supplies for the army and fleet, financial rewards for the men, and for Scipio powerful proof to all of his leadership, military skills and favour from the gods.[10]

Even so, the proconsul was almost at once called on to calm a quarrel among his own soldiers, overwrought and emotional after their victory. The customary mural crown (a gold coronet) for the first man to scale the walls was disputed between Q. Trebellius, a centurion supported by Sempronius Tuditanus, and a fleet marine, probably an officer, named Sex. Digitius, backed by Laelius – a dispute fervid enough to threaten a physical clash between factions. The quarrel has even bolstered critics of Polybius and Livy: neither mentions marines scaling the sea walls in the final attack. So Polybius could be accused of suppressing Laelius' and his fleet's contribution so as to magnify Scipio, and Livy of being too slavish a follower of Polybius (despite all his added non-Polybian touches), only to let slip the truth now from some other source.

The suspicions are not needed. With no stopwatches or cameras, no one could have worked out the precise timing of two separate actions at two clash points half a kilometre or more apart, with New Carthage in uproar in between. Trebellius and Digitius more likely were two of Scipio's selected task force, Tuditanus and Laelius their normal commanders. Scipio solved the issue in sensibly predictable fashion. He announced that, after making an inquiry, he was satisfied that both soldiers had jointly been first. Rancour subsided.[11]

It was, in turn, good public relations to meet the three hundred Spanish hostages held in the city and promise that they would be free to return home. All of them, adults and children, were naturally of high and even princely rank, such as the wife and daughters of Mandonius, brother of the Ilergetan king Indibilis from northern Spain. As Polybius tells it in unusually lively fashion, Mandonius' elderly wife first asked for the women hostages to be properly treated, and Scipio promised her that they would receive generous supplies. The princess replied with dignity:

'You do not rightly follow my words, general, if you think we are asking you about our stomachs.' Realizing that they feared rape, he at once took steps to ensure proper protection for them.

The story is believable, though no doubt Scipio took care to have his solicitude well advertised. In turn, admirers like Laelius and Polybius could use it later to show how he could relate to people in need or distress, foreigners and Romans alike. In the same vein, he sought out and freed any Saguntine slaves or prisoners who were held at New Carthage – a practice he would follow when he took other Spanish cities, as grateful envoys from Saguntum later assured the Senate.

A much more famous incident soon followed. Polybius' version is straightforward. Some young Romans had noted a particularly beautiful girl among the prisoners and brought her to Scipio as a gift, 'knowing that Publius was fond of women'. (The young men were probably military tribunes, with ready access to their commander.) Scipio thanked them, saying that she would have been just what he wanted, had he been a private citizen, but as commander he could not accept the gift. He restored the girl to her father, helpfully adding that the father should marry her to a local citizen of his choice.

Livy's account is a romantically charged revision that makes the girl the fiancée of Allucius, a young Celtiberian lord (implicitly she is now a Spanish noblewoman). Scipio summons Allucius as well as her parents and kinsmen and restores her to them. When the family insists on thanking him with a gift of gold, he presents that to Allucius as a dowry. Overwhelmed, the young lord soon returns with 1,400 horsemen to join the Romans. All this is too fanciful to be believed (and Allucius and his horsemen are never heard of again).

Noticeably, in both narratives the girl and her family are nameless extras and the focus is on the magnanimous Roman. Polybius' account can still be believed – including its hint that Scipio was a far from faithful husband. Scipio's self-denial on this particular occasion was no doubt carefully publicized to reassure New Carthage's citizens, and others beyond, that he was a conqueror with principles. Of course, nothing rules out that he may instead have taken up quietly – now if not already – with some other, less noticeable Spanish girl. Livy's florid version, meanwhile, served as inspiration for many seventeenth- and eighteenth-century plays, operas and paintings – canvases by Tiepolo and Joshua Reynolds among them – that celebrate the 'continence of Scipio'.[12]

While capturing New Carthage struck a severe blow against Carthage's strategic and political position in Spain and flagged a stunning reversal of Roman fortunes there, an anticlimax followed. Laelius was sent off to Rome with the eminent Carthaginian captives to announce the victory. Scipio put his soldiers and sailors through a hard and healthy regimen of drills – such as 6-kilometre cross-country runs by infantry in armour, and battle games at sea for crews – and set the artisans of New Carthage to work making fresh munitions.

There is a chance, too, that he now experimented with army organization: grouping the thirty *manipuli* of each legion into ten *cohortes*. Each cohort held one maniple of front-line *hastati*, one of the legion's middle-line *principes* and one of the third line's *triarii*, for a notional total of 210 infantrymen. They are first heard of, as a known quantity, two years later in his battle at Ilipa. Cohorts allowed a legion more flexible manoeuvring with larger units, though maniples remained in being until Caesar's time at least.[13]

Scipio must have spent some further months seeing to all these tasks. Once he judged everything in order, he left a strong garrison in the city and set off with his main land and sea forces, and with the freed Spanish hostages, to return to Tarraco.

4
Baecula and Ilipa

Even though New Carthage was taken in spring, there were no further military operations during 209. As just mentioned, Scipio's activities in and around the city must have taken several months more. The war was on pause until the next year: Scipio presumably decided that his forces were not yet strong enough to confront the enemy's. His father and uncle had been overwhelmed, two years before, by the same trio of generals and armies; clearer intelligence about them (he perhaps reasoned) was necessary before he made a new move. This decision proved justified.

It became obvious that none of those generals would be going on the offensive. They made no move even to recover their lost capital. Nor did they try to take advantage of most of the Roman expeditionary army and fleet being far from the northeast, by dispatching Hannibal's brother over the Pyrenees to Italy, even though Hannibal kept demanding it. This apathy is hard to understand – and how they explained it to Hannibal and Carthage hard to guess – unless their sources of information were so defective that they thought Scipio's and Silanus' armies much larger than they were. It was the same sort of apathy that all three had practised after liquidating the elder Scipios in 211. The strategic initiative stayed with Scipio.

On his way back to Tarraco, the proconsul was met by obsequious delegations from Spanish towns and peoples keen to declare friendship – an indication of how obnoxious the Carthaginians had made themselves in Spain's eastern parts. A crowd of excited Spanish lords then gathered at Tarraco over the winter to be charmed by Scipio.

Notable among them (says Polybius) was Edeco, king of the Edetani, an east coast people. On receiving his ex-hostage wife and children from

Scipio, he flattered the proconsul by calling him a king and used his influence to bring more peoples in the region over to Rome. All the same, Edeco never reappears in later events (nor does his people), and Polybius may overstate his importance. In reality, the most powerful rulers in eastern and northeastern Spain were the Ilergetan brothers Indibilis and Mandonius, whose territory centred on the fortress town of Ilerda but stretched over most of the middle Ebro valley.

These two had been keen allies of the Carthaginians from the start of the war. Indibilis (in Polybius he is 'Andobales') had played a major part in the defeat and death of Scipio's own father two years earlier. Now, insulted by Hasdrubal the Barcid, forced to hand over their womenfolk as hostages and gouged for money, he and his brother withdrew their troops to wait on events. It was this example that other peoples allied to Carthage then followed. It put Hasdrubal, in particular, in a difficult position.

Whatever issue divided the three Carthaginian generals, it still persisted. Neither the Barcid Mago nor the non-Barcid Hasdrubal were on speaking or, it seems, communicating terms with their nominal superior – an unusual situation for multiple Carthaginian commanders, and odder still when two were brothers. As the Barcid faction was dominant in Carthage's politics – Carthage's commander-in-chief was their brother and Hasdrubal, son of Gisco, was their most powerful political ally – the breakdown in relations could not be solved by recalling or demoting any of the three. So Hasdrubal the Barcid was left on his own against Scipio.

Scipio prepared to move south again in 208. Laelius had returned from Rome with the satisfying news that his *imperium* and Silanus' had been indefinitely confirmed by the Senate (and a day's thanksgiving ceremony decreed for the victory at New Carthage). As enemy naval forces no longer existed in Spanish waters – something Scipio knew, a further sign of good intelligence sources – he could strengthen his army by drafting suitable men from the fleet. This more than replaced the casualties in the attack on New Carthage. That city continued to be safely held by a Roman garrison; nothing more is heard of it until 206.

Sometime in the first half of 208, Scipio left Tarraco to cross the Ebro at the head of some 30,000 horse and foot, this time without the fleet but again with Laelius as his deputy. He aimed to seek out Hannibal's brother Hasdrubal. Silanus again stayed to hold the northeast, a task that was humdrum but essential. On the march the army was met by Indibilis and Mandonius, who thus declared their change of allegiance. Their reward was not only a formal alliance but the return of their womenfolk to them. For Scipio to bring these princesses along, he must have been expecting the Ilergetan lords to appear – this despite the risk that once their wives and daughters were restored, they might desert him as they had Hasdrubal. He was confident enough to run the risk. The two lords did briefly leave, but only to gather their fighters and rejoin the Romans on the march. Like Edeco earlier, they flattered Scipio by addressing him as a 'king' – meaning not a territorial monarch but a special grandee like themselves. Scipio studiously ignored the flattery, or so Polybius says. Whether Edeco, and young Allucius if he really existed, joined the army too is not reported, but with the Ilergetans Scipio's forces probably grew by another 5,000, if not more.

Hasdrubal's strategy was uninspired. He took up a position in southern Spain and waited. It would have been more intelligent for the Carthaginian generals to let Hasdrubal keep Scipio busy while the others came up and trapped him in a replica of their 211 victory (Scipio feared just that). Perhaps this was still Hasdrubal's hope, but the idea was beyond his colleagues. Scipio and his allies were able to advance unopposed from Tarraco.

Their march, 650 kilometres (400 mi.) or more from there to northeastern Andalusia, must have taken at least three weeks, moving probably past Saguntum, across the open plains of La Mancha and then southward either through the pass of Despeñaperros (today's A2 route), or via the corridor further east between the Sierra Morena and the rugged Sierras de Alcaraz and de Cazorla – locations where intelligent cooperation between the enemy armies could have done to him what they had done, and probably in the same regions, to his elders. Hasdrubal instead preferred to encamp outside a place called Baecula, in the upper Baetis (Guadalquivir) valley, and wait for Scipio.

Baecula was near the silver-mining city of Castulo (thought to be close to modern Linares), incidentally the home town of Hannibal's wife. The battle site has usually been identified with a large hilltop beside Bailén, a town famous for a Spanish victory over the French in 1808 and well placed to meet an army moving south into eastern Andalusia. All the same, another candidate for Baecula has now been proposed, a hilly area outside Santo Tomé 75 kilometres (47 mi.) further east, beside the Cazorla range. There, quantities of Roman and Carthaginian military items (such as spear points, javelin heads and plentiful boot nails) have been excavated, together with mainly local Iberian coins but also scattered Carthaginian and Roman ones, and all are dated to this period by their finders. The very plentiful Roman remains, though, outnumber the Carthaginian ones: an unusual feature for a victorious Roman battlefield. They may mark Santo Tomé instead as where one of the elder Scipios had made his last stand three years before. That would leave the Bailén region as the likelier one for Baecula, Scipio's first field battle.[1]

After a short cavalry skirmish when the Roman army approached, Hasdrubal shifted to a second position on higher ground. This was a broad plateau with two levels (Livy's description is fuller than what we have of Polybius', but plausible). Hasdrubal was protected by difficult slopes both in front and to left and right, and behind by a river. Neither Polybius nor Livy mention numbers, but the Carthaginian army is thought to have been only about 25,000 strong against Scipio's 35,000 if not more. This would explain why Hasdrubal chose so defensive a position. He plainly reckoned that the Romans would have to attack him up the steep ground in his front, as he judged the rest of his perimeter inaccessible. At the same time (we are told), he was equally prepared in case of a defeat: he would retreat with as much of the army as he could and make for Italy. He must have reasoned that a victorious Scipio would not pursue – and in this, at least, he would be proved right.

The strategic and political situation does not say much for Hasdrubal as a general or as governor of Carthaginian Spain. He had lost control of his nominal subordinates, failed to boost his own military strength and turned previously faithful Spanish allies into enemies. He now had to rely on Scipio to attack him, no doubt gambling that he could inflict losses brutal enough to terminate this second Roman invasion and clear his own way to join Hannibal.

Scipio encamped near Baecula and spent two days judging the terrain and its challenges. Even though Hasdrubal was clearly operating on his own, the risk obviously remained that Mago and the son of Gisco, or even just one of them, would see sense and arrive with reinforcements. In any case, more delay was out of the question, for the Romans had no supply depots and must forage daily. Moreover, inaction could lose their new Spanish allies' support (as had happened ruinously to Scipio's elders). On the third day he launched his attack.

Conventional battle tactics – for instance the Roman army's at Cannae – put the heavy infantry in the centre, the cavalry on either wing and the light-armed fighters ahead of the infantry. The young proconsul deployed his men differently. Part of his light-armed force (his *velites*) and a select body of heavy infantry pushed their way up Hasdrubal's frontal slope to attack the troops – Numidian cavalry and Libyan light infantry, according to Livy – on the plateau's lower sector. The Numidians, incidentally, were led by the same prince, Masinissa, who had helped destroy Scipio's father and brother three years before. At the same time, Scipio formed up his legions and Latin and Italian contingents in two columns, one under his own command and the other under Laelius'. Oddly, Indibilis' fighters or other locals are not mentioned in the fighting.

Hasdrubal, watching from his camp on the upper level, held his main army back until he saw the Roman assault below him gaining the upper hand, as the rest of the Roman light-armed now reinforced their comrades. Whether he could see Scipio's legions forming up in the distance is not clear. There may have been woodlands in places to give the Romans cover. In any case he became preoccupied with marshalling his own soldiers to exit camp and join the fray ahead.

Now Scipio's column moved off, swinging to the right, and Laelius' to the left – not to join in the frontal assault but to head for the plateau's flanking slopes and climb them. The relentless training and physical exertions he had put the troops through now proved their worth. As soon as the infantry reached the top, Scipio's first and then Laelius', they charged into the flanks of the Carthaginian army.

Hasdrubal had neither foreseen this manoeuvre nor, as a result, done anything to guard his flanks. His cavalrymen could have done so, but, apart from the Numidians whom Livy mentions in the front line, his horsemen (like Scipio's Spanish allies) are conspicuously missing from the narratives. The enemy cavalry must have lost formation (or fled) as confusion spread through their army. With his front and both flanks collapsing, Hasdrubal sounded the signal for a general retreat.

Livy claims that the two roads down from the plateau had been blocked by Roman troops, but even if this is correct – Polybius does not mention it – Hasdrubal still managed to extricate up to half his army, much of which had not been engaged at all. He and it marched away at speed. Polybius and Livy take him from the battle site, over the river Tagus and towards the Pyrenees all in the same sentence, but in reality this must have taken some weeks even though Scipio did not pursue him. He was still not too far away some days later, when he joined his two colleagues for a no doubt acrimonious war council.[2]

Scipio's losses are unknown but cannot have been very many. Hasdrubal's casualties are not clear. Supposedly 12,000 enemy prisoners were taken, 2,000 of them cavalry; and, adds Livy, another 8,000 men had been killed. These figures look overblown, but perhaps 12,000 killed or captured – about half the Carthaginian army – is a plausible total.

Baecula was a limited victory. Nonetheless, it confirmed that the Romans now had a general able to win victories in ways too inventive for opponents to forecast. His refusal to pursue Hasdrubal was unconventional, but rational. He reckoned that if he did, Mago and the son of Gisco would finally decide to intervene to save Hannibal's brother, and this would be a combination too big to defeat. He was right – they were already on the way but, typically, too late.

Next day, Scipio told the Spanish prisoners they were free (the Libyans and Numidians, by contrast, would be sold as slaves, the usual fate of captives). He also found himself greeted by envoys from the towns and peoples of the upper Baetis river, on the same day if Polybius and Livy are right. They must have been waiting in the neighbourhood to see who would win. Like Edeco and the Ilergetan princes earlier, these spokesmen congratulated him with the acclamation of 'king', noisily joined in by the liberated prisoners. Again this was flattery, not a call for him to become their sovereign.

This time, though, with his own army looking on, Scipio took notice. Phrasing his words rather like when declining the offered girl, he told the Spaniards that he wanted to be kinglike and be called so, but not to be or be called king. Instead, 'call me general' – *strategos* in Polybius' account, in Livy's *imperator* – for so, he added, his soldiers had already dubbed him.

If Scipio did say *imperator*, it marks the first recorded time the term was used: a term with a long and pregnant future, first for victorious generals and later for rulers of the Roman Empire. It was just an informal coinage in 208 – *imperare* means to command – and *imperator*, or its common Greek equivalent *autokrator*, does not appear elsewhere for Scipio, not even in his and his brother Lucius' letters to Greek states twenty years later. But the first person to use it, in any known document, was his brother-in-law L. Aemilius Paullus as governor in Spain in 189. Paullus may have remembered this incident and started a portentous fashion.

Polybius lavishes praise on Scipio's nobility of soul in rejecting, now and later, the chance to be a king (kingship being 'the greatest good a man dare pray to the gods for') and revealing his steadfast devotion to country and duty. The praise, though, is overdone. Scipio had no use or even concept for being any kind of king in Spain, and no way – even had he fantasized about it – of becoming one at Rome. The irony is that his achievements did contribute, indirectly and unwittingly, to making something even grander than kingship become established at Rome, long after he was dead.

Livy tells of Scipio questioning Massiva, a captured young Numidian lord, and learning that he was nephew to Masinissa. He at once sent him honourably back to his uncle. The story may be true, for such gestures did occur at command levels in war; it would happen to Scipio's own son in another war. If so, it was the first tentative step in a relationship between Roman general and Numidian prince that would have critical consequences for them, for Rome and for Carthage too. Masinissa, as it happened, was also related (a brother, it seems) to the Massylian prince Naravas, whom Hamilcar Barca had long ago taken as his son-in-law. The irony of history made Scipio's coming new friend a kinsman by marriage of Carthage's greatest general.[3]

But Baecula, fought in summer 208, was followed by another surprising hiatus. Scipio marched back to Tarraco along the route he had come, unfollowed by Mago or the other Hasdrubal. He sent a body of troops to the edge of the Pyrenees to keep an eye on Hasdrubal, who eventually crossed the western side of that range with a new army to winter in southern Gaul. But in Spain there was no more campaigning until 207. The other two generals still had no wish to try to retake New Carthage or march north to pen Scipio behind the Ebro.

According to Livy, the Carthaginian three had met after Baecula (we are not told where) to work out what to do. While Hasdrubal the Barcid agreed to march for Italy at last, the other Hasdrubal was to regroup in southwest Spain near the ocean but avoid battle, Mago should sail to the Balearic islands to recruit fresh mercenaries, and Masinissa would use his cavalry to harass Rome's allies in the north and protect Carthage's. Livy may be right about these decisions – Polybius' account does not survive – but they are not the whole story. Masinissa made no known movement out of southern Spain. Mago may have brought back Balearic recruits, but the islanders were lightly equipped (though powerful) wielders of slingshots, not trained or trainable infantry. More importantly, Hanno, a new general, arrived from Carthage with reinforcements, and when Livy's narrative returns to Spain for the year 207, Hanno and Mago are in central Spain recruiting more Celtiberian mercenaries. The Celtiberians, whose lands lay largely in central Spain, were the toughest and most professional of the peninsula's warlike peoples – although, as Scipio's father and uncle had found, not always the most loyal.

The new year 207 brought to Tarraco Scipio's brother Lucius, to be another lieutenant to the proconsul along with Laelius and Silanus. Scipio quite likely had sent for him. Lucius had no special military talents, but aristocratic families had to foster their members' careers. Lucius would prove tough, efficient and dependable. Scipio no doubt looked forward to one day becoming a consul, and would wish his only brother to achieve the same. Military service was essential for this, to bring sufficient *gloria* – though in the end Lucius had to wait until 190 for his consulship.

To curb Mago's and Hanno's Celtiberian recruiting, Scipio despatched Silanus with 10,000 foot and 500 horse. By then the two generals had gathered a small Spanish army alongside their own. Silanus moved fast through mountainous country, probably the Sistema Ibérico, which parallels the Ebro south of the river and separates the Mediterranean coast from the Castilian Meseta inland. The enemy, surprised in their camps, were easily disposed of. Some were killed; most fled. Mago decamped with some infantry and cavalry and did not stop for ten days until he reached his colleague Hasdrubal at Gades (Cádiz) on its island. The hapless Hanno, though, was captured before he had a chance to fight.

Scipio followed this side action with a return march in full strength to the Baetis region. Livy probably echoes Polybius in stating that he now hoped to finish the war in Spain. Neither Mago nor Hasdrubal, son of Gisco, had shown impressive generalship. Carthage's Spanish allies north of the Baetis river and around New Carthage had ended their support; many were siding with Rome, though we have no names. Scipio could reckon that defeating the last remaining enemy forces would have the same effect on the south's Spaniards. How large his army was is not reported, nor Hasdrubal's (who was now definitely Mago's operational, and maybe his official, superior). But Hasdrubal found a way, inglorious but practical, to frustrate the incursion: he avoided battle. Probably he knew, or thought, he did not have superior enough numbers. Instead he turned to a passive strategy, parcelling out his troops as garrisons among cities still loyal. Again, we have no names of these.

This stymied Scipio. It was useless to try capturing or winning over a series of fortified centres – and could expose him to attack if the troops became bogged down – when his essential target was the enemy's field army. He might have tried forcing Hasdrubal's hand by borrowing a Hannibalic tactic, ravaging the farms, woods and fields of southern Spain's fertile countryside. But this would antagonize the Spanish communities he wanted to win over. Instead he decided that he should retire once again to Tarraco.[4]

First, though, he detached his brother Lucius with a strong force to attack an important city in the prosperous region south of the upper Baetis. Livy calls it 'Orongis', probably the same as an 'Aurinx' he recorded in one of the elder Scipios' campaigns. Most likely its real name, distorted by Livy's sources or later copyists, was Aurgi (today Jaén), at the foot of an imposing mountain bloc, the Sierra de la Pandera. The aim must have been to counter any impression of weakness that his withdrawal might make. Lucius forced the city to yield after an energetic assault and carried off the Carthaginian garrison as prisoners.

Another benefit from the action may have been an offer of alliance from a regional king named Culchas or Colichas, described as lord of 28 towns. If not now, Culchas must have made his offer during the following winter, for when Scipio came south early the next year, Culchas sent 3,500 soldiers to the Roman general – a total that suggests that his towns were mostly large villages. His territory perhaps lay in the countryside around pro-Carthaginian Aurgi; in crushing this centre, L. Scipio may have done the king a favour he was happy to return.

Scipio's otherwise unproductive campaign in 207 in Spain contrasted with events in Italy. Hasdrubal the Barcid had crossed the Alps to enter Cisalpine Gaul in spring, then in early summer he set out from there to join his brother in Apulia – only to distract himself for some time trying to take Placentia on the river Po. Hannibal, closely watched by Roman armies, remained in Apulia. Hasdrubal's couriers to him, outlining the younger brother's plans to advance further south, were captured by the consul commanding in Apulia: the same C. Claudius Nero whom Scipio had superseded in Spain three years before. Nero made a bold decision with fateful consequences.

He took a select force north at speed to link up with his colleague M. Livius Salinator, who was shadowing Hasdrubal in Umbria. Hannibal continued totally unaware and immobile in Apulia. On 22 June, at the river Metaurus near Fanum Fortunae (now Fano), the consuls defeated and killed Hasdrubal and destroyed his army. Hannibal famously learned of the disaster only when the returning Nero had his brother's severed head flung to one of his outposts. Nero's march north – a manoeuvre of Hannibalic, not to mention Scipionic, resourcefulness – ended any hope of reinforcements for Hannibal and left him beached in southern Italy, almost irrelevant to the wider war.

In Spain, the next year would prove decisive. Its course of events is not totally clear. Only excerpts from Polybius' work survive, while Livy narrates a very large variety of actions during 206, extending from the Battle of Ilipa to Scipio's triumphant return to Italy. Yet a contrary view, that Ilipa was fought in 207, heightens the difficulties more than it eases them. With some analysis, an acceptable sequence of events can be fitted into 206, especially if his return home took place during the winter of 206–205.

Scipio was turning thirty and eager to finish affairs in Spain. He was now convinced that the war could be ended by invading Africa, leaving Hannibal behind in Italy – and, of course, that he was the general to do it. His opponents in Spain, too, had decided to fight at last. Hasdrubal, son of Gisco, spent the winter of 207–206 raising more troops, to a total of 50,000 infantry (so Livy says) or 70,000 (Polybius), with 4,000–4,500 cavalry, some of them Masinissa's Numidians. He had even acquired 32 elephants, no doubt from North Africa. With these imposing forces he moved to encamp on a plain near a line of hills and a town that Polybius' text calls 'Elinga' and Livy's text 'Silpia'. There he chose to wait for the Romans.

Scipio had now crossed the Ebro, aware of Hasdrubal's preparations, and advanced through central Spain to cross the Sierra Morena itself, or between it and the more easterly Sierra de Alcaraz, collecting Spanish allied troops en route. He halted near Castulo and Baecula, where Silanus rejoined him after taking charge of Culchas' 3,000 foot soldiers and 500 riders (Culchas himself preferred a prudent absence). Though unhappy with all the native allies – as before, he suspected their loyalty if it came to a pitched battle – he moved out to face Hasdrubal and Mago. He had 45,000 infantry and 3,000 cavalry in all, the Roman, Latin and allied Italian contingents totalling rather more than half. When he sighted Hasdrubal's camp, he pitched his own camp on a rise close by and began planning for battle.

Just where the battle was fought is debated. Conventionally it is called Ilipa and identified with a town so named (now Alcalá del Río) a few kilometres north of Hispalis (Seville) on the lower Baetis. This, though, would mean that Scipio marched 250 kilometres (155 mi.) from the Castulo area along the right bank of the Baetis, risking Trasimene-style attack from the often steep slopes of the Sierra Morena that would have edged his right flank, and needing to cross several large tributaries of the Baetis (the Rumblar, Jándula and Guadiato among them) – opportunities ignored by Mago's and Masinissa's cavalry. These held back their assault until he was camping opposite their own position.

Polybius and Livy mention no long march or river crossings. Instead they imply that Elinga/Silpia was not far from the Castulo area. Neither Elinga nor Silpia are otherwise found in ancient Spain, despite copious road lists, inscriptions and local coins; one or both must be later manuscript copyists' mistakes. 'Ilipa' is a modern surmise – with more difficulties.

Various towns in southern Spain named Ilipa, Ilipula, Iulipa and Iluipa are recorded on inscriptions and coins, some at still unknown sites. Ilipa near Hispalis, called Ilipa Ilia in Roman times, was one. Another Ilipa, or the like, may have stood on the northern side of the Baetis not far from Isturgi (now Andújar) about 40 kilometres (25 mi.) west of Castulo. In Pliny the Elder's regional survey of Spain (in his *Natural History*), the list of cities east to west along the Baetis includes an 'Ipasturgi' or 'Ipraisturgi', another copying error that scrambles together a real Isturgi with, it seems, an Ipra, Iluipa or other Ilipa not far east of Isturgi. This stretch of the Baetis has level terrain on either side, edged in turn by low hills. Somewhere on those fields, near the Rumblar river and its junction with the Baetis-Guadalquivir, may lie the site of the battle that broke Carthage's rule in Spain.[5]

After driving off the enemy's cavalry attack on his first day, Scipio waited on each of some further days while, late every afternoon, Hasdrubal drew up the Carthaginian army to offer battle. Scipio then deployed his own army but refused to advance. Nor did Hasdrubal, obviously preferring to receive attack rather than launch it. Each time, in standard fashion, his infantry, disciplined Libyans from Carthage's subject territories, formed the centre and his Spanish allies and mercenaries the wings. The Carthaginian cavalry and elephants positioned themselves in front or skirmished forwards. Scipio matched this array: Roman, Latin and Italian infantry in the centre, Spanish allies on either wing, with cavalry and the light-armed *velites* in front intermittently skirmishing and returning. But then on the day he chose for battle, he activated a boldly – and dangerously – reverse line-up.

The army must have been well rehearsed during the previous winter, because Scipio planned to put it through an extraordinary sequence of manoeuvres. First, the Roman and Italian infantry would deploy as his two wings and the Spanish allies as his centre. This was not the only surprise for Hasdrubal. Instead of waiting until late afternoon, the Romans took an early breakfast and marched out as the sun rose. When the cavalry and *velites* surged ahead to launch missile attacks on the half-asleep enemy camp – they can hardly have done much damage – Hasdrubal reacted in haste. He gave his troops no time to eat, sent out his cavalry and light-armed against the assailants and ordered immediate general deployment onto the plain. The dust from the skirmishing between the two armies at first kept him and his officers from realizing that the Roman battle line had changed drastically. When they did, it was too late to reverse their own.

This was just the beginning of Scipio's sequence of tactics, feasible because his now veteran soldiery had been thoroughly trained in four years under his command and because the Spanish allies forming his centre – even though less drilled and less trusted – now showed their worth. He let skirmishing go on at some length to make the hungry and thirsty enemy suffer the mounting heat of the day. Livy claims that it went on until the seventh hour – around one in the afternoon – but this looks exaggerated, for the Roman army too (even though fed) was experiencing the same heat in full armour. But finally Scipio recalled his cavalry and *velites*, ranged them on the wings behind his infantry and sounded a general advance. Though it was not a fast one.

Hasdrubal, unsure of what to expect, stayed in position. Where his colleague Mago was is not recorded. While Scipio's Spaniards kept to their slow pace, at about 4 *stadia* (800 metres or so (2,625 ft)) from the enemy his heavy infantry on either wing now faced about into columns of march. With Scipio and (probably) Laelius leading the right wing, Silanus and Marcius the left, their columns moved laterally away from the Spaniards forming the centre. Alongside the infantry wings trotted the cavalry and *velites*. This opened a gap of some size on either side of the still advancing centre. The Spaniards must have been carefully coached during the previous days, and been ably led now by their officers: they showed no alarm as their allies marched steadily away. Scipio was executing one of the most dangerous manoeuvres in combat: dividing his forces in face of the enemy.

As the head of each infantry column neared Hasdrubal's puzzled and immobile Spanish wings, it smartly wheeled once more – Scipio's column to its left, Silanus' to its right – to become once again lines ready for fighting. Now they closed in on the enemy wings. The accompanying cavalry and *velites* had carried out their own wheel, too, apparently before the infantry reformed into lines, to hurl javelins and other missiles at the Carthaginian elephants. Once these became unmanageable from panic and pain, they posed as much danger to Hasdrubal's troops as to their Roman attackers. Many or most may have lumbered off the field to escape. What had become of the Carthaginian cavalry is not reported, but most likely it was routed along with the elephants, or gave up the fight and rode away.

As battle developed on both Hasdrubal's wings, his stationary centre watched Scipio's Spaniards slowly approaching. Hasdrubal dared not turn the Libyans to help his Spanish wings or order them forward against the approaching enemy. Either move would open gaps in the very centre of his position. But when, after a strenuous struggle, his Spanish troops' resistance ebbed on either wing, Hasdrubal must have given the signal by trumpet and bugle for withdrawal from the field. The entire Carthaginian army began as orderly a retreat as its various contingents could manage.

Hasdrubal the Barcid had done this with some success at Baecula. But his namesake's soldiery swiftly collapsed into a disorganized mass as the men retreated further, seeking higher ground. Then they broke up in rout when the victors redoubled their attacks. Most of the shattered survivors made it back into their camp, where the gods (Scipio's piety notwithstanding) seemed to take pity on them. A huge thunderstorm erupted to put an end to fighting and drive Romans, Italian allies and allied Spaniards back to their own camp.

Scipio's tactical mastery in the battle and the firm discipline of his soldiers, including the Spanish allies, had no Carthaginian counterpart. Hasdrubal, son of Gisco, was as mediocre a general as Hasdrubal the Barcid (and Mago the Barcid was no better). Scipio even so took immense risks. Keeping the infantry motionless under the hot sun risked wearying them nearly as much as the enemy, even though they had taken food before dawn. Separating both wings from his centre in three different stages – moving away to right and left, then wheeling into columns for forward advance, and then their pivot back into lines of battle further and further away from the barely advancing Spanish allied centre – caused growing gaps in his array that an agile opponent could have exploited. Good luck thus played its part in his victory, and good luck, *felicitas*, was (as Cicero would later stress) an essential element in a great general's formula for success. Its reward at Ilipa to Scipio and Rome was total: Carthage on that day lost Spain.[6]

5
The Fall of Carthaginian Spain

Polybius' account of the aftermath of Ilipa no longer exists, and Livy's is fuzzy in places. But Livy shows that the aftermath was not going to be limited like Baecula's. Scipio did not attack the enemy camp next morning, but some of the Carthaginians' surviving Spanish troops began to desert. The next night, Hasdrubal and Mago led the rest of their army further away, but Scipio at once gave chase with local guides. His cavalry and *velites* cut off the enemy's access to a ford or bridge to the southern, more open terrain of the Baetis valley. As the desperate Carthaginians and their remaining allies marched along the river's northern banks, hoping to reach the distant Atlantic coast, harassing pursuit by the Roman cavalry and light-armed slowed and then stopped them.

This was the end of the broken army. The Roman infantry came up and cut it to pieces, killing or capturing all but 6,000, who escaped with the two generals up to a steep line of heights. The pursuit may have lasted more than a couple of days, if the battle was fought somewhere close to the Baetis, for near Hasdrubal's and Mago's refuge the Baetis was navigable for ships. Their refuge was inaccessible to the Romans but had no water. Hasdrubal had sent word on to Gades and, despite Scipio blockading his makeshift camp, was able to flee aboard a ship sent from there. Livy says ships, but no other passengers went along – not even Mago, though Hasdrubal did then send the ship back for him. By then Scipio had left, after giving Silanus 10,000 foot and 1,000 horse to keep up the blockade.

For the Carthaginian generals to desert their last loyal troops was too much for the Numidian Masinissa, who had remained with them throughout. He secretly contacted Silanus, who allowed him and his remaining followers to abandon the blockaded heights. Masinissa followed Hasdrubal and Mago to Gades, but with plans to change sides as soon as the time was ripe. Meanwhile the last of the trapped Carthaginian army surrendered or dispersed.

Scipio had left the region – for Tarraco, Livy says, and his march took seventy days. This is not easy to believe, partly as it makes the chronology of the year hard to follow and partly as Livy's narrative is not quite consistent. The enemy remnants could hold out on their arid heights for just a few days (a point Livy himself makes), and once they gave up Silanus supposedly went to Tarraco to report to Scipio. With his smaller force and no opposition en route, Silanus would hardly take as long as seventy days to reach Tarraco – yet he found his superior already there. Then, according to Livy, Scipio left Tarraco to march at speed south to New Carthage for a brief mission over to North Africa, and on returning to New Carthage led operations against recalcitrant Spanish cities. A further series of busy activities followed.

With so much still to do, Scipio is not likely to have taken ten weeks on a return march from the middle or lower Baetis to Tarraco, even if the distance is a sturdy 800-odd kilometres (500 mi.). Livy's numeral may be a mistake, his own or a later copyist's. The proconsul may perhaps have left his brother Lucius in command of the main army, and with a small escort hastened ahead faster. Still likelier, he and the army marched not north to Tarraco, but southeast from the Baetis to New Carthage: a trip of 500 to 550 kilometres (310–340 mi.). If so, it was to New Carthage that Silanus came to report, and then it was to Tarraco that Scipio sent him with some of the army to control Spain's northeast. Livy's version, Silanus given charge of New Carthage and L. Marcius left at Tarraco, is probably another slip.[1]

From New Carthage, Scipio sailed over probably to Siga, the port and chief city of western Numidia (Takembrit, near Rachgoun in Algeria), in the hope of striking an alliance with Syphax, king of western Numidia's dominant people, the Masaesyli. Laelius had made a preparatory trip a little earlier and received a cordial reception. Syphax was able and ambitious. The Masaesyli had a long-standing enmity towards eastern Numidia's chief people, the Massyli, ruled by Masinissa's family. They had already fought a back-and-forth war, Syphax seizing some Massylian territory, Masinissa retaliating to drive him out of his own kingdom, Syphax regaining it after Masinissa was sent to Spain by the Massylian king to campaign with the Carthaginians there.

Because of Masinissa and his kinsmen's close links with Carthage, Syphax in turn had made friends with Scipio's father and uncle around 212. They had sent over a Roman centurion named Statorius for a time, to train his infantry fighters. The connection had obviously broken since then. Scipio was prepared to risk putting himself in the Numidian's power to revive it.

His voyage from New Carthage, maybe first coastwise to the gulf of Almería and then directly south for another 200 kilometres (125 mi.) across the Mediterranean, took perhaps two days of easy sailing. To Scipio's and Laelius' surprise, their two quinqueremes found seven others, from Gades, already anchored in the port. Hasdrubal, son of Gisco, had also arrived, to woo the very flattered Syphax. As guests of the king, the two generals treated each other graciously, even reclining together on the same couch for the banquet laid on by their host. Livy waxes lyrical over how Scipio's straightforward and affable personality charmed not only the barbarian monarch but the Carthaginian aristocrat. It was far from rare for leading Romans, and no doubt others (for instance merchants), to have contacts, even friendships, with Carthaginian equals. Hasdrubal need not have been the first of Scipio's, nor would he be the last.

Livy adds, almost offhandedly, that the proconsul then struck a treaty with Syphax before leaving on a more stressful return trip to New Carthage (contrary winds made it take four days). In spite of Scipio's affability, the 'treaty' cannot have gone much beyond expressions of mutual goodwill. Neither he nor Syphax sent each other military aid, Syphax did not become formally a friend or ally of the Roman people, and within a year or two Hasdrubal had won him for Carthage.[2]

Military and political conditions in southern Spain were still unsettled, especially south of the Baetis in the populous and prosperous regions between that river and the southern sierras. Livy soon mentions, casually and abruptly, that Roman soldiers were wandering through them, as well as camp-servants and traders. Some towns were already allied to Rome, or at any rate were pro-Roman – most likely swayed by

Lucius Scipio's campaign in eastern Baetica in 207, then by the aftermath of Ilipa. The wanderers were harassed by pro-Carthaginian, or simply opportunistic, centres like Astapa (in Roman times known as Ostippo; modern Estepa, 110 kilometres (70 mi.) east of Seville).

There were Roman scores to settle, too. Settling them revealed a more ruthless Scipio than Syphax's cheerful guest. The townsmen of Ilugo (Polybius calls it Ilurgeia), probably Santisteban del Puerto, 60 kilometres (36 mi.) northeast of Castulo, had once been friendly to Rome but in 211 had murdered survivors of the elder Scipios' disasters who were seeking refuge. Scipio and Laelius marched from New Carthage 300 kilometres (185 mi.) northwest to Ilugo (Livy implausibly claims they took only five days) and stormed it, against furious resistance from the doomed townsfolk. Scipio at one point had to threaten his wavering troops that he would climb the walls by himself. The steep hill that still dominates modern Santisteban, complete with medieval fortress, held out longest but was taken by Libyans, deserters from Carthage's service who had joined the Romans: a noteworthy reminder that every ancient army suffered its share of deserters (Hannibal's in Italy among them), and many were readily received into their opponents' ranks.

After Ilugo was in his hands, Scipio with deliberate indiscrimination had his troops slaughter everyone they met. Children did not escape. He then burned Ilugo to the ground. The atrocity was not an indulgence in personal revenge (neither of the elder Scipios had died there) but an amoral act of public policy. It was meant to teach Spaniards that Rome had a long memory both for good and, no less, for ill. It was also implicitly a message: Rome had not liquidated Carthaginian rule in Spain to leave the Spaniards to manage their own affairs. This policy would not become official for years yet. But some Spaniards, notably the Ilergetan princes Indibilis and Mandonius, were already suspecting that they were exchanging one set of foreign masters for another.[3]

Scipio took care to follow up the killings at Ilugo with generosity at Castulo. His subordinate L. Marcius had been sent to keep watch on the place until Scipio himself could arrive. Castulo had not murdered Roman soldiers in 211 but had changed sides. Now its leading citizen Cerdubelus could see there was no future in continuing to be pro-Carthaginian: when the proconsul arrived, Cerdubelus had the city gates opened. The

Carthaginian garrison and its commander Himilco were marched off into captivity.

Scipio returned to New Carthage and there held rites and ceremonies to fulfil his vows, undertaken probably in 210 as mentioned earlier, to honour his father and uncle. Gladiator contests fought by freeborn Spanish volunteers were included. Marcius, meanwhile, had been sent into western Baetica to make the cities and peoples there aware that Rome was now the hegemonic power. Astapa would not comply: the entire population voluntarily perished rather than face punishment – so Livy's firmly Roman version tells it – for their banditry. The rest of the region more sensibly accepted the new situation.

Livy has Marcius then return to New Carthage and be promptly sent out again with some troops towards Gades, while Laelius with seven ships sails for Gades too: this because deserters from there have come to Scipio offering to betray the city. The details of this new mission do not ring quite true, especially because Livy reports Marcius himself receiving the offer to betray Gades when encamped near that city later. In any case, the story makes him traverse southern Baetica twice: first from Astapa in the lower Baetis area to New Carthage, an approximately 550-kilometre (340 mi.) march; then from New Carthage back towards Gades (some 600 kilometres). These criss-crossings would have taken him two or more months, as he was marching with troops, and are hard to fit into what was left of 206 BC. Rather more likely, Livy doubles Marcius' movements across Baetica through misreading a source, or maybe in trying to combine two sources' varying versions. If so, then Marcius was still in western Baetica when Scipio sent couriers to him with the order to move on Gades. Marcius would also have been told that Laelius was on his way by sea. The reason was that Hannibal's brother Mago was gathering a small army at Gades for a last stand.

While waiting somewhere near that city for the plotters to act, Marcius – one of the ablest, yet least celebrated, junior commanders in the war – swiftly intercepted and annihilated Mago's lieutenant Hanno as that officer was gathering Spanish recruits. But the plot to betray Gades had itself been betrayed. The plotters must have been Carthaginian officers of rank, for instead of killing them, Mago put them on a ship bound for Carthage. Laelius damaged the squadron escorting it as the enemy sailed past his anchorage at Carteia (opposite Gibraltar), but he and Marcius then agreed it was time to return to Scipio, leaving Mago to be dealt with later.[4]

They found Scipio in crisis. He had fallen seriously, and for a while it seemed mortally, ill. Stress, climate, infection or even diet may have struck him down. The news spread fast through eastern Spain. The Ilergetan lords Indibilis and Mandonius, trusting in his death, struck out at other peoples in their region who were friendly to Rome. Worse, a mutiny erupted among Roman and Italian allied troops quartered at Sucro, a coastal town on the river Júcar, 58 Roman miles (65 kilometres/39 mi.) south of Saguntum and perhaps near modern Sueca in Valencia province.

When they had been sent to Sucro is not mentioned; Livy implies a long time before and says they numbered 8,000. It is very improbable, though, that Scipio could afford to leave the equivalent of two legions – nearly a third of his total Roman and Italian numbers – on garrison duty while he was still campaigning. They must have been sent after Ilipa, or even after the fall of Ilugo, and they probably were many fewer than 8,000.

These stationary troops, says Livy, had grown demoralized and missed having opportunities for plunder. But he lets them mention in a short speech that they also wanted to receive their overdue pay and go home. Unpaid arrears amid lengthy service were a constant complaint in ancient armies. Polybius in an excerpt stresses how aware Scipio was of the problem (Livy barely notes it), but he blames it on the Spanish allies for being irregular with money contributions – the first we hear of these. As it was normal for soldiers' pay to be sent from Rome, the explanation most charitable to Scipio would be that the costs of warfare over in Italy had choked off that income.

The soldiers' action was not really a mutiny but a strike. They did expel their military tribunes, and their leaders Albius and Atrius, one a Roman and the other an Italian, made the mistake of using *fasces* (the bundled rods and axes of elected Roman magistrates) to uphold their authority, outraging Scipio and later Livy. But they maintained discipline, Livy has to admit, and were ready to negotiate on their grievances. As soon as he recovered from illness, Scipio sent other tribunes to Sucro to promise the men fair treatment – once they came to New Carthage.

What followed showed him to be as much a master of double-dealing as were (in Romans' eyes) the Carthaginians. The Sucro men's fears were eased by hearing that the army at New Carthage would march out against the Ilergetes the day after they arrived. When they did, they received a convivial welcome. But during the night their 35 principals, including Albius and Atrius, were seized. Next day, all 35 were publicly flogged and then beheaded in the marketplace. Their comrades, surrounded by the rest of the army with weapons drawn, had to watch. But there were no other reprisals. Scipio knew the troops had genuine complaints. Mass punishments would lower his army's strength and could alienate other units that also had grievances but had stayed obedient. Instead, he gave the men a long and severe lecture, at any rate in both Polybius' and Livy's telling. The former mutineers were not only forgiven but, importantly, were paid their arrears. Scipio's reputation, like his health, was consolidated.[5]

The problem of Indibilis and Mandonius was quickly solved, though probably not as fast as Polybius and Livy claim. Supposedly, Scipio took only ten days to reach the Ebro, 470 kilometres (290 mi.) north of New Carthage. But even if this was slower than his claimed seven-day dash to that city in 209, it is just as hard to believe unless again some or all of the move was aboard ship. After that, a more believable four days then brought him in sight of the enemy somewhere north of the Ebro.

The Spaniards were encamped on a slope of a narrow valley we cannot identify. After winning a brisk skirmish between his *velites* and Indibilis' light troops, next morning Scipio defeated the Spanish army with an ingenious double manoeuvre: Laelius with the cavalry circling behind the nearby hills to strike their riders in the rear, Scipio himself attacking their foot soldiers. Most of the enemy army was destroyed, at a cost of 1,200 Roman and allied dead and over 3,000 wounded: sizeable losses (as Livy notes). But soon enough, Mandonius appeared – apparently that same day – to throw himself and his brother on the proconsul's mercy. Scipio no doubt knew that their promises of future loyalty and good behaviour were essentially worthless but, anxious now to settle affairs in Spain and return home to stand for the consulship of 205, he opted to give Mandonius a stiff lecture and inflicted no penalties, apart from exacting money to pay his troops.

He then raced south again, catching up with L. Marcius after sending him ahead. How long this latest journey took is not reported, but to Gades from the northeast was (and is) more than 1,000 kilometres (620 mi.). Even with a lightly equipped escort it would not have been less than three weeks, unless Scipio used his fleet and coasted down from Tarraco to Carteia or to the mouth of the Baetis. Near Gades he met messengers sent from the island city by Masinissa, agreed to a secret meeting and a few days later came face to face at last with the Numidian, a man only three or four years older than he was.

Livy rhapsodizes: how spellbound Masinissa was by the proconsul's majestic bearing, flowing hair and youthful vigour; how impressed Scipio was with the prince's leadership qualities. In reality, the meeting must have been restrained though cordial. Masinissa had been a major player in the destruction, only a few years before, of Scipio's father and uncle. He was also an enemy of Syphax, whom Scipio wanted to win over. Nor could he promise much – only that he would change sides once he got home. Scipio cautiously accepted him as a prospective, if yet uncertain, ally. Masinissa, it turned out, would find affairs at home too disrupted and dangerous for him to be useful as an ally for a long while, and only after nearly losing his life.

Gades declared for Rome when Mago sailed from there to raise soldiers in Africa. Failing in a pounce against New Carthage and finding himself then locked out of Gades – an insult he repaid by luring its chief magistrates out and crucifying them – he obeyed orders from Carthage to go to Italy with more troops. His mission's purpose was of course to help Hannibal. Paradoxically, Mago instead took sizeable forces to Liguria in northern Italy, fought a useless mini-war there for nearly three more years and finally perished of battle wounds in 203 when sailing home to Carthage, around the time his brother was recalled from Italy too. But already in 206, with the youngest Barcid's departure from Spain, the last embers of Carthage's once splendid Iberian empire flickered out. Everyone knew it was thanks to the leadership genius of Scipio.

After the colloquy with Masinissa, Scipio set out for Tarraco. It was perhaps on this march, on a plateau near the lower Baetis where the river turns southwards, that he founded a settlement for long-service veterans who wanted to stay in Spain. He named it Italica. Close to the then small riverside town of Hispalis (present-day Seville), Italica was to flourish spectacularly. One day it would be the family seat of two notable Roman emperors Trajan and Hadrian.[6]

Reaching Tarraco, Scipio gave Marcius and Silanus charge of Spanish affairs – two official replacements, for him and Silanus, were yet to arrive from Rome – and sailed for home. It was near the end of 206, or even early in 205. His squadron of ten ships bore him, Laelius and other officers, quantities of war booty and an appreciative embassy from restored Saguntum. Winter was not usually good for ships, but his journey was calm, and he knew that in the new year he would be consul.

6
Consul and Proconsul

Scipio met the Senate in the temple of Bellona, Rome's goddess of war, just outside the city wall and directly beneath the Capitoline Hill. Though an *imperium*-holder, he was not a magistrate in office, so could not cross the formal boundary of the city, the *pomerium*, before resigning his command. His report on five years of military command must have been electrifying even to well-informed senators – in Livy's summary,

> how many pitched battles he had fought, how many towns he had forcibly taken from the enemy, how many peoples he had brought under the sway of the Roman people. He had gone to Spain against four generals and four victorious armies [actually three each], and in those lands had left not one Carthaginian.

With Hannibal still in the field in southern Italy, Scipio was incontestably the man to win the war.

Scipio hinted that for his achievements he merited a triumph, the great parade through the city that was the apex of a general's career. But he did not push the case. It would have meant the Senate awarding a triumph to someone who had not held a higher magistracy, a novelty sure to trigger criticism – in fact extra criticism, for Scipio already had detractors. Instead, the conqueror of Carthaginian Spain entered Rome as a private citizen, to deliver huge quantities of booty in silver to the republic's treasury, the *aerarium*, to visit once more the Temple of Capitoline Jupiter and there to sacrifice no fewer than one hundred oxen as fulfilment of vows he had taken after quelling the Sucro mutiny. Now if not before, he was reunited with Aemilia and their boys, the first time they had seen him in five years.[1]

The consular and other elections for 205 were quickly held. The outcome for the consulships was predictable. Scipio and his old friend the *pontifex maximus* P. Crassus were elected by an unusually large assembly of voters agog to see Rome's new military hope. It was a foregone conclusion that when the new consuls' *provinciae* (areas of action) were decided, Crassus would have the war theatre in southern Italy. Hannibal was caged there, in Bruttium – now more a headache to Rome than a menace. As *pontifex maximus* Crassus could not go abroad, and the leader of any expedition overseas plainly had to be Scipio. Scipio wished to propose Africa as his *provincia*.

The plan alarmed very many of his fellow senators. A less bold and obviously much safer policy was to cooperate with Crassus in south Italy in a pincer strategy against the troublesome Hannibal. An extra worry was Mago, still at large with ships and soldiers – he had wintered in the Balearic island of Menorca – and very possibly aiming, many thought, to cross to south Italy. (We have seen that he did something else.) Scipio's clear intention to propose Africa led to a dramatic confrontation in the Senate at the end of March, when the new consuls opened debate about the state of the republic, the war and assigning *provinciae*.

Opponents of the invasion scheme were led by the aged but still spirited Q. Fabius Maximus. The speech that Livy gives him in the debate is in sophisticated Augustan-age rhetoric, but Livy had not only Polybius to draw on (we do not) but Roman contemporaries of the events like the soon-to-be historians Q. Fabius Pictor, who was probably present, and L. Cincius Alimentus, who may have been. Certainly the speech ably sets out the arguments that Fabius Maximus without doubt made.[2]

The Delayer, who as dictator and in three later consulships had faced and often frustrated Hannibal at the height of the war in Italy, viewed Scipio as too young, too self-confident and arrogant (and he may have had doubts about Crassus, equally young and with no military experience). He judged his own work unfinished – and endangered – if Rome did not concentrate efforts on the enemy at home. To launch an invasion of Africa would run a mortal risk, like Regulus' catastrophic foray fifty years before, during the previous war with Carthage; and disaster in Africa would re-empower Hannibal in Italy. Livy gives him a concluding barb that must sum up many others' attitude in early 205: 'I think that the armies have been raised for the protection of the City and Italy, not for consuls to take them over to any part of the world they choose with king-like arrogance.'

Scipio, of course, put his own case in reply. Livy's version is again a composition, but again can have drawn on earlier records. It certainly reflects the only arguments open to the new consul. He was fully confident of his ability to defeat both the Carthaginians in Africa and then Hannibal when he was forced to return there from Italy. To operate only in Italy meant dragging on the war. Crassus (who in fact would have their mutual friend Q. Metellus, now a proconsul, as his operational colleague in Bruttium) was fully able to contain Hannibal meanwhile. In effect, Scipio asked the Senate to trust him.

How little its majority trusted him was made clear soon enough. Senior senators – men who had fought Hannibal themselves as officers and magistrates – were angry over a report, quite possibly correct, that he meant to put the invasion proposal directly to the people, should the Senate refuse to authorize it. When another eminent ex-consul and veteran commander, Q. Fulvius Flaccus, asked him bluntly whether that was what he intended, Scipio concisely – and, for some, arrogantly – replied that he would do what was in the interest of the republic.

The discussion became so testy that the plebeian tribunes intervened, in effect to warn Scipio that they would not let him bypass the Senate. Scipio, properly chastened, asked for time to talk matters over with Crassus, and it may have been thanks to Crassus that a compromise was found. Next day the Senate met again, to assign not Africa but Sicily to Scipio – but with permission to cross to Africa 'if he judged it to be in the interests of the state'. Crassus received Bruttium, with Q. Metellus as his operational colleague (Metellus was already operating in the south).

Scipio thus got what he wanted, but it was at the cost of sharp ill-feeling from other powerful senators. After putting on a set of public games (so completing his Spanish vows) he had to levy fresh troops, as his veteran army in Spain had passed to the new proconsuls there. He was fully aware that he faced trouble from his peers.

Some forces were already available. Sicily, cleared of Carthaginians and restored to Roman control four years before, was held by two veteran legions: none other than the survivors of Cannae eleven years before – sent to Sicily, paradoxically, as moral punishment for surviving. Joining them in 212 and 210 were the survivors of two other southern victories of Hannibal's. The exact numbers are not recorded but – Romans, Latins and Italian *socii* together – must have come to 20,000 or more. These troops had borne the brunt of fighting in Sicily, climaxing in the great sack of Syracuse under Marcellus in 212 and then the consul Valerius Laevinus' destruction of Acragas two years later. The men had appealed to be allowed home, but the Senate was unrelenting. Now they would be the core of Scipio's expedition to Africa. But, after the wear and tear of a decade's campaigning, they were not enough for a venture as perilous as this.

Normally a consul at the outset of his command would levy two fresh legions of conscripts or volunteers, complemented by roughly equivalent units supplied by the *nomen Latinum* and the Italian *socii*. Ships, crews and naval equipment were drawn from coastal Italian *socii*. Crassus did not need to hold a levy because he would take over the army of another proconsul in south Italy, L. Veturius Philo (Metellus' fellow consul in 206), and cooperate with Metellus. Invading Africa, by contrast, required – as past experience showed – more than two legions.

Yet Scipio realized it was no good asking the Senate for authority to levy more. His critics' argument must have been that the state was too worn down by thirteen years of war in Italy, Spain, Sicily and Greece to afford a further drain on manpower. The point was flimsy. The republic had fewer legions in the field by 205 (twenty including the Cannae men) than in many previous years: as many as 23 in 207 and up to 25 in 212–211. Senators unwilling to vote Scipio more troops need not have been merely spiteful, all the same, but calculating. If he were limited to the Cannae legions in Sicily, he might well have to focus on south Italy after all, the theatre most critical in Fabius' and others' eyes.

The looming rebuff over levying troops contrasted with the Senate's ready vote to send substantial and costly offerings to the gods at Delphi, in Greece, from the plunder that Scipio had taken at Ilipa (a 90-kilogram (200 lb) gold crown and 450 kg (1,000 lb) of objects in silver). One of the two envoys chosen was his cousin M. Pomponius Matho, a concession perhaps, but it did not ease the problem of troops. Scipio solved the problem straightforwardly. He called for volunteers.

Seven thousand recruits responded from all over central and northern Italy. Many of these must have been men with military experience. He had also asked for voluntary naval contributions to build, equip and crew up to forty warships to escort the army's transports. Again the response was enthusiastic. Livy, very unusually, includes a catalogue of the goods that various communities, Roman and allied, across Etruria, Umbria and central Italy, offered. Though probably selective (and sometimes doubted), the details look acceptable: iron for making weapons, actual weapons, sails, timber, construction tools, corn, crews and marines. He adds that 45 days after the first trees were felled, a fleet of twenty quinqueremes and ten quadriremes was ready to sail. Only later did the consul find that, thanks to this speed, the new ships' timber was still too green. He had to beach them to dry out when he reached Sicily. Luckily, the province itself had thirty existing and well-seasoned warships for ready use.[3]

Sometime in early summer, Scipio sailed south with his new forces. As always, Laelius was with him. Other officers included L. Scipio once more; L. Baebius, a middle-ranking aristocrat; and Q. Pleminius, a man of unknown background (perhaps a family friend) whose inclusion Scipio would come to regret. His next tasks were integrating his volunteers with the veteran legions in the island and putting them all through the drill regimen he had developed in Spain. They would need to be highly trained if they were to face Hannibal on his home ground one day.

Careful as always about his own safety in battle, he also organized a special company of three hundred young volunteers. As Livy and others tell it, he summoned that number of young Sicilian aristocrats for cavalry service – to their (expected) dismay. When he offered to release them on condition they donated their fully equipped steeds and weapons and trained their replacements, they promptly agreed, and thus he outfitted his own volunteers cost-free. Livy assures the reader that this corps went on to serve splendidly in battle. If true (some do think it too neat to be true), it was a typically artful Scipionic stratagem.[4]

Where all this happened is not reported, but it was probably at Panormus (Palermo), one of the island's largest and most prosperous cities. The newly made ships were beached there, so it would have been convenient to billet the troops in the city and neighbouring towns and train them on the coastal plain and surrounding mountains. Grain was requisitioned from the province's communities, allowing Scipio to stockpile his own supplies for the invasion. Meanwhile, Laelius was given command of the thirty seasoned warships and sailed to raid Carthage's African coasts.

Scipio next travelled to Syracuse, Sicily's largest Greek city though currently not its wealthiest – it had been ruthlessly sacked by the unforgiving Marcellus only seven years before. Still, it was recovering enough energy to offer amenities and culture that the consul appreciated. He had to concern himself too with problems of governance, as Sicily – especially the communities that had sided with Carthage, like Syracuse – continued troubled even after the warfare ended. He earned plaudits by deciding for some Syracusan landowners in a bitter dispute with newcomers from Italy, who had seized their properties in 211 and ignored a Senate order to return them. Scipio set matters right, 'feeling his first priority was to safeguard the integrity of the state', as Livy puts it. No doubt he made sure that his attitude was widely known. Livy adds that it made all the Sicilians even keener to help his military preparations. No less keen, surely, because the sooner the expedition left for Africa, the easier the burdens on them.

Laelius' raid around the northern port of Hippo Regius (Annaba, Algeria) lasted several days and struck panic into the Carthaginians at home. This was partly due to the large quantity of plunder his men amassed, partly too because at first the Carthaginians believed that Scipio was in command and the invasion had begun. They had known it would happen, once they learned of him arriving in Sicily. Astonishingly, all the same – if Livy can be trusted – it was only after the raid that they began serious preparations to fight on home soil: raising an army, sending appeals to Syphax and supposedly offering the king of Macedon (who at that moment was ending his own war with Rome) lavish funds to invade Sicily or Italy.

Livy must overdramatize the facts, for soon he reports the Carthaginians sending off warships, money, nearly 7,000 further soldiers and even seven elephants to Mago in Liguria, hoping somehow to keep Scipio busy. When he did at last cross to Libya the following year, organized Carthaginian military forces were conspicuous by their absence. Laelius' raid showed him how vulnerable Carthaginian Africa was to a determined invader. And he may well have felt further reassured once he learned that the general in command at home was none other than Hasdrubal, son of Gisco.

Laelius brought back not only plunder but news of Masinissa. The Numidian prince had come to see him just as the raid was ending and urged some pertinent points: Scipio was acting too slowly, the Carthaginians were demoralized, Syphax was busy at home and in any case could not be trusted – but Masinissa promised to bring vigorous help (even though he was currently exiled from his kingdom). The invasion should be speeded up.[5]

These urgings made sense. Delay gave the enemy valuable extra time. Scipio's troops, says Livy drily, were so excited at the likely plunder from Africa that they were eager to sail. They were fully trained, it was summertime, fleet and armaments were ready. Selling the plunder would add to Scipio's war chest. Provincials and Romans alike expected action. But then, in Livy's words, the 'major scheme was put on hold by a lesser one'. Scipio let himself be distracted – ironically, by Hannibal.

The Greek city of Locri, on the toe of the Italian peninsula facing Greece, had gone over to Carthage after Cannae and was garrisoned by a body of Hannibal's troops. Pro-Roman Locrians were living in exile at Rhegium by the Sicilian straits, 100-odd kilometres (60 mi.) to the west. Now some city Locrians, including craftsmen employed by the Carthaginians, were captured outside the city by Roman patrols and taken across the mountains to Rhegium. They told the Locrians exiled there that they had the trust of the garrison and, if ransomed and sent home, could betray the city. As soon as the ransom was arranged – the captives must have been valuable to their home town – the exiles sailed from Rhegium to Syracuse to alert Scipio.

Locri was an important coastal centre, perhaps Hannibal's best remaining port for contact with Carthage. In 215, the only reinforcements he ever received from home had landed there. Scipio thought it too important to pass by. Rhegium had a Roman garrison, so he sent two of his military tribunes, M. Sergius and P. Matienus, to take 3,000 men from there and advance on Locri. He also wrote to his subordinate Pleminius to command the enterprise. Pleminius was probably at Messana, opposite Rhegium, keeping watch on the straits, and took some of its garrison with him.

The thrust at Locri had a half-success: the main citadel was seized, the Carthaginian troops retreated to a secondary one on the other side of the city and the townsfolk declared for Rome. But the Carthaginian commander, another Hamilcar, sent word to Hannibal for help. Pleminius sent the same appeal to Scipio. Both generals acted quickly. Hannibal was positioned further north, near Croton and Cape Lacinium (Capo Colonna), where he had just set up an inscriptional memoir of his campaigns to date. His army was suffering from sickness, perhaps the common military problem of dysentery, but he marched nonetheless. It was 170 kilometres (105 mi.) to Locri, a four-day march via the coast.

Scipio in turn moved up to Messana. He deputized his brother Lucius to look after Sicily while he crossed to Italy with a small squadron and troops. He was still at sea when Hannibal's forces encamped by a river called the Bulotus, near Locri (probably now the Torbido, about 10 kilometres (6 mi.) to the north), and sent Hamilcar orders to assail Pleminius' citadel next morning, so that Hannibal could take the Romans by surprise on its other side.

There followed – in Livy's telling – one setback after another for him. Hamilcar obediently began his attack inside Locri before dawn. But when Hannibal arrived outside, he realized that he had not brought along scaling ladders and so could not climb the walls. Instead, he arrayed his army nearby (on the flat coastland, maybe) – to intimidate the Romans, says Livy – and rode up to the walls to see how things stood. Then a missile shot by a catapult from the citadel brought down one of his Numidian guards. He promptly pulled the entire army back, to encamp out of range and have his men construct ladders. In the city, Hamilcar stopped his own attack. If this account is accurate, Hannibal was certainly out of normal form (perhaps unwell, like so many of his troops).

Around mid-afternoon, Scipio's fleet arrived. Livy specifies that his entire force (size unstated) was able to disembark and enter the captured citadel before sunset. Hannibal, surely not too far off, did nothing to block them, still less try an attack. Perhaps his campsite lacked a view of the arrival and could not hear the sounds; perhaps his troops were suffering badly from their ailment. Hamilcar noticed nothing either, so could not alert his general. Instead the double Carthaginian attack on the citadel (and now Hannibal had ladders) again waited for dawn.

Scipio's answer was to open the gate and charge out before the attack could be made. Taken aback, Livy writes, and losing a couple of hundred troops, Hannibal called off his men, sent a message to Hamilcar's force to see to their own safety and after nightfall marched away, with Hamilcar and his troops scrambling after him after firing their own citadel.[6]

Scipio had won a small but handy victory – his first – over the Carthaginian who for thirteen years had terrorized Rome. Livy, alert to its symbolism, tells the episode in detail and adds dramatic daubs: Hannibal frightened by his near-miss from a missile, then deterred on realizing that Scipio was present. Exaggeration, perhaps, but clearly enough the Carthaginian had botched an opportunity to harm, capture or even kill the general most able to win the war for Rome. As for Scipio, he had knowingly risked that Hannibal would not attack the citadel directly but try to blockade it and trap him inside.

The consequences for the hapless Locrians were harsher than Scipio intended. Of course he put their pro-Carthaginian leaders to death, brought home the exiles and told the chastened townspeople that they would have to answer to the Senate for defecting from Rome in 215. But then he left Pleminius in charge and sailed back to Messana with the reinforcements he had brought. The troops now at Locri were partly the ones who had come over with Pleminius and partly the others brought by the tribunes Sergius and Matienus. These were well disciplined. Not so Pleminius' men, who quickly turned to violence, rape and looting in the occupied city. When the tribunes tried to stop them, Pleminius' soldiers and their own fell to blows. The infuriated commandant then had Sergius and Matienus brutally flogged – only to be set upon by the tribunes' equally infuriated troops, who thrashed him and his attendants, then mutilated his nose and ears.

Scipio was still at Messana. He sailed back to Locri, saw what had happened and not only exonerated the badly injured Pleminius but had Sergius and Matienus imprisoned, giving orders to send them to Rome. He then left for Syracuse. Pleminius, humiliated, 'insensate with rage' (in

Livy's words) and no doubt with pain too, at once had the two tribunes savagely tortured to death in public and their corpses flung out to rot. His and his men's criminal treatment of the Locrians redoubled, even to the point of pillaging their universally revered temple of Proserpine.[7]

Scipio ignored it all. So did his colleague Crassus in northern Bruttium, though Crassus at least had the excuse that the Roman forces there, along with Hannibal's, were being racked by disease. The two consuls were expecting, correctly, that they would be continued in their *provinciae* for the coming year as proconsuls. The elections for 204, supervised by Q. Metellus (recalled from the south and made dictator for the purpose), produced another Cornelius, a Cethegus, as patrician consul, and as one of the praetors Scipio's cousin M. Pomponius Matho, who was then appointed to govern Sicily. Possibly less agreeably, one new quaestor was M. Porcius Cato: thirty years old, attached to Fabius Maximus and already firmly traditionalist – which meant critical and even suspicious of foreign (especially Greek) tastes and those attracted to them. He became the quaestor assigned for 204 to none other than proconsul Scipio.

At the same time, Scipio faced fresh controversy. Spokesmen for the desperate Locrians travelled to Rome to complain to the Senate about their mistreatment and his indifference. Uproar followed.

Livy describes it maybe too imaginatively, but the crucial points must be correct. Again Fabius Maximus took the lead. He called for Pleminius to be brought in chains to Rome for trial and a different garrison to be sent to Locri. He denounced Scipio's manners and morals and declared him a virtual tyrant (he may have known that Scipio admired Syracuse's ruthless tyrant king of a century before, Agathocles). A litany of accusations was unleashed: leaving his province without being authorized, letting his legions' discipline degenerate in Sicily, opting to wear a Greek cloak and sandals and to loaf about in the gymnasium and wrestling yard – and read books – instead of focusing on the war. Likewise all his officers. Fabius wanted him recalled and relieved of command.

Livy comments that some of the complaints were true (he does not say which). Fabius' demands were loudly supported in the Senate. Fortunately for Scipio, his friend Q. Metellus was at the time in Rome; he persuaded the Senate to a more temperate – and more disingenuous

– decision. Matho the praetor would take a commission of ten senators, plus two plebeian tribunes and an aedile, to question the proconsul in Sicily or, if he had already sailed, in Africa; and, if he were found to be responsible for the atrocities at Locri, to bring him back. If not, not.

With cousin Matho in charge of the commission, and with Africa soon to be invaded, the outcome was foreseeable. To start with, Pleminius was arrested along with 32 accomplices. Where, and who ordered the arrests, was varyingly told in Livy's sources. Not necessarily on Scipio's orders, therefore. As he was no longer in Italy, more likely Matho and his commission authorized it. At Locri they made, or anyway promised, full restitution to the citizens – who in turn were careful to stress that they were certain Scipio had had nothing to do with the outrages. He was a man (they conceded, diplomatically and truthfully) 'whom they would rather have as a friend than a foe'. This feeling Matho and his commissioners plainly shared. Mightily relieved, says Livy, they sailed on to Syracuse and Scipio.

He was ready for them. His army in battle array executed manoeuvres, his fleet in the Great Harbour performed a model sea fight, his arsenals and depots packed with munitions were opened for display. The visitors (we are told) had nothing but awestruck praise for everything they saw and hastened back to Rome to say so. Fabius was – temporarily – silenced.[8]

Meanwhile, Scipio found that envoys from his old dinner host Syphax had come to Syracuse. The king had by now made himself master of eastern Numidia, seizing the kingdom of the Massyli just after Masinissa had taken it over from his own usurping kinsmen (one of them, incidentally, married to a niece of Hannibal). Masinissa was reduced to holding out in the mountains between the city of Cirta (Constantine) and Hippo Regius, which explains how he could ride to the coast to meet the raiding Laelius.

Whether or not Syphax knew of his rival's contacts with Scipio, he let himself be persuaded by Hasdrubal, son of Gisco, to choose Carthage instead of Rome. The much defeated but resilient Hasdrubal was now Carthage's chief general in Africa and, in practice, the city's home leader. As well as a persuasive tongue, he had an extra attraction to offer the king: marriage to his daughter, the beautiful, cultured and today still famous

Sophoniba (Saponbaal in Punic). Polybius himself insists that she was the decisive factor in bringing Syphax into the Carthaginian fold. The king's envoys now advised Scipio to give up his invasion plans, his hoped-for ally having joined the Carthaginian alliance. To avoid making him their enemy too, the king helpfully suggested, Rome should carry on the war as before – outside Africa.

Of course, Scipio was not minded to listen. He gave Syphax's envoys a letter calling on him to respect the two men's ties of hospitality and the friendship Syphax as king had with Rome. Then he turned their obvious presence in Syracuse into a plus. They had come, he falsely informed the troops at a parade, to add Syphax's voice to Masinissa's, to urge a prompt start to the invasion, and he would comply. The fleet and army were ordered to assemble at Lilybaeum, the fortress port on Sicily's west coast (today Marsala). He also summoned Matho to meet him at Lilybaeum to finalize preparations. Rome's second invasion of Africa was about to start.

7

Scipio in Africa: Utica and the Great Plains

Livy could not be sure how large Scipio's army for Africa was. His sources, he wrote, ranged unsatisfyingly from 10,000 foot and 2,200 horse to well over 32,000. Another of them, Coelius Antipater, was so sceptical of all estimates that he refused any of his own. Still, Livy himself reports Scipio winnowing the Cannae legions of unfit personnel and replacing these with his 7,000 volunteer recruits, to create two extra-large legions of 6,200 infantry, each with a regular 300-strong cavalry complement. With these came the Latin and Italian allied forces in Sicily (likewise pruned, presumably). Italian allies usually matched or outdid their Roman counterparts in strength: if so now, Scipio should have had around 25,000 infantry and 2,000–2,400 cavalry. The forty warships had their own marines, a few thousand more. This was no great armament for invading Africa, especially as Scipio had lost any support from Syphax. He would have to rely on whatever the exiled Masinissa could bring in. But if he had misgivings, he kept them from everyone, except maybe Laelius.

Laelius was not Scipio's only thoroughly experienced officer. Another was of course L. Scipio, and so too L. Veturius Philo, who had been consul the year before Scipio. M. Cato the quaestor was another: abrasive, but vigorous. The expedition was due to leave in midsummer. Scipio took pains to make sure everything was in perfect order, ready for sailing from Lilybaeum. Livy, alive to its significance – it was the first step in Rome's march to continental empire – describes the preparations in detail.

The army would sail in four hundred transports, each with rations and water for 45 days (including fifteen days' worth of cooked food). Forty warships escorted the transports, Scipio and his brother leading twenty on the right flank, Laelius and Cato the other twenty on its left. Scipio thought it necessary, via two spokesmen per transport, to warn the soldiers to maintain silence aboard ship and not get in the sailors' way. At night, warships were to show a single light, transports two and either flagship three.

At dawn on the day for departure, in a rite important to the proconsul, to the other participants and to the huge crowd of spectators around the port – Lilybaeum's townspeople, delegations from towns all over Sicily and the soldiers remaining with Matho in Sicily – Scipio from the deck of his flagship prayed to the gods and goddesses of the seas and lands to favour the enterprise. The elaborate prayer in Livy's narrative, though certainly his own composition, must reflect Scipio's gist: that the gods should favour the enterprise, bring the army home safe – and laden with booty – and allow him to punish the Carthaginians for the harm they had inflicted on Rome. This was a predictable formula for a Roman general starting out on campaign. Scipio then solemnly cast into the sea the raw innards of a sacrificed animal as an offering and ordered a trumpeter to give the signal to sail.[1]

The landfall he had decided on was Emporia, the very prosperous coastal region along the east coast of ancient Libya, from below the Cape Bon peninsula down to the Gulf of Sirte. Today this is the east coast of Tunisia, where these towns or their successors (many of them holiday resorts) still stand. Several Phoenician- or Carthaginian-founded towns stood there, notably Neapolis (now Nabeul), Hadrumetum (Sousse), Leptis (Lamta) and Thapsus (Ras Dimass), but none big enough to pose a threat to an invading force. From Hadrumetum it was four or five days' march northwest to Carthage, from Neapolis and its neighbourhood half that. Communicating with eastern Numidia, Masinissa's country, would be via territory mostly cultivated and also far enough from Carthage to lessen the risk of interception. Scipio may not have known that Masinissa, after regaining the Massylian kingdom, had just been expelled again by Syphax – or perhaps did know that, to escape his rival's vengeful attentions, the fugitive king had moved to areas inland from the Gulf of Gabès.

Seas in a Mediterranean summer were not always benign. Squalls, storms and winds could blow sailing fleets in unwanted directions. Twelve years before, a Carthaginian fleet dispatched to help anti-Roman rebels in Sardinia was carried off by hostile winds to the Balearic Islands, and by the time it did reach Sardinia the rebellion had been quashed. Scipio's armada found it could not make his intended landfall either. Over the three-day journey dense fog came down, lifted and came back, while the friendly wind dropped overnight to return at dawn and then dropped again the following night. In the fog the hundreds of ships came repeatedly into peril of colliding. The African coast and Cape Bon were sighted, but, with only sun and stars as guides – and these blanketed much of the time by fog – sailing southward proved impossible. One of Livy's predecessors, perhaps the excitable Coelius, told a lurid story of violent storms almost sinking the fleet and finally forcing the men to abandon their flooded ships and scramble ashore in rowboats. This would have reduced the invasion to a shambles, and Livy rightly disbelieves it.[2]

That Emporia was not in fact Scipio's destination, only a piece of disinformation directed at the enemy while he aimed all along for Utica's

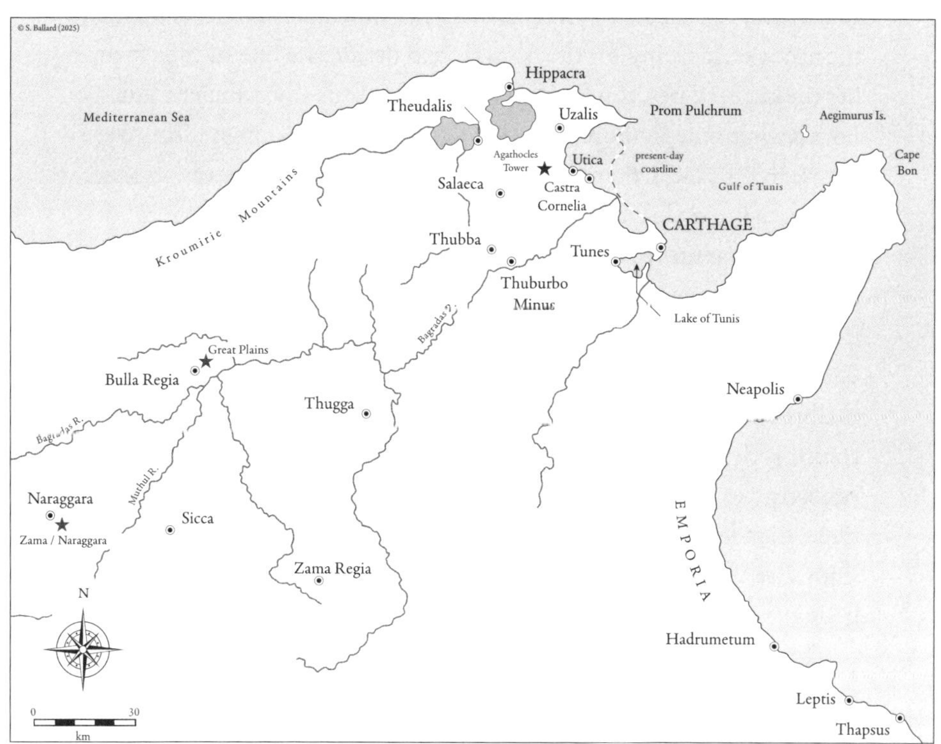

The North African campaign, 204–201 BC.

neighbourhood, is often held. But the northern districts of Emporia, around Neapolis and Hadrumetum, were within less than a week's march from Carthage, virtually bereft of protective forces, populous and fertile (as Livy stresses). Sicily was within a few days' sail – if the weather did not play up there as elsewhere.

Landfall near Utica, more or less in sight of Carthage and within easy reach of Punic naval attack, was much more risky – or would have been, had the Carthaginians' defence been fit for purpose. Noteworthily too, once he did land there Scipio did not move against Utica for weeks, even after Masinissa joined him. Instead he spent the time raiding and looting the countryside between Cape Farina and, to the northwest, Hippacra. It looks as though he had to rethink his plans.

In any case, he must have suffered seriously anxious moments before his fleet emerged from fresh fog as the third day dawned. It found itself close to the long and narrow headland of Cape Farina, a day's sail north of Carthage. The headland's name for Romans was Promunturium Pulchrum, Fair Cape. Scipio seized on the good omen and disembarked the army, encamping on the coastal strip beside the line of hills forming the cape. (The shoreline has moved outwards since ancient times.) For the first time in more than half a century, large Roman forces were ashore in Libya. Carthage lay only 60 kilometres (37 mi.) away, its sister city Utica just 27 kilometres (17 mi.).

There was no opposition. In spite of coastal lookouts, the alarm from Laelius' earlier raid and the Carthaginians' supposed reaction, and likely informants like Syphax, the home authorities led by Hasdrubal, son of Gisco, had done almost nothing to ready Libya militarily. This was virtually criminal neglect. Hasdrubal was not even at Carthage but in the countryside, trying to collect recruits for an army and sailors for the navy. Appian gives him 6,600 horse and foot, a plausible but surprisingly small force, then less plausibly has him purchase 5,000 slaves to crew the warships. Events were already showing that his generalship at home was no better than it had been in Spain.

The only other military forces available were in Carthage itself, and not many even there. Worse, if Livy is right, these were hasty levies. The Romans had time to disembark, set up camp and unload their equipment, while crowds of panic-stricken refugees even more desperate than during Laelius' raid rolled across the green and populous landscape of coastal Libya. Carthage itself was put on high alert, the authorities fearing that Scipio might strike at the city directly. All they could do at the moment was to send out a small cavalry force under a young aristocrat named Hanno, to reconnoitre and (optimistically) harass the enemy. At the same time, Hasdrubal sent off urgent messages to his new son-in-law Syphax, imploring troops. But serious resistance needed time. Hasdrubal must have wondered whether Scipio would grant it.

In effect, Scipio did. Although young Hanno's small cavalry troop was easily routed, with him among the dead, the Romans did not march on Carthage or even its small neighbour Tunes, where Tunis the modern city stands. Scipio sent his warships down the coast to blockade Utica, then devoted time to the congenial Roman activity of plundering and ravaging. A satisfying benefit was the capture of 'quite a prosperous town', unnamed – a subject Libyan one, according to Livy, so perhaps Uzalis (El Alia), notable probably then as now for its fine olive groves. Soon the proconsul collected no fewer than 8,000 locals, both free Libyans and slaves, to be sent off with other booty to Sicily.[3]

At this point, Masinissa arrived. He had only a couple of hundred riders with him (Livy rightly discounts other claims – Coelius again? – of up to 2,000), but these were more than the mere two who had helped him escape the clutches of Syphax's son Vermina some months before. Livy claims that the Romans were overjoyed to have him with them. This is surely historian's hindsight. Not only had Masinissa been accessory to the deaths of the elder Scipio generals seven years before, but two hundred cavalrymen were small support against the thousands that Syphax was gathering. More Massylian cavalry did perhaps come in over the next few days or weeks (to judge from his exploits in the next battle). At home – so he no doubt assured Scipio – support for him was building. If Scipio had misgivings, he did not show them.[4]

Yet Scipio's overall strategy was open to question. When readying the invasion he may have planned on military aid from Syphax, now master of nearly all Numidia, or at least his neutrality, which would have left only Hasdrubal to be dealt with. But Hasdrubal had adroitly turned the tables. Scipio then lost any advantage of surprise by not moving fast against

Carthage – in contrast to Agathocles a century earlier, who did. His aim from the start, it is usually argued, was to make Utica his base for further operations. In fact, he did not move against even Utica for several weeks. Instead the army spent its time – aside from routing feeble enemy feints – ransacking the fertile countryside inland from Cape Farina, dragging off loot and locals for transport to Sicily and destroying what could not be taken. They also looked for Roman and Italian war captives working the fields to free them. But rescuing these and ravaging broad swathes of northern Libya were hardly the purpose of bringing an army and fleet to Carthage's heartland.

Scipio may now have reckoned or at any rate hoped that the enemy would be so alarmed at his coming that Hasdrubal would march against him with hastily levied and readily defeatable forces, while Syphax at least stayed neutral or hesitated. Carthage could then be besieged and forced to seek terms before Hannibal could return from Italy (where the commanders were under orders to keep him in place). By contrast, lengthier and more roundabout operations heightened the risks seriously. The invaders were dangerously exposed on both sea and land. As noted earlier, numbers were not massive – even if some more Massylian cavalry followed Masinissa's arrival – and the fleet stood at an open anchorage with the Carthaginian navy barely a day's sail away. Hasdrubal and Syphax were busily organizing armies inland. Communications with Sicily were vulnerable to any vigorous Carthaginian naval strike.

Scipio nonetheless had several advantages. He was totally self-confident, and he was facing not Hannibal but Hasdrubal, son of Gisco. Syphax, despite his new alliance, was anxious to broker peace rather than commit fully to war. As for the enemy navy in its well-stocked harbourage, it showed no interest in the invaders for the next twelve months. On all the evidence, it was far from seaworthy when the Romans landed at Cape Farina; the first we hear of actual preparations to attack them by sea comes only during the following winter – after months of enemy operations in Carthaginian Africa.

Scipio now heightened the pressure, moving south from Cape Farina to encamp one Roman mile, about 1.5 kilometres, from Utica. The camp was probably on a narrow northern sector of a ridge now named Jebel Menzel Roul, in those days a seaward projection of northern Libya's uplands. (It now lies some distance inland.) On the same ridge, at the water's edge, stood Utica itself.

Some weeks must have passed since the landing, but it was still summer. So much grain had been gathered in that available granaries were full. A new officer, Hanno, son of Hamilcar (not a Barcid), had been appointed at Carthage to local command, no doubt with Hasdrubal's approval, and the latter's recruitment efforts had produced a cavalry army of 4,000. Two hundred riders were young Carthaginian aristocrats, handsomely equipped and keen to strike their first blow against Rome. Most of the rest were Numidians, perhaps a mix of mercenaries and of riders sent by Syphax.

Livy felt sure that this corps, its commander and the battle it soon fought were different from the earlier Hanno's fatal skirmish. For some of his sources, and likewise Appian and many moderns, only Hanno, son of Hamilcar, was genuine. But it would make sense – even for the insouciant Carthaginians – to have sent out a reconnaissance force, the earlier Hanno's, as early as possible. Its destruction, and Scipio closing in on Utica, called for a stronger body to do the same. Commander-in-chief Hasdrubal was still absent, building up his army amid messages of mounting desperation from the home authorities. The sizeable new cavalry corps might at least inhibit the rampaging Romans.

But the second Hanno's effort was as undermanned for its task as his predecessor's. He himself quickly realized this. Instead of reconnoitring he rode to Salaeca, a town 15 Roman miles from Utica, and installed his cavalry there, horses and all. Where Salaeca stood is unknown, but at or near the modern village Ain Ghellal looks a good possibility, 19 kilometres (12 mi.) west of Utica's site across the fertile countryside. Scipio was disdainful at the news: 'Cavalry housed in summertime? Let there be even more of them so long as they have a leader like that.'

Before dawn next morning he had Masinissa lead his Numidians over to Salaeca to taunt the enemy out, while Scipio after a careful pause drew the Roman cavalry from camp, to wait hidden from view behind the Menzel Roul ridge, about 6 kilometres (just under 4 mi.; 30 Greek *stadia*) west of Utica. He probably took position close to where the ridge slopes down and the larger Jebel Douimis rises. A tower there, according to Appian built by Agathocles, may or may not be a small (and today perhaps extinct) ruin standing on the narrow ground between the two ridges.

At dawn, Masinissa duly enticed the surprised enemy out of Salaeca, then carried out a fighting retreat for two or three hours over a dozen kilometres. This suggests he now had more than his original two hundred riders, who would have been overwhelmed by twenty times their number. Once he and his pursuers passed Agathocles' tower, Scipio sounded the charge from behind Jebel Menzel Roul. Caught on all sides – Masinissa turned and struck them head-on, the Romans in flank and rear – Hanno's men died with their commander, or became prisoners, or fled. Hanno's two hundred fellow aristocrats were killed or captured. Scipio took care to lavish praise and gifts on the victorious troops, and especially on Masinissa himself now that the Numidian exile had proved his reliability.[5]

The proconsul felt secure enough to march through the countryside inland from Utica, capturing (and, naturally, looting) Salaeca and other places and over seven days 'spreading the terror of war far and wide', as Livy puts it, before returning to the coast. Appian's fanciful tale of how Hasdrubal without Syphax ambushed Scipio and Masinissa, only to be roundly defeated and lose most of his men (some falling off a cliff), can safely be judged a Coelian or similar concoction – if not one by Laelius or Scipio himself after the war. The expedition's transport ships, bringing new supplies from Sicily on the same day that he and Masinissa had dealt with the second Hanno, soon took on a fresh haul of captives and booty for the return trip. There was still no sign of Hasdrubal, nor did Carthage's magistrates and senate venture to send out a third observation force. Instead, and at last, they started work on refurbishing the Carthaginian fleet.

Scipio decided to close in on Utica. As Livy tells it, this was when he decided to make it his base of operations. He likely reckoned that if Hasdrubal and Syphax came on the scene with forces too strong for him to confront, and if the Carthaginian navy finally joined in, Utica would form a secure stronghold over the winter. (And at worst it would be an evacuation point more defensible than an open beach.) So he blockaded its small harbour with his warships, encamped the army just outside the city's walls and brought up siege engines – some manufactured in camp by artisans brought with him – for assaults.

The assaults were repeated by land and sea over forty days, but they failed each time. Appian, this time credibly, insists that the defenders inflicted plenty of damage on both the siege machines and the warships. By the end of the forty days it was probably mid-autumn, with cooler days, nights becoming chilly and the sea dangerous. Worse still, Hasdrubal and Syphax were at last approaching. Scipio called off the attacks.[6]

He knew that his current encampment by the city, on a low spur of Jebel Menzel Roul, vulnerable on every side, would not be safe. He transferred his forces instead to the neck of what was then a narrow headland about 3 kilometres (nearly 2 mi.) to Utica's east, a site afterwards called Castra Cornelia (today Qa'lat al-Andaluus, an inland ridge and town looking seaward over green fields). The fleet was beached alongside, the crews lodging in the ships or, rather likelier, under canvas alongside. There the Romans awaited the enemy.

Anticlimax followed. Hasdrubal and Syphax set themselves up 10–12 kilometres (as much as 7½ mi.) south of Castra Cornelia on a pair of low hills – Hasdrubal's nearer than Syphax's to Castra Cornelia – just south and west of the small modern town of Protville. The river Bagradas (Medjerda) did not flow through the district as it now does, but further south. There the two armies stayed, neither attacking the Roman encampment nor facing attack by Scipio. In fact both Polybius and Livy afterwards mention a truce existing, though not when it was made or what its conditions were.[7]

Polybius, and then Livy echoing him, give Hasdrubal 30,000 foot and 3,000 horse. That or near that would be a plausible total, since some months earlier he reportedly had 13,000 and had been busy since then recruiting more. He even (we learn later) had fourteen war elephants. But Syphax's supposed 50,000 foot and 10,000 riders are unbelievable and should be shaved to maybe a third of those numbers. A total enemy strength of about 45,000 infantry and 8,000 or 9,000 cavalry would better fit Livy's figures – probably from Polybius, whose figures are lost – for casualties later on. Scipio, having left a garrison in Salaeca, perhaps also in Uzalis, was much outnumbered even if he faced a more economically estimated 54,000. His new position was more secure than the old, but if the enemy went on the offensive the Romans would still be at major risk.[8]

Why Hasdrubal continued inert we are not clearly told. He may still have felt insecure about Syphax – ally and son-in-law though Syphax now was. Scipio, according to Polybius, certainly thought he could detect signs that the king might yet change sides. He hoped that the infatuation with Sophoniba had faded (Africans being seen as quick into lust and equally quick out of it) and with it the king's interest in fighting for Carthage. A practical, maybe formal truce was made while Scipio and Syphax exchanged a number of messages, obviously with Hasdrubal's approval, about possible peace terms.

Syphax seems to have been genuine in offering talks, and Hasdrubal too. Syphax made it clear he would not dump either his wife or his allies, but urged peace on the basis of joint withdrawal, Hannibal from Italy, Scipio from Africa; each state would keep what it currently held elsewhere (in other words, Carthage would give up its Spanish territories). This implied but left unsaid that Hannibal's brother Mago would end his forlorn campaign in Liguria. In effect, Syphax and Hasdrubal wanted a compromise peace – though Syphax kept quiet about Masinissa's kingdom, for reasons not hard to guess. A peace based on his compromise would of course turn into another war sooner rather than later, a reality Hasdrubal no doubt understood even if his royal son-in-law did not. The Carthaginians may have reckoned it would be worthwhile if it gave them a few years to recover and, with Hannibal back home, a fair chance of victory next time.

Scipio was not genuine. He made no offers of terms himself but kept hinting that he might (or else might not) agree to Syphax's. He was playing for time, partly until he could be sure his proconsulship would be prolonged for at least another year and partly to push his irresolute opponents further off their guard while he probed their positions. His envoys to Syphax surely knew this, but they were excellent diplomats. On some or most occasions one was Laelius; L. Scipio and L. Baebius probably took part too, though Scipio may have varied the spokesmen he sent. (Cato the quaestor had already left, apparently sent to Sardinia to expedite supplies promised from there – and happy to leave Africa, as his opinion of both Scipios was lower than ever.[9])

When sailing conditions returned, Scipio received welcome fresh supplies from not only Sardinia but Sicily and even Spain: more grain to store in his granaries – he had to set up new ones, though Livy does not say where – plus 12,000 tunics and, perhaps for religious rites, 1,200 togas. Increasingly sure he would not be attacked at Castra Cornelia, he sent his spokesmen several times to Syphax attended by drably clad slaves, different ones each time. In reality they were veteran soldiers (half of Scipio's troops were Cannae survivors). One was Statorius, the senior centurion who years before had spent time with Syphax training his soldiers, and the military writer Frontinus tells of Laelius having to stop him from chatting with Numidian friends he recognized.

The spies strolled about Syphax's camp unhindered while their 'masters' negotiated with him. They studied every feature: the soldiers' huts, made of reeds and branches woven together (plainly it was a mild winter); the large number bivouacked outside the camp's defences; where its entrances and exits were; where and how often sentries were posted. They learned too that Hasdrubal's camp was not much better built, with local wood and branches. It was as easy, that is, to set on fire as Syphax's.

Not only the two enemy commanders but their experienced subordinates could, and should, have expected that the visiting 'attendants', even if real slaves, could pick up useful bits of information while ambling around. This seems not to have occurred to any of them. More than once, Laelius and his negotiating colleagues passed several days as guests among the Numidians, exploiting Syphax's insouciance. The charm that Scipio had worked on him and Hasdrubal in their meeting at Siga two years before may have been strong still.

Early in spring 203, Scipio learned from Rome that his command as proconsul had been extended by the Senate and people, and not just for a year but 'until the war in Africa should be completed'. Even though this would not stop one consul after another, in 203, 202 and even 201, from trying to take over his command to earn their own *gloria*, he could now be sure of full backing at home.

The next step was tricky. He must both show Hasdrubal and Syphax that he was ready for a new campaign and yet convince them that he really preferred peace. Late in March or early in April he sent 2,000 troops over to reoccupy the knoll outside Utica where the army had encamped for a time. With much ado (to draw his opponents' attention), he had his warships made ready and moved siege machines onto them. All this activity was pretence that he planned a fresh assault on Utica – a pretence so successful that his own troops believed it. The detachment's real task on the knoll was to deter the city garrison from making a sortie against his camp after he had taken the rest of the army from it.

Shortly after, he sent envoys once again to Syphax's camp. They told the king that the proconsul was at last ready to agree to his proposals, so long as the Carthaginians were equally ready. They added that they were under orders not to return to Scipio without a firm answer. Syphax, overjoyed, at once dispatched this message over to the Carthaginian camp. As before, no one was concerned to see the envoys' shabby servitors taking leisurely walks this way and that while their masters waited with the king. Syphax was still more elated when Hasdrubal's approval was brought to him. He confirmed the settlement on behalf of them both, and the Romans left to report to their general.

It was still morning. At Castra Cornelia, preparations for a very different response were under way. Scipio convened his war council to confirm his plan of attack. A second group of envoys was waiting at Castra Cornelia for the earlier group to return, and once these reappeared their replacements were sent off with a new, different and disconcerting statement for Syphax: Scipio did want to accept his terms, but his council opposed them. They did not say – it was left to the king and Hasdrubal to infer – that for Scipio the truce was now over.

This was chicanery. Even if some of his council did want to reject the peace terms (more likely none did), Scipio could have overruled them. Nor did his final spokesmen explicitly tell Syphax that the truce was over. Scipio left open the impression, even if a slight one, that he was open to more persuasion. Of course, he was not under an obligation to warn the enemy of imminent attack, but his handling of the talks and their denouement made some Romans uneasy later.

Livy reflects it. His account has Syphax and Hasdrubal confirming their wish for peace and Syphax sending a messenger to Scipio to say so – though Livy, like Polybius, records the Roman envoys to Syphax saying they could not depart without an answer. But the king adds 'certain unjust items' (unspecified) via his messenger, and these terms, says a relieved Livy, justified Scipio in wishing to end the truce. Even so (the historian continues), Scipio sent yet one more message to Syphax: he must break with the Carthaginians if he wished to keep out of the war. Of course there was no reply from the king.

There is no need to believe all this illogical fiction. It was plainly concocted later, an extra shield for Scipio against accusations of ill faith. His actual prevarication, about being the sole advocate at Castra Cornelia for peace, must have looked too weak to some.

At midday, Scipio assembled his most experienced military tribunes and told them what he planned. The troops should eat an early dinner and be ready to march; then, when the trumpets in the usual way sounded the hour for the camp's nightwatchmen to take up their stations, the legions were to march out, except the garrison to be left in camp. By nightfall all preparations were complete. At the end of the first watch of the night (around nine o'clock), Scipio set the troops in motion southward.

Syphax and Hasdrubal, oblivious, had spent the afternoon and evening discussing Scipio's volte-face and, necessarily, how best now to restart military operations and force battle on him. As Polybius implies, they took for granted that they held the initiative. They still had no observers out in the countryside, not even to monitor Scipio's supposed preparations against Utica. Security in both camps stood between lax and non-existent. When night came on, some of their soldiery opted for sleep, others for drinking and socializing.

Around three in the morning – towards the end of the third watch – Scipio halted within sight of the Carthaginian camp. Laelius with half the legionary troops and Masinissa with his Numidians were detached to move silently against Syphax's a few kilometres to the west. There Masinissa positioned his men outside its entrances; then Laelius' men moved in to set the perimeter huts on fire. In the dry conditions the blaze spread frighteningly fast. Syphax and his soldiers at first took it to be accidental, but could not put it out. Men who ran for the exits found themselves surrounded by fire – and, if they made it through, were cut down by attackers. Others were trapped inside the camp, some still in their huts, to be burned alive.

The appalling flames and uproar roused Hasdrubal's camp. Again he and his men supposed an accident had happened. Some set out across the fields to help, others came out to watch in fearful fascination. Scipio was waiting. His troops fell on the unarmed and bewildered men as they emerged, while other troops moved around the camp's edges, turning the flimsy structures into bonfires. Chaos and panic again spread fast. Soon burning, dying and dead animals and men piled up around and outside the exits and in the camp's narrow pathways.

Over maybe a couple of hours, the two armies that had threatened Scipio were almost completely annihilated. Dawn lit up a horror landscape: burned, slaughtered or dying men, horses and mules piled up amid the smoking wreckage of the two enemy camps. 'Of all the brilliant exploits performed by Scipio, this seems to me the most splendid and the most adventurous,' writes Polybius, directly after detailing the gruesome results of the attacks. Like many admirers of warrior-heroes, Polybius could narrate, without deploring, the pain and death that Scipio, Hannibal and others inflicted on their opponents.

Reportedly 40,000 Numidians and Carthaginians died. There were prisoners – 5,000 of them, including high-ranking Carthaginian officers and eleven senators. Even 2,700 Numidian horses and the half-dozen surviving elephants were rounded up. The victors captured too a vast quantity of weaponry along with, Livy itemizes, 174 'military standards' (all probably found in armoury shelters separate from the encampments). Scipio had no use for the weapons and burned them as a pious dedication to the god of fire, Vulcan, who had been so instrumental in his victory. It had cost him, if we can cautiously believe Appian, one hundred men killed.[10]

The few thousand Numidians and Carthaginians who had escaped their comrades' catastrophe were in desperate flight, most of them injured. Scipio launched an immediate pursuit. Hasdrubal took 2,500 foot and horse with him to a nearby town that Appian calls 'Anda' – a name unknown and most likely a mistake for Thuburbo Minus, today Tebourba by the river Medjerda, 35 kilometres (22 mi.) southwest of Utica. Syphax was nearby at Abba, as Polybius calls the place (Obba in Livy): possibly a Thubba identified at Chouigui, just north of Tebourba.[11]

The leaders refused to be cowed by their calamitous defeat. They gathered together what troops they could and were heartened by the arrival, at Abba, of a 4,000-strong body of hired Celtiberian warriors. These must have landed at Carthage from Spain a few days before but, luckily for them, had not reached the camps in time to be set on fire. Syphax received pressing pleas, too, from the magistrates at Carthage to stay loyal, pleas (say Polybius and Livy) redoubled by his wife, though this may be a fancy since bringing a wife on campaign would have been decidedly unusual.

The two defeated leaders did not spend a long time in the area. Scipio and Masinissa were in pursuit, so they moved further west. Wisely or unwisely, Scipio did not keep up the chase. He stopped to capture Hasdrubal's first refuge; it surrendered, and then he seized two others (Abba probably one), which he let his troops loot. After that, he marched back to Castra Cornelia to relaunch the siege – 'as though the war against Syphax and the Carthaginians had been finished', is Livy's surprising and perhaps surprised comment.

Scipio's insouciance prolonged everything. Had he pressed the pursuit, he would probably have made short work of the demoralized and outnumbered forces remaining to Hasdrubal and Syphax. That would have strengthened the voices for peace already making themselves heard at Carthage. Leaving Hasdrubal and Syphax the leisure, instead, to regroup and rearm recalls Scipio's similar lack of interest in exploiting his victory at Baecula with a relentless pursuit of Hasdrubal the Barcid, a misjudgement he did not make after Ilipa.

Appian tells a complicated story of Hasdrubal now being condemned to death by the authorities at Carthage – to be replaced as general by one Hanno, 'son of Bomilcar' – but refusing to yield and continuing with Syphax to recruit new troops, including slaves. Though sometimes believed, Appian undermines his own story by forgetting to mention the battle on the Great Plains that followed: he goes straight on to the later naval attack on Scipio's fleet and then the romantic episode of Masinissa and Sophoniba. His Hasdrubal stays active, on the sidelines, until well into the following year. A Hanno, son of Bomilcar, did exist – in fact he was a nephew of Hannibal's and had served under him in Italy – but if there is anything to the story, his appointment occurred later, as we shall see. Most of Appian's other reportage on Hasdrubal has to be disregarded.

Supposedly thirty days after they fled from the coast, Hasdrubal and Syphax, with 30,000 troops, took their stand near the middle Bagradas river, in a district called the Great Plains: a fertile countryside 150 to 200 kilometres (93–124 mi.) from Carthage, between today's Bou Salem and Jendouba. On a hillside just north of Jendouba, the imposing ruins of the Roman city of Bulla Regia still look out over the broad plains as its Libyan precursor did in Scipio's day. If organizing this new army had taken only a month, the two leaders had proved themselves remarkably effective – in recruitment and logistics at least. Polybius' thirty days may in reality refer to the period once they reached the Great Plains and there gathered recruits, arguably after retreating from Abba and 'Anda'.

Why they chose a position so far inland is not obvious. Scipio was harassing Utica again, and he could threaten Carthage itself unmolested. He might now (for all they knew) obtain extra forces from Sicily or Italy. None of these actions Hasdrubal and Syphax could obstruct. Perhaps their recent catastrophe made them fearful of approaching Castra Cornelia too soon, whereas several days' march inland would both be a buffer against surprise attack and allow time to build up fresh forces, especially as it was nearer to eastern Numidia. And then if Scipio could be drawn inland, and this time be beaten, it would annihilate the invasion; perhaps even convince Rome to accept a reasonable peace at last.

Scipio was still making no progress against Utica. He was perhaps only performing a gesture, hoping to entice back his opponents. But at the news that Hasdrubal and Syphax had a new army ready on the Great Plains, he left a garrison in camp and marched to find them. Even if Masinissa now had a sizeable force of enthusiastic Massyli, encouraged by his shared triumph at the camps, Roman and Numidian numbers can hardly have been larger than the enemy's and most likely were smaller. Scipio took his two legions, or at least one and some elements of the other (Polybius later writes 'legions', plural), and probably too most of his Latin and Italian troops and most of the cavalry – on estimate, about 20,000 men, leaving about 6,000 to 8,000 (including the warships' marines) to hold Castra Cornelia, Salaeca and any other captured towns, seconded of course by the plentiful ships' crews. Masinissa can scarcely have added more than 10,000 foot and horse; perhaps fewer.

Scipio was probably aware (from deserters at least) that the only troops both experienced and untraumatized whom he and Masinissa had to face were the just-arrived Celtiberians. Livy terms Hasdrubal's Carthaginians 'new soldiery', meaning raw recruits, and Syphax's Numidians 'rustics': a description not in Polybius' account but likely accurate enough. Scipio did not intend to give their training or morale time to improve. After another surprisingly – or exaggeratedly – speedy march of just five days, he and Masinissa came in sight of the enemy camp. They stopped on a hill 30 *stades* distant (about 5.5 kilometres or 3½ miles), then the next day moved down to pitch camp barely 7 *stades* from the opposition. Two more days passed, marked only by cavalry skirmishes. On the fourth day, both sides closed for combat.

Polybius and Livy treat the battle very succinctly; Appian and Cassius Dio completely ignore it. But Polybius' account (and so Livy's) is full of puzzles. Scipio's battle array, we read, took the regular Roman format: legionary infantry as his centre in their three lines – *hastati, principes, triarii* – with 'his Italian cavalry' as the right wing, Masinissa's Numidians as the left. These faced 'the Carthaginians' of the enemy's right wing and 'the Numidians' forming the left. Polybius' description necessarily implies a single legion facing the Celtiberians, and that the enemy wings were formed of horsemen only.

This order of battle cannot be complete: no sign of a second legion, Roman cavalry or Italian allied infantry, and no enemy infantry except the Spanish mercenaries. But one legion on its own would mean that only some 6,000 Roman infantry were present (Scipio's legions were extra-large), while Polybius' mention of only 'Italian cavalry' would leave all Scipio's Roman cavalry and allied infantry back at Castra Cornelia. All this would imply that the combined Roman and Numidian army was only 10,000–12,000 strong.

That is not the only implausible feature. If the only enemy infantry were the 4,000 Celtiberians, the rest of that army's 30,000 troops (or even if 20,000, as lower estimates claim) would have included 10,000 cavalry or more, plus unusually large swarms of light armed fighters. These disproportions would be hard to believe, especially as all but the Celtiberians were easily chased away when Scipio's and Masinissa's far fewer horsemen charged. The solution must be that, accidentally or by intent, Polybius and then Livy left out other contingents, in both armies. Scipio had both legions with him: so Polybius afterwards shows with a reference to 'the Roman legions'. He surely had most or all of the Latin and Italian infantry too. Thus he could deploy Roman *and* Italian infantry to face (we must infer) Carthaginian and Numidian infantry – not cavalry – on both flanks of the Spaniards. And as Polybius does record, one legion in its three lines faced the Celtiberian mercenaries, and in both armies cavalry formed the wings.

Once fighting began, the hostile cavalry were quickly disposed of. It looks as though the (inferred) Carthaginian and Numidian infantry standing beside the Celtiberians collapsed quickly too. In the centre, the men from Spain kept fighting even after the rest of their army dissolved. At first they had only the opposing legion's line of *hastati* to face. But once their flanks were exposed, Scipio had the second and third lines, *principes* and *triarii*, move outward and then forward to strike those flanks, a move reminiscent of his manoeuvre at Ilipa.

Triarii, a legion's oldest and most experienced soldiers, numbered half as many as each of the other two lines, and this should be true even of Scipio's enlarged legions. Such inequality would make his twin flanking attack unbalanced – 2,000 or so *principes* against one flank, half as many *triarii* against the other. Perhaps it did not matter much in practice; or perhaps for this battle he had formed the *triarii* of both legions as the third line of the legion attacking the Spaniards. The manoeuvre itself was a typical Scipionic tactic, another variant of his skill in unexpectedly outflanking an enemy.

And then, to judge from hints in Polybius and Livy, it was completed with another. By now his other legion and Italian infantry had routed the Carthaginians and Numidians they faced. Some of these victors should now have been free to turn and join the attack on the Spaniards. Polybius insists that these warriors' dogged and doomed resistance kept the Romans from pursuing the rest: in other words, Scipio and Masinissa now concentrated all their forces on the Celtiberians. Livy in turn describes these as 'surrounded on every side'. They were hemmed in not only on their flanks but now in their rear. The few not killed were captured.[12]

Syphax fled west with his remaining cavalry, but within a day Laelius, leading a Roman task force of cavalry and *velites*, and Masinissa with his men were in pursuit. Hasdrubal, trailed by his remaining troops, made his way to Carthage – where he disappears from Polybius and Livy. Maybe now he was sacked as general and replaced by Hanno, son of Bomilcar, then hounded to suicide by embittered Carthaginians (even if Appian, much less plausibly, stretches these events into the following year). The new Hanno, though, made little mark on events, outside Appian's implausible rivalry between him and his ousted predecessor.

Scipio made his way back to the coast with the bulk of his army, plus a train of plunder and prisoners. The towns along the middle and lower Bagradas river opened their gates or were forced to open them, adding to the plunder and spreading fresh alarm. This aggressive return march must have taken several days, maybe two or more weeks. Efficient as usual, he sent ahead his hauls of loot and captives under escort to Castra Cornelia. He and the rest of the army crossed the hills that border the landward side of Carthage's peninsula to take Tunes (present-day Tunis) at the western end of the Gulf of Tunis. A small but strategically sited town with a line of high hills behind it, this had already served as an operations base for enemies, including, over just the past century, Agathocles, Regulus and the rebels of the Truceless War fought three decades before. Less than 25 kilometres (15½ mi.) from Carthage itself and visible from there, Tunes' position enabled an occupier to cut the metropolis off from its hinterland. Scipio, after twelve months, was doing to Carthage something that Hannibal over fifteen years had never managed to do to Rome.

At Carthage, panicked demands to summon Hannibal home redoubled. If Polybius and Livy are right, now the city acted to strengthen its walls and other defences. Inexplicably then – it is hard to believe – Carthage's fortifications had earned no or minimal attention even after the traumas of Laelius' coastal raid in 205 and Scipio's landing the previous summer. Nor, during the days and weeks of Scipio's absence inland, had it apparently occurred to the authorities – who for months had a new fleet ready in the city's enclosed ports – that his absence should be the right time to attack his warships helping to besiege Utica. Only now, when he was virtually visible at Tunes, was the naval commander (Appian calls him Hamilcar) ordered to sail out with his one hundred vessels. This inertia, already verging on incompetence, was promptly compounded with fecklessness.

Scipio could see the fleet emerging from the ports and realized why. He at once set his troops in motion for Castra Cornelia. But Utica was 40 kilometres (25 mi.) from Tunes: even a forced march there cannot have taken less than ten hours, and it probably took more. The Carthaginian navy had about the same distance to sail or row and so could have fallen on its enemies – there were Roman transports as well as warships moored outside Utica – well before Scipio arrived to take charge. Livy notes the paradox: had the Carthaginians struck at once, they would have found everything in hurried confusion; instead they chose to sail slowly up the coast by day, then spend the night at the harbour beside Cape Farina. Only after sunrise did they form in line of battle to challenge the Romans.

By then Scipio had matters in hand. His warships were too few to take on the enemy's, so he had them close in to the shore between Castra Cornelia and Utica. Then he grouped the much more numerous transports in front of them, three or four deep, as shields. The crews took down ships' riggings to lash transports together, with spaces between some to let small boats come and go. This ingenious naval fortress was manned by a thousand soldiers with a plentiful supply of javelins and other missiles. The tardy Carthaginian fleet, thwarted of a sea battle, decided to attack the transports' wooden wall. Despite the missiles raining down from those ships' higher decks and the harassment of Scipio's small boats, the attackers won a success. Crewmen flung poles tipped with grappling hooks to snag ships; their efforts tore the first line of transports open, and half a dozen were towed away.

To the stressed population in Carthage it came as an unhoped-for and encouraging victory, but reality quickly returned. Their fleet did venture out again at various times, but it tried no new assaults. Nor did it try to stop ships and supplies coming to and departing from the beachhead. Before long, Scipio with part or most of his army marched back to Tunes to resume blockading Carthage. The long-demanded recall of Hannibal was still held up, perhaps by political jockeying – Barcid faction members versus critics anxious to ensure he did not come back as a dictator – or a mere paralysis of will.

Soon after reopening the blockade, Scipio found himself in an episode fraught with future fame. Masinissa and Laelius had defeated Syphax in a battle near Cirta, his capital (on 22 June, according to the Augustan poet Ovid), had taken him prisoner and Cirta had surrendered to Masinissa. Almost Masinissa's first action as its new lord was to marry Sophoniba, ignoring her hapless husband and a furious Laelius, who saw her as a Roman prisoner of war.[13]

Not long after this news reached Tunes, Laelius and Masinissa arrived with their prisoners, Syphax included. Scipio treated his former ally with courtesy, though the fallen king would still have to go to Italy with the other prisoners. Syphax blamed his change of alliance (Livy and others claim) on his infatuation for his wife and warned Scipio that the same would happen to Masinissa. Scipio hardly needed the advice. He shared Laelius' disapproving view of the hasty nuptials and claimed Sophoniba as Rome's captive.

The claim is hard to justify in law or logic. Cirta had surrendered peacefully (to Masinissa, not Laelius), and the queen was not a military figure. His real concern, no doubt, was what Syphax supposedly voiced: that she would seduce her new spouse back to Carthage's side. Masinissa himself had fought for Carthage and helped kill Scipio's father and uncle only a few years before. Now, though, his military support was essential to Scipio's invasion.

Livy's telling of the episode immortalized it. His Masinissa is a headstrong and amorous youth, Sophoniba a beautiful and dignified young woman: for Masinissa it is love at first sight. (By contrast, another tradition made him, not Syphax, her original betrothed.) Scipio then admonishes him in almost fatherly tones against falling a slave to passion, and stresses that Sophoniba along with the rest of Syphax's realm had become not Masinissa's possession but Rome's: a questionable claim on both counts. The ardent youth blushes, weeps and then, to save her from humiliation, sends Sophoniba a dose of poison. With a sad reproach she drinks it, leaving Scipio to handle a young lover wild with grief. He eases Masinissa's sorrow by publicly acclaiming him as king and loading him with royal gifts.

More should be seen in these doings than a romantic story of impulsive love thwarted. Masinissa was 35 years old and not a rash youth. Sophoniba's father was Carthage's leading citizen after Hannibal and had been its chief general in Africa. Masinissa would know that Hannibal was coming home to confront Scipio. He could not be sure that Scipio would win. Renewing a tie to the Carthaginian elite, with whom he already had links, could seem a politic move for the future of Numidia and himself – if Scipio would let him do it.

Scipio in turn could not discount the risk of a change of heart, and he needed Masinissa and his Numidian cavalry. His personality and leadership proved strong enough to convince his ally to break off the new marriage, with recognition as king easing the rebuff (as Livy carefully notes). Masinissa saved face further by sending poison to Sophoniba, even though this was a noteworthy rebuff to Scipio, who had wanted her for his muster of illustrious captures. Whether she obeyed the death order as willingly as Livy, Appian and other ancients insist may be wondered.[14]

Nothing suggests that Scipio felt regret or pity for her enforced death. His one concern about Sophoniba was that she should not jeopardize Masinissa's loyalty to Rome. If he could not send her off to Rome like Syphax, he quite likely felt that she was better dead. Now he turned back to larger matters. Masinissa was sent back to Numidia to bring the Masaesyli, Syphax's people, under control. With Syphax's capable son Vermina still holding out, the task would take time – probably longer than Masinissa or Scipio foresaw. Next, Laelius was ordered to sail to Italy with envoys from Masinissa and with Syphax and other important prisoners, to inform the Senate and people of his chief's successes.

Divesting himself of his most trusted and ablest lieutenant shows that Scipio did not expect more fighting, at least for the rest of 203. He returned to Tunes with most of his army to strengthen its fortifications and press the blockade of Carthage. Once there, he received welcome news. The Carthaginians were ready for peace at last.

8
Zama and Peace

The fall of Syphax, perhaps too Hasdrubal's death if it happened about now, left the leaders of Carthage with few choices. Hannibal, with Carthage's only remaining army, was under watch by a consul and his legions in Italy. Scipio stood at Tunes, blocking all food and goods that the Carthaginians normally relied on from their hinterland. Their authorities' response to the crisis was peculiar.

It was dual. Envoys came over to Tunes to request talks for peace. At more or less the same time, other envoys set sail to order Hannibal to return to Africa – with his army. The contradiction in logic cannot have been lost on Scipio. Whatever peace terms he might work out with the city leadership risked being thrown aside when Hannibal arrived. On the other hand, his own situation was delicate. He may have known from friends and kinsmen at home that Servilius Caepio, the consul shadowing the inactive Hannibal in Bruttium, had thoughts of sailing across to Africa and, as consul outranking a proconsul, taking over the command. Continuing support for Scipio was not guaranteed if a virtual military stalemate dragged on. By contrast, if a firm peace could be concluded, even an unwilling Hannibal should find it hard to revive hostilities; or so at any rate Scipio might calculate.

The envoys were the thirty senior senators who formed the inner council of Carthage's senate, the body that (Livy writes) had the chief influence in the senate's affairs. Most must have been former magistrates and generals. They may even have included two or three leading aristocrats, such as a very elderly Hanno, nicknamed the Great, who for most of his life had been the Barcid faction's chief opponent – powerless, but too eminent to be silenced. Some very likely were acquainted with Roman aristocrats, including Scipio's family. They nonetheless caused some surprise (and maybe some disdain) by prostrating themselves on the ground before Scipio and his council of officers and even kissing their feet. Livy supposed, perhaps rightly, that this was an ancestral Phoenician act of submission. But as no envoys from Carthage are recorded doing it in any negotiations before now, it looks as though the obeisance was revived to impress Scipio.

When they spoke, the envoys put all the blame for the war on Hannibal and his supporters. This was a piece of submissive fiction – a symbolic prostration to match the physical – as it was Rome that had declared war on Carthage fifteen years before. Blaming the Barcid family and faction was all the more specious when many, or most, leading Carthaginians since the days of Hannibal's father – and therefore most of the current senate and its inner council – must have been supporters and beneficiaries of the Barcid era. (A year later, a leader of the opposition faction would admit, in effect, that it had been powerless throughout the war.) But the thirty envoys had to make a token effort to deflect blame, no matter how glaringly implausible, in pleading for mercy.

Scipio offered terms that, though not mild, were not extreme. The Carthaginians must hand back prisoners of war, deserters from Roman armies and runaway slaves (standard stipulations by victors). As was found out a year later, there were 4,000 Roman and Italian prisoners still held in the city. The Carthaginians must pull their forces out of Italy and Cisalpine Gaul – in fact they were about to do this anyway – and must keep out of Spain and 'all the islands that lay between Italy and Africa'. Scipio of course meant the main islands, Sicily, Sardinia and Corsica; probably those further west, too, the Balearic isles and Carthage's own colony of Ebusus (Ibiza). Yet this was not a new blow, for all of them had been out of Carthage's reach for years. So was Spain. These terms simply required the Carthaginians to recognize reality.

It was much harsher to enact that they should keep only twenty warships and surrender the rest. In effect, Scipio was signalling the end of Carthage as a naval power. He demanded goods and money too: half a million bushels of wheat, 300,000 of barley and 5,000 talents of silver. The grain must have been for his troops and crews, but the silver more likely was to be paid over when peace was concluded. It was the equivalent of 30 million of Rome's recently introduced silver *denarii* – a very large sum. Appian adds some other provisos (no mercenaries to be hired in future and Masinissa to be recognized as ruler also of Syphax's kingdom) but, given Appian's erratic quality in narrating the war, those look more like imaginative extras.[1]

Scipio gave the Carthaginians three days to consider. They could not haggle or plead for changes. They returned on the second or third day, to confirm that Carthage agreed to everything and would promptly send other delegates to Rome to seek ratification. As Scipio had promised, this brought about a full armistice, while he put one of his officers, Q. Fulvius Gillo, in charge of conducting the Carthaginian peace mission to Rome. All the same, he did not let the ceasefire extend to allowing a full flow of provisions into the city. Like the Entente allies after November 1918, he saw keeping the enemy hungry as a military asset, especially with Hannibal preparing to return. It proved a costly miscalculation.

The attacks on Utica stopped with the armistice. While everyone waited for word from Italy, the wheat and barley Scipio had called for were delivered and soon used up, so before long he was awaiting two sizeable new supply shipments from Sardinia and Sicily. This must have been after the harvests there had been gathered, and so in August or early September 203. He can hardly have been unaware that meanwhile Hannibal was readying his departure from Bruttium, even though he could not be sure when that would happen – or if it would, as Rome's forces in south Italy were still under firm orders to keep him there.

Laelius meantime reached Rome with his eminent prisoners and reported the events in Africa to a delighted Senate and people. Masinissa's recognition as king was confirmed and the captured Numidian lords freed (except Syphax himself, now interned at Alba in the hills near Rome) to win him popularity with Syphax's people. Then a few days later the new embassy from Carthage arrived under Gillo's escort. They brought along some prisoners of war plus some deserters and runaway slaves. The prisoners must have been Romans and Italians, probably of rank. The deserters' and runaways' fates would of course be the opposite of release: death for the former and re-enslavement for the latter.

The Carthaginian envoys were soon received by the Senate. At this point Livy's account – Polybius' does not survive – becomes bizarre and self-contradictory. Most of the envoys he describes as young men, and they behave with unseemly self-assurance. They denounce Hannibal as the sole author of the war, urge that therefore the peace treaty made in 241 should still hold and ask the Senate to return to the status quo that that treaty set up. Pressed on this extraordinary (not to say preposterous) proposal, quite different from their authorized mission, they profess to be too young to remember details about 241.

Senators react equally strangely to this farrago, in Livy's telling. Scipio's friend Q. Metellus urges that the victorious Scipio be authorized to negotiate peace in Africa – as though Scipio has not yet done what he had in fact just done. Valerius Laevinus, another ex-consul, denounces the envoys as spies and calls for Scipio to press on with the war. More bizarrely still, Laelius, called in for comment, agrees with Laevinus, telling senators that 'Scipio thought that the only hope of peace lay in Mago and Hannibal not being recalled.' As Livy has earlier mentioned Carthage recalling them, in effect he means that Laelius, like Laevinus, thought the war should continue; this would obviously imply that Scipio held the same view. Yet Livy himself, again a few pages earlier, recorded precisely the opposite proviso by Scipio: the brothers must vacate Italy. Finally, the browbeaten envoys are sent away empty-handed. The peace is rejected.

This fantastical scenario makes Laelius overturn – in Scipio's name, at that – the peace settlement that Scipio had set up. Scipio's actual terms of peace have disappeared. The story implies a stunning rebuff to him from the Senate: this at the instigation of his own close friends, Laelius included. By further implication (though it seems to escape Livy), Rome thus remains at war with Carthage. Yet in Livy's own narrative, Scipio afterwards blames the Carthaginians for restarting hostilities – for by then the historian has gone back to Polybius, who was plainly not his source for the above scenario. Livy also tells us later that the renewal of warfare caused consternation at Rome.

The solution is obvious. For the Senate's reception of the envoys, Livy turned to a source different from Polybius, one offering an invented mini-drama that made for better theatre: arrogant, verbally specious Carthaginians routed by sternly untrickable Romans. But Polybius' account has to be the right one. The Senate and people did ratify Scipio's terms, and the news reached Scipio soon after, not from a returning

Laelius but probably by a fast ship. Then two events changed the situation. One of the supply fleets he was awaiting fell into the hands of the Carthaginians, and Hannibal landed in Libya.[2]

The larger fleet, two hundred transports from Sicily commanded by a propraetor, Cn. Octavius, was unluckier than the hundred from Sardinia. Those had arrived safely; Octavius' convoy ran into an autumnal storm as it neared the African coast, one rough enough to beach laden ships on the western shore of Cape Bon, others further north on the rocky shoals of Aegimurus island (now Zembra) – all in sight of a hungry and restive Carthage. With the ships abandoned by their crews, and many of these taken prisoner, crowds outside and even inside Carthage's senate building pushed the authorities into ordering admiral Hamilcar to sail across the bay with fifty warships and tow the transports in.

Scipio was understandably furious. He at once deputed three officers, L. Baebius, L. Sergius and L. Fabius, as envoys to sail by quinquereme from Castra Cornelia to remonstrate at Carthage. Not only were the looted goods (and ships) Roman property, and the crews freeborn seamen, but the armistice period had not expired: so the envoys pointed out, in no moderate terms, to both the senate and the people's assembly. But they found the Carthaginians in a changed mood. These now knew that Hannibal and his army were on their way, in fact had landed on the east coast near Hadrumetum. News that the treaty had been formally ratified at Rome – a fact announced to the Carthaginians by Baebius and his colleagues – made no difference. The three undiplomatically truculent envoys had to be rescued from crowd violence and put back on their quinquereme.[3]

They were not out of danger. Hamilcar's war fleet, or some of it, was now moored at Cape Farina (perhaps watching Scipio's), and as the Roman ship came in sight of Castra Cornelia, three of his triremes set out to try to sink it. It managed to run aground near foraging Roman soldiers, but only the envoys and a few of the crewmen survived the attackers' missiles.

This piece of treachery against ambassadors, a moral outrage by every ancient code, was at any rate the story from the Roman side. It may have originated from Scipio's own reports home, reinforcing his claim that renewal of war was a deliberate enemy plan and the Carthaginians were shameless armistice violators. Had the attack on the ship been done only by a trio of rogue captains, saying so would weaken the outrage. Yet it may have been true. Hamilcar launched no follow-up provocations – he disappears from history after this – and the ensuing renewal of military action was launched by Scipio to minimal resistance. Even without the attack he would probably have acted, for his true motive was not a short-lived (or invented) item of treachery, but the presence of Hannibal.

The timeline of events turns fuzzy. Both Polybius and Livy compress it into a few generalized remarks. Appian supplies improbabilities, seconded by Cassius Dio's Byzantine epitomator Zonaras. There are just a few time-pointers. By now, late autumn in 203, Hannibal certainly was in Libya; our sources make that clear, at least. The decisive battle that followed in 202, misnamed Zama, coincided – if we believe Dio via Zonaras – with an eclipse of the Sun, which can be dated by astronomy to 19 October that year. Not long afterwards, Syphax's son Vermina, coming too late to help Hannibal, was defeated somewhere inland on the first day of the Saturnalia festival (says Livy). This fell on 17 December each year in the Roman calendar. The calendar, though, was administered erratically by the pontiffs during much of the third and second centuries BC. Thus 17 December 202 is now calculated as falling in late November, probably 25 November. As for the October eclipse, this was at best only limitedly visible in North Africa. So its claimed panic effect on the combatants looks like a later fancy – but possibly a fancy by someone who knew that the battle happened in October, knew of the eclipse (thanks to a scholar at Alexandria?) and dramatized them happening together.[4]

In other words, nearly a year separated Hannibal's arrival in Libya from the final campaign. The conundrum is obvious. Why, on returning to rescue his homeland from ruin, did he delay battle for so long – and why did Scipio let him? Not only Livy but Polybius too are strangely vague about the interval, though Polybius' vagueness may be due to his Byzantine excerptor's clumsy scissors. Still, an outline of events can be reconstructed.

Before the Carthaginian envoys returned from Rome under escort, Scipio marched inland from the coast on a punishment expedition. With Laelius still absent escorting the envoys, he left L. Baebius (one of his nearly lynched spokesmen) in charge. Soon Baebius sent him word of the

Carthaginian envoys' arrival at Castra Cornelia, adding that they were in fear of their lives because of the fleet-plundering. Scipio ordered they be sent home unharmed: a proper, and propagandistically neat, example of how to treat ambassadors. He then continued attacking and sacking inland towns and enslaving their populations, a *chevauchée* punitive and profitable together. He was at the same time sending repeated messages to Masinissa in Numidia, urging the king to return with a strong army, not to mention with the Roman contingent Scipio had lent him. Intent on subduing all he could of the Masaesylian kingdom (Vermina was still at large), Masinissa ignored him.

Laelius and his group came back accompanied by fetial priests. So it seems from a fragmentary piece of papyrus surviving from a lost, and perhaps early, history of these events. *Fetiales*, and their counterparts on the opposing side, formally exchanged the oaths necessary to sanctify a treaty. The Carthaginian envoys at Rome had no doubt been qualified to do the same there. Of course, by the time all the returnees reached Castra Cornelia, the armistice had broken down. That explains why none of our surviving literary accounts mention the persons whom, the papyrus fragment says, 'they [the Romans at Rome] sent out to render and take the oaths'. A year later, when peace finally was made, Livy does assure us that fetials went from Rome for the task.

The same broken fragment includes an enigmatic comment. 'Repudiating the oaths they sent out men bearing, instead of peace, war.' If this means that the Carthaginians formally rejected the treaty they had sworn to, it would be an extra detail to add to Polybius' narrative – not a contradiction of it (as often thought). But more likely, it is the unknown author criticizing – or having Scipio and his council criticize – the looting of the beached supply ships and the claimed attack on Scipio's spokesmen. It would be easy for a pro-Roman writer, echoing Scipio, Laelius or some other informant, to stigmatize the looters as agents of Carthage's magistrates and senate, authorities intending to negate the treaty as soon as they knew of Hannibal's safe and armed return.[5]

Hannibal had escaped Italy, to the intense annoyance of the Senate in Rome. Roman fleets patrolled the seas, and the consuls were supposed to keep him in Bruttium – yet he gathered, or was sent, enough transports for several thousand troops and embarked these at Cape Lacinium without being noticed, stopped or chased. How and where he gained the transports is not known. Polybius and Livy avoid the question; Appian claims, not very plausibly, that he built his fleet himself, but most probably the Carthaginians sent the needed vessels over. (They still had five hundred seagoing vessels a year later.) Scipio's men could not have avoided seeing this from Tunes, but, if they did, he did not try to stop the Carthaginian transports. With only a few dozen warships, and maybe admiral Hamilcar still on watch, he would not risk another setback at sea.

Hannibal was lucky a second time, too. Autumn could be dangerous or even lethal to seafarers, as Octavius' supply fleet's calamity showed, but he and his army made the trip safely, although winds as unhelpful as Scipio's the previous year carried them to Leptis on the east coast, not far south of Hadrumetum. Hannibal himself owned an estate further south again, near Thapsus. That the Senate had wanted him kept in Italy was one of the war's most plangent ironies. Just as his arrival in 218 had been unwanted, so now was his departure. Scipio by contrast, it is clear, was confident he could defeat Carthage's most renowned commander. Rather than march directly against him while Hannibal and his veterans were establishing themselves at Leptis and environs, he left them alone.

Nor did Hannibal challenge him before late in 202. The winter of 203–202 closed down operations by both sides. It freed Hannibal to work at building a new army capable of taking on Scipio's and Masinissa's veterans. He needed horses for his cavalry arm – having had to leave the ones in Italy – and more troops than just his own veterans, as well as food and other supplies. He probably did gain a reinforcement of at least a few thousand more soldiers: what was left of his late brother Mago's forces, defeated in northern Italy during 203 and recalled to Carthage. Though a Roman fleet intercepted some of this returning flotilla near Sardinia, most of the ships escaped to reach Carthage. Hannibal's army at the battle of Zama included the Ligurians and other troops it brought. But Mago had been badly wounded in his last battle and died off the Sardinian coast. This left Hannibal the sole survivor of Hamilcar Barca's three military sons.

At some stage, maybe in 202, he also gained a welcome contingent of 2,000 cavalry led by one of Syphax's kinsmen, lord of a small Masaesylian tribe in western Numidia (in Polybius he has the Greek-sounding name Tychaeus). The recruiting efforts ranged more widely too as he looked to hire new mercenaries and – a sign of desperation – even levy Carthaginians. No surprise if all this took time.[6]

Even now it would have been possible to negotiate a peace. Polybius and Livy report Hannibal later telling Scipio that Carthage would accept Rome holding Spain, Sicily and all the other islands between Italy and Africa, and guarantee never to wage war for them. In effect, almost in wording, this was the same territorial settlement that Scipio had dictated in the recent, now abrogated treaty. It would not have been unthinkable, either, to work out the same (or even a larger) war indemnity. And with Syphax nullified, Carthage could have recognized Masinissa, a leader with good Carthaginian connections, as Numidian king without losing face. Hannibal would have returned to Carthage to be a leading peacetime citizen (as he still did in the end); Scipio to Rome to celebrate a splendid triumph and be Rome's most eminent citizen (as he too did); Carthage would have begun a new life as a limited North African state enjoying steadily growing post-war prosperity (this did happen after 201). The thousands of lives lost at Zama would have been preserved.

Neither side was interested in making the effort. Scipio and Rome were bent on a total victory for total submission. Not to obliterate Carthage, true, but to ensure it would never pose another threat. Hannibal and Carthage still hoped to salvage some of the city's past Mediterranean power and avoid becoming merely a hapless Roman client. Both needed a final battle. Each had his reasons.

During spring and summer 202, Scipio left Cn. Octavius in command at Castra Cornelia and continued his forays into the Libyan heartland to sack, loot, burn and kill. He refused towns' and communities' offers of surrender and pleas for mercy, claiming as before that it was punishment for the looting of his fleet and the attacks on his envoys. Of course, the Libyan peoples he attacked were not responsible for either act. It was a transparent pretext for a terror campaign to force the Carthaginians to fight or yield.[7]

He may well have had a specific reason for trying to push the pace. At Rome, both new consuls, M. Servilius Geminus and Ti. Claudius Nero, were keen to replace him in the African command. They began agitating for this as soon as they took office in March, and they brushed aside both

Q. Metellus' arguments against it in the Senate and even a decree by the people reconfirming Scipio. The Senate authorized them to cast lots in the usual way for military commands, and *provincia* Africa fell to Nero. Supposedly he would co-command there (Servilius, less glamorously, had to look after Italy). He then set about readying transports and warships. Cousin to the C. Nero who had helped destroy Hannibal's brother at the Metaurus, he was ambitious for glory of his own.

A Senate resolution ordered that Scipio should still be in charge of peace talks, but Ti. Nero no doubt felt that, once on the spot, as consul he could pull rank – or at least win a share of the military and diplomatic renown. In the end slowness, bad weather and incompetence would stop him from getting any closer than Sardinia, but Scipio could not foretell that. It was in his own interest (and Rome's) to inflict the final blow on Carthage before Nero arrived and interfered. All he needed now was Masinissa with strong Numidian forces.

Hannibal could calculate just the opposite. Unless somehow absolutely cut off from all information from Italy through Greek and other traders, or deserters from Scipio's forces, he may have learned in spring 202 about the moves at Rome to sideline Scipio. For Hannibal, any other Roman commander would be easier to handle and certainly easier to defeat. It was, then, in his and Carthage's interest not to hurry into combat; rather to wait and meanwhile train Carthage's last army.

This situation changed late in 202. Ever louder calls for action came from the authorities at Carthage: Scipio's destructive rampage through Libya was creating almost frantic fear in the city. By late summer, Hannibal may have known that no one would be arriving from Rome (or Sardinia) in Scipio's place. Probably too, he had a promise of military support from Syphax's son Vermina. Where Vermina was is not known, but Syphax's original territory around Siga in Numidia's west looks likely. In October, if we may trust Zonaras' dating, he set out from Hadrumetum to find the Romans.[8]

Scipio himself was in the western parts of Libya. Neither Polybius nor Livy describes his movements in detail. One reason for being 200-plus kilometres (125 mi.) from Castra Cornelia and Tunes was to link up with Masinissa, who at last was ready to cooperate and was gathering troops. But Masinissa could have come to the coast as he had done before.

So another reason for Scipio stationing himself in the west may have been to draw Hannibal away from Carthage and the coast. Defeating him far from the city would make another recovery virtually impossible. The Romans too would be cut off from supplies or succour if things went wrong, but Scipio was plainly confident that things would not. After all he had already done the same to fight at the Great Plains.

Hannibal first stopped at a town Polybius calls 'Zama', five days' march from Carthage: almost certainly Zama Regia (its name in Roman times), at modern Seba Biar near the city of Siliana. It lay a good 180 kilometres (112 mi.) inland from Hadrumetum. Hannibal and his army must have taken five or six days, and with hard marching too over hills and valleys, to arrive there. From Zama he sent out a trio of spies to find and probe Scipio's position. Where the Romans were sources do not say, but certainly between Sicca (El Kef) and Cirta, as Scipio was impatiently waiting for Masinissa. The spies were promptly caught. Famously, the proconsul confounded expectations. Though the usual treatment for spies was mutilation or death, Scipio had them taken round his camp to inspect everything, then fed and told to report back to Hannibal what they had seen. There is no need to suspect the story: Scipio quite likely knew, from Herodotus and other authors, how the Persian king Xerxes had done the same with Greek spies centuries before. More than an act of showy mercy, it was a piece of dramatized bravado plus calculated misinformation. The spies would not report seeing Masinissa and his reinforcements – he had not arrived yet.

A still more famous episode followed. While at Zama, Hannibal had decided he must meet Rome's young general. A herald – a formal envoy whose function and person were sacred – was sent to Scipio to propose a face-to-face conference. Scipio, perhaps flattered, surely intrigued, agreed to have it in a few days' time. The day after the herald left, Masinissa at last arrived. He brought in 4,000 cavalry and 6,000 foot soldiers, much to his ally's relief. The two now advanced to a town called Naraggara, pitching camp on a hilltop close to a useful stream. Hannibal in turn soon arrived on a nearby hilltop – a waterless one, much to his troops' frustration, as they had to dig wells. From Zama to a hilltop in Naraggara's neighbourhood would have taken his army three days at most – maybe two as Hannibal was eager for a showdown. As often suggested, he may have been hoping to bring the enemy to battle before Masinissa reinforced them. Scipio had been careful to avoid that happening.

Naraggara, which must be a native Libyan name, is known from Roman evidence: a country town in broad, undulating landscape, now Sakiet Sidi Youssef on the border with Algeria – 32 Roman miles (47 km/29 mi.) west of the bigger city of Sicca. Hannibal in turn set up camp on the waterless hill only 30 *stades* away, less than 6 kilometres. Polybius' name for the town where Scipio and Masinissa encamped is Margaron, and he implies but does not flatly state that the ensuing battle was fought near both camps. Whether Margaron is a Greek version of Naraggara, or denotes a different place, is one issue in the constant controversies over the battle, which Hannibal's brief biography by Cicero's friend Cornelius Nepos (but no other ancient source) calls 'Zama'.

The landscape around Sidi Youssef is generally judged too hilly for a large battle. The nearest extensive plain, today called Draa el Metnan, is 15 kilometres (about 10 mi.) southwest of El Kef and a good 25 kilometres (15½ mi.) southeast of Sidi Youssef. It is therefore the main contender for battlefield honours. A newer challenger is much further east: the plain below Kbor Klib, a massive stone-built ancient monument on a ridge 56 kilometres (35 mi.) east of El Kef and 17 kilometres (10½ mi.) southwest of Siliana. The monument, complete with battle friezes, funeral chambers and shrines, could have been set up (its advocates argue) by Masinissa later to commemorate the victory over Hannibal. Yet this is far from certain. Other studies date Kbor Klib 150 years later, to the age and maybe the agency of Julius Caesar during his civil wars.[9]

Sceptics of Naraggara rely partly on Appian's mention of supposedly important cities – Partha and Cilla – in pre-battle operations. There is a problem with this. These supposed cities do not appear anywhere else in ancient North Africa's ample written and archaeological evidence. Naraggara, by contrast, was a real ancient place in an identifiable location. Its environs can be defended cautiously as the battle area. Nor is Draa el Metnan necessarily the only nearby ground broad enough, or the only flat ground edged by hills for armies' camps. On the eastern edge of Sidi Youssef there is sizeable space, and not far away – over the Algerian border – another extends outside the town of El Haddada.

The next day the two generals met. That they did is sometimes doubted on one ground or another: that generals did not normally stage a pre-battle rendezvous, or that this one was invented to mirror other storied interviews – Croesus' with Solon, Alexander's with Diogenes the philosopher and Porus the Indian king (after defeating him), and with the Persian Darius III as he lay dying from a traitor's knife. All the same, none of these earlier meetings pictured commanders before battle. Nor does a striking saying or poignant drama mark Scipio's and Hannibal's. Writers keen for something more memorable, for instance Appian and whatever source he used – not to mention Silius Italicus in his epic poem – sought real drama by making Scipio and Hannibal, and then Hannibal and Masinissa for good measure, fight hand to hand during the battle. Militarily unconventional though the meeting near Naraggara was, it was between two very unconventional generals.[10]

Each rode down from his camp with a small escort and an interpreter, halted the escort and went forward with only the interpreter. Hannibal and Scipio both knew Greek, but personal and public dignity made each keep to his own language. What they said comes to us, as usual, through the rhetorical prisms of Polybius and Livy. (Appian and others have just one-sentence or two-sentence summaries.) Livy, unsatisfied with Polybius on this matter, gives Hannibal an elegant speech more than two and a half times lengthier than in Polybius and only occasionally echoing his. The Livian Scipio follows with one not much longer than Polybius' version but again oratorical.

In Polybius, the older man (Hannibal was now 45) lectures the younger like a mentor about the changeable ways of fortune, points to himself as a prime example, and urges Scipio to accept his offered terms rather than chance everything on a battle. The role of fortune (in Greek *tyche*), a commonplace in ancient rhetoric, exerted a special fascination over Polybius. Whether it did the same to Hannibal is not known, and in making him mention it Polybius hints that part, perhaps most, of the homily in his account may be as freely composed as it is in Livy.

Nonetheless, both concur on Hannibal's territorial concessions for peace – virtually identical to those that Scipio's treaty had dictated. Neither Polybius nor Livy has him speak of Carthage paying an indemnity, limiting its navy or handing back prisoners and deserters. This may be true. Had he offered virtually everything that was in the previous treaty, there would have been no reason for Scipio to reject it. To put forward purely territorial concessions, though – granting Rome regions it already controlled and leaving Carthage able to repair its African hegemony and naval strength – was effectively to waste Scipio's time. If he was underwhelmed that would be no surprise.

The historians have Scipio answer with his own uncompromising lecture, warning his opponent that the tables have turned and Carthage faces only a stark choice – accept Rome's (that is, Scipio's) terms, or fight. Livy softens him slightly: if Hannibal agrees to reparations for the looted supplies and the attacks on his spokesmen, there is a chance for fresh talks; otherwise, it is war. This small concession is no doubt Livy's own touch to illustrate Scipio's moral moderation. In reality, Carthage would have had to give up much more – in effect give up being a serious Mediterranean power – to end the war, as both men knew. Scipio closes with sharp concision: 'Either hand over control over yourselves and your country, or fight and win.' The conference ended.

Scipio no doubt knew that, win or lose, Carthage's prospects were bleak. Defeated, it would be merely a satellite dependent of Rome, and Hannibal's own career (and maybe life) would be over. Annihilating Scipio and Masinissa might convince Rome to make peace, but Hannibal surely knew that, much more likely, it would unleash a relentless response. Carthage, with most of its resources lost, all its allies gone and its finances drained, and with sixteen Roman legions still in arms and all Italy back in Rome's grip, would still face a desperate struggle.

For Scipio and his men the prospects were as clear, and more immediate. To be defeated, far inland in foreign territory, against an embittered and desperate enemy meant annihilation: death for many, slavery for the rest. Scipio himself, with Laelius and the other officers, could expect – and probably would wish – to die fighting like Hasdrubal the Barcid, rather than become humiliated captives like the previous Roman invader Regulus. Defeating Hannibal, by contrast, would mean everlasting glory, not to mention the rewards of plunder and a triumph, and for Rome the mastery of the western Mediterranean world.

Fifty years later, Polybius was so alive to the momentousness of the clash that he characterized it in even grander world-historical terms:

never did two braver armies or two more successful and brilliant generals contend, or Fortune hold out a more splendid prize – the mastery of not only Africa and Europe but every land known to history. Scipio, we can be sure, did not see the coming contest as quite so extravagantly coloured, though no one knew better the gravity of the crisis facing the expedition.

The morning after he and Hannibal met, the two armies deployed to fight. Their strengths are not clearly known. Having had to leave troops at the coast as before – but perhaps fewer, now that he had the urban Carthaginians' measure – Scipio was at the head of at least 20,000 or so Roman and Italian infantry and 1,200 to 1,500 cavalry. Neither Polybius nor Livy state numbers, while Appian gives Scipio rather more infantry (23,000) plus 1,500 horse. His source for these figures is unknown and they look optimistic: Scipio had not been sent reinforcements from Italy, and casualties and illnesses over three campaign seasons must be allowed for. If nevertheless Appian is accurate, maybe the garrisons left at Castra Cornelia and Salaeca were chiefly marines and sailors, as suggested earlier. Masinissa's Numidians then brought the total allied army to between 31,000 and 34,000.

Hannibal led forces that were diverse. The toughest infantry element was his own veterans: most of them Bruttians and Lucanians from southern Italy, the rest Africans and Spaniards still surviving after sixteen years' hard service. Another element was a mercenary force 12,000 strong (Polybius' figure), of Ligurians, Gauls, Balearic islanders and Mauretanians. The Ligurians and Gauls must have been from his brother Mago's evacuated force. The other mercenaries were troops recently hired; some, just possibly, recently unemployed Greek or Macedonian mercenaries, a basis for Livy's false story of the king of Macedon – at peace with Rome since 205 – sending thousands of royal troops over to help.

Hannibal's remaining contingent was a body of Carthaginians and Libyans. Scipio's scouring of so much of the countryside would have uprooted Libyan communities and driven refugees away to safer places, including Emporia and Byzacena by the east coast, where recruiting agents were busy. Carthaginian citizens living there and others able to make their way from the blockaded metropolis could also have been recruited (or conscripted). Regions of the hinterland not raided by the

Romans, like Byzacena, Emporia and perhaps the Cape Bon peninsula, could supply what Polybius terms Carthaginian cavalry, no doubt made up of Libyan horsemen as well as actual Carthaginian citizens. The rest of the cavalry were Tychaeus' Numidians. Hannibal had acquired more than eighty war elephants, too, more than he had ever had in past campaigns. But whatever the animals' training at Hadrumetum, none had yet taken part in a real battle.

Appian's total for this army – 50,000 infantry and cavalry – could be reasonably correct. The army certainly outnumbered Scipio's. So Polybius believed, quite possibly from a Carthaginian source. In the pep talk that he reports the Carthaginian giving his veterans before battle, Hannibal tells them to look at the enemy and mark how many fewer they are. It is not likely that he was also counting in Scipio's light infantry (the *velites*) or Masinissa's Numidians. In the final phase of combat (writes Polybius again), Hannibal's veterans from Italy and the combined *hastati*, *principes* and *triarii* attacking them were nearly equal in numbers as well as valour. If Polybius, and his user Livy, mean literally these legionaries alone, that would make Hannibal's veterans number about 10,000 to 12,000. If Scipio's Latin and Italian infantry should be counted in too (they are ignored in the narratives, as they often are by sources), Hannibal's veterans would total twice that. This looks like the better solution, though far from certain. With 20,000 or so veterans, the 12,000 mercenaries, no doubt at least as many Carthaginian and Libyan recruits and about 4,000 cavalry, Hannibal should indeed have been at the head of nearly 50,000 men.[11]

His deployment was conventional: three infantry lines, one behind the other, and cavalry on the wings. The elephants were put ahead of the infantry front line. The three lines showed the variety of his forces: mercenaries forming the first; local troops the second, perhaps half a *stade* (100 m/328 ft) further back; and veterans the third. This, Polybius notes, stood one *stade* further back again. The Carthaginian cavalry held position on the right, Tychaeus' Numidians on the left. With no ambush or stratagem planned, and it seems no reserves, his intention was to fight a hard battle of attrition using his superior numbers and elephants. He would wear down the enemy, if possible scatter their cavalry, then strike a final blow.

Scipio deployed his infantry in their usual three lines: *hastati* in front, then *principes*, lastly *triarii*. The Latin and Italian contingents must have formed part of this array. As usual the cavalry squadrons formed up on the flanks, Laelius' Roman and Italian squadrons on the left, Masinissa's Numidians on the right. Where the proconsul himself was on the field we are not told, but we may envision him riding with his three shield-bearing guards between and around the legionary lines to direct and exhort.

The infantry, though, were not arranged conventionally. Normally a legion's thirty *manipuli* (its companies) formed the three lines in a chess-board pattern, so that the spaces between maniples in one line were covered by the maniples of the line behind. Scipio formed up all three lines of maniples in files, leaving wide lanes between them. In effect, he arranged them as cohorts. He then filled the lanes with his light-armed *velites*, who normally would be skirmishing ahead of the legions. Where Masinissa's foot soldiers were is not mentioned, but, as Numidians were mainly light-armed fighters too, some or most were likely stationed with the *velites*. These atypical arrangements had the enemy elephants in mind.

The unconventional layout soon proved its worth. Some Numidian riders on both sides were already skirmishing; then serious action began when the elephants charged at the front line of *hastati*. Scipio's trumpeters and buglers erupted harshly to signal the coming attack – a cacophony that spooked some elephants into turning tail just as some of Tychaeus' riders were coming up in support. As these Numidians were flung into disarray, Masinissa launched his own cavalry charge. It spread confusion and then panic through all the enemy's left wing. Meanwhile some other elephants, goaded by missiles and blows from the agile *velites*, began lumbering down the lanes between Scipio's maniples. They trampled over many of their tormentors but soon fled from the fighting over the fields. Still others swung aside over the open ground between Hannibal's mercenaries and Scipio's *hastati*, then were chased off the field by missiles – but their stampede disorganized the Carthaginian cavalry on Hannibal's right wing enough to give Laelius his opportunity. Like Masinissa, he sounded the charge.

The elephants' attack thus proved a deadly farce. Not only did the untried and frightened animals disappear from the field, but before long both of Hannibal's cavalry wings fled in rout, pursued by Masinissa and

Laelius. Admirers of Hannibal want to see this as a deliberate plan: to pull the more numerous Roman cavalry away from the battle and crush Scipio's outnumbered infantry through superior numbers. If so, it was a dangerous gamble – and in such a gamble Hannibal had no need of an elephant corps at all, especially one unused to battle.

Cavalry sacrifice was likely not what he wanted. Cavalrymen, and in his earliest battles elephants too, had played roles critical for victory. Now, it would have been better to loose his elephants against Scipio's and Masinissa's riders, not the Roman infantry, and leave the two armies' infantry to clash until his own cavalry were free to join in. Instead, the Carthaginian army's elephants and horsemen were all put to flight.

One grinding infantry clash after another followed. First Scipio sent forward the *hastati* and their unmentioned Latin and Italian comrades against the waiting mercenaries. As they neared the enemy, the steadily marching troops beat their swords on their shields and shouted their war cry, to be answered with 'indiscriminate and peculiar' yells (Polybius disdainfully writes) from their polyglot foes. In hard hand-to-hand fighting, these did some damage to their attackers but soon began to be forced back as Scipio's troops, their ranks keeping solid order, pushed with their heavy shields and slashed with their two-edged swords.[12]

The attacking *hastati* cannot have been more than 8,000 strong – and could have been fewer – against the 12,000 mercenaries. But the legionaries and their comrades were, nearly all of them, veteran survivors of years of warfare in Italy, Sicily and Africa. Behind the front line the *principes* moved up to heighten morale, no doubt taking over the war cry and the clanging of shields. Not so the Carthaginian and Libyan recruits of Hannibal's second line: without orders, maybe unnerved (as Polybius claims), they would not move even as casualties piled up among the mercenaries. A frightening idea sprang up among these: they had been left to be slaughtered. Some furiously turned from fighting the Romans to clash instead with the recruits, who fought back. Others began leaving the ranks for open ground.

Extraordinary confusion fell across the battlefield: Carthaginian and Libyan recruits duelling with mercenaries of their own army, then clashing with the Romans' front line as it came up, only to be shattered in their turn by the inexorable *hastati*. So Polybius tells it, then Livy following him – an account so bizarre that not every reader has believed it. Yet if what happened was different and more straightforward, for instance the *hastati*, or *hastati* and *principes* together, cutting to pieces first the mercenaries, then the recruits, there was no reason for Polybius to fake a much more fanciful version. Nor for any of Livy's other sources to do it.

One further and crucial point stands out. As he watched half his infantry army break up in violent chaos, Hannibal did nothing. Scipio cannot have believed his luck. The first and second lines of the Carthaginian army collapsed, many of the men dead or dying on the ground amid shattered or shed armour and weapons. Survivors plodded back to Hannibal's massed ranks of veterans but were barred by levelled spears from joining them – another strange-seeming decision, but to Hannibal they looked worse than useless for the coming climax. They may have taken refuge further to the rear, or fled to their hilltop camp. Hannibal and his veterans stood effectively alone – but fresh, ready and equal in numbers – to meet Scipio and his army, the *hastati* battered but unbroken, *principes* and *triarii* and their allied cohorts unscathed.

Another unconventional episode in this convention-defying battle now happened. Neither side closed with the other. The ground between was littered with dead men and broken weapons and wet with slippery blood. Hannibal's veteran front stretched further to right and left than the ranks of the Roman front. Scipio in effect declared a pause – trumpets and bugles sounded the recall, the *hastati* obeyed, and camp-servants and *velites* sought out the wounded to bear them off to the rear. Hannibal's moment had come: to attack, outflank the Roman infantry as vulnerable without cavalry as at Cannae, and crush Scipio in a reverse Ilipa. But, confident in his troops' strength, or suspecting a Scipionic trick, Hannibal waited.

Scipio did have a riposte, but not a trick. With his *hastati* keeping their central position, he swung his second and third lines to form up on their left and right. To make each new line of equal strength (as *triarii* numbered half as many as *principes*), probably half the maniples of *principes* and *triarii* moved to merge, form line and then march out left and right to take their stand flanking either side of the *hastati*. As always, the Latin and Italian allied cohorts must have replicated this manoeuvre. The Roman army now formed a single line, some ranks deep, more or less the same length and strength as the enemy's. Then Scipio sounded the advance. The legionaries crossed the bloody field of the earlier struggle and struck at the Bruttians, Lucanians and Hannibal's oldest surviving veterans.

How long the fighting went on is not stated, but it did last long. Scipio and Hannibal did not engage directly in the fighting (Appian's and the poet Silius' fancies of them duelling are imagination), but, as in other battles, they kept watch on how it went forward. Eventually the drumming hooves of approaching horses signalled the end. Masinissa's Numidians and Laelius' Romans, having driven the enemy cavalry far enough from the battlefield, came back to fall on the Carthaginian rear, and Hannibal's third and last line disintegrated.

Scipio had turned against him the tactics of Baecula, Ilipa and the Great Plains, and matched the envelopment Hannibal had used to conquer at Cannae. Yet he might not have won had Hannibal seized at least two opportunities: to send his second line to reinforce his first (while his veterans' presence kept the rest of the Romans in check), and to launch a final assault with the 20,000 or so veterans while Scipio was reordering his formations.

The unstinting praise that Polybius lavishes on Hannibal, and which Livy echoes, is overdone. Putting elephants in front of the army to disrupt the enemy's ranks no doubt looked fine as a concept, but it had failed dismally. Using his first two lines to weary the Romans and blunt their swords, and holding his veterans back for a decisive fresh blow, had not worked either, though it came close. Scipio owed much, too, to his adversary's earlier failure to recruit cavalry in enough numbers and experience to stand up to Masinissa's and Laelius' squadrons. Arguably, the outcome of Zama was due as much to Hannibal's now blunted brilliance as to Scipio's tactical mastery – and to the relentless strength of the men of Cannae.

Reportedly 20,000 of the Carthaginian army were killed and almost as many taken prisoner. The figures may well be exaggerated, but it was all the same the end of Carthage's last army. The prisoners no doubt included not only survivors among Hannibal's veterans but men from the first and second lines too, surrendering or rounded up. Polybius reports over 1,500 of Scipio's men dead, and very likely the wounded were at least as many: a serious cost to a Roman army of only 22,000 or so. Appian puts Numidian losses at rather more than Scipio's, a much heavier proportion of Masinissa's force. To both leaders the losses were worth it. In practice, the war was over.

Hannibal and a few companions left the field to ride for two days and nights back to Hadrumetum. There he managed to collect some troops, but he knew it was time for peace. Before long he was back in Carthage, for the first time (as he told the Carthaginians) since leaving 36 years before. Appian's further fantasies – Hannibal raising a new army 6,000 strong, the Carthaginians striving yet again to gather supplies to fight on, reviling his advice to make peace, then driving aristocrats out of the city – are not to be believed.[13]

After the battle Scipio seized Hannibal's camp with its contents, opulent according to Livy. Livy may exaggerate; in marching across country to find and fight the Romans, Hannibal had had little need for fancy and costly baggage. With the prisoners and battle spoils the proconsul returned to Castra Cornelia. The propraetor in charge of Sardinia, P. Cornelius Lentulus, had arrived with a fleet of quinqueremes, transports and plentiful supplies. Scipio at once sent Laelius on to Rome to announce victory and ordered Octavius to march down to Tunes with the returned, even though weary, troops. He himself sailed his enlarged war fleet boldly south for Carthage.

His confidence was justified. A single Carthaginian ship lavishly adorned with symbols of submission, white woollen garlands and branches of olive, rowed out from the city with ten of Carthage's highest-ranking senators aboard. Appointed on orders from Hannibal, they must have been the two current *sufetes* and the rest former *sufetes*, members of the inner council. Appian names their leaders as Hanno the Great, the leading and long-standing enemy of Hannibal and his dominant faction, and his associate Hasdrubal, nicknamed the Kid. That was, probably enough, why they were selected – to prove Carthage's genuine wish for peace and also (if the peace was crippling) to deflect blame from the Barcids. They sailed up to Scipio's flagship to proffer Carthage's plea.

His reply was that a formal embassy should await him at Tunes. Then he sailed the fleet round into the Lake of Tunis (much more open then than today) as an unmissable demonstration of total military triumph.

After that he returned to Castra Cornelia and, maybe a day or two later, marched for Tunes.

On the way he received word that Vermina, Syphax's son, was in the area. Just what the tardy Numidian prince thought he could achieve, weeks – perhaps now a month – after Hannibal's defeat, is hard to see, even though he had a sizeable force (Livy's narrative implies over 16,000 men, chiefly riders). He proved no great problem. A task force of some infantry and all the Roman cavalry went out from Tunes (commander unreported) and annihilated the Numidians somewhere in Carthage's hinterland. Like Hannibal before him, Vermina barely escaped with a few followers. The date by the out-of-kilter Roman calendar was 17 December, the first day of the Saturnalia festival: as mentioned earlier, corresponding apparently to a correct 25 November.[14]

Thirty senators from Carthage waited on Scipio at Tunes. They may have been again the thirty of the 'inner council' who had negotiated with him a year earlier. He read them a stern lesson about how treachery – the sack of Saguntum, the attack on his transports – deserved no leniency, then promised that nevertheless Rome would be generous. His new peace terms did combine sternness with mildness, though some members of his council wanted Carthage treated much more brutally – even its total destruction. Many, like Scipio himself, had lost kinsmen in battle and had seen much of Italy and Sicily ravaged by the long war. Pretty certainly there were demands for Hannibal himself to be seized like Syphax.

Scipio overruled objections. One of his motives, conceded by Livy, was to avoid being superseded at the last moment by some ambitious successor who would take on the glory of concluding peace. He may even have learned from friends at Rome that at least one candidate for the coming year's consulships, another Cornelius Lentulus, had just such an ambition. Averting this was not only a point of personal pride. For Carthage and Hannibal to be left free to renew the fight against some other – any other – commander was a valueless risk. Another motive, military and simple, was to avoid the cost and possibly even the failure of besieging Carthage, a city as strongly fortified as Rome. (Rome would encounter exactly this problem half a century later.)

Scipio supposedly liked to say afterwards that Ti. Nero's greedy ambition, and then Cn. Lentulus', kept him from finishing the war by annihilating Carthage. But if he did say it, it may only have been a testy response to the critics who infested his later years. At the time, he much more likely aimed for a firm but not vindictive peace that would end any chance of Carthage becoming a threat again, without new costs in Roman lives and treasure and with his reputation as bringer of victory unassailable.[15]

The terms he laid down, again permitting no negotiation, mixed the temperate with the harsh. He began mildly: the Carthaginians would keep their independence, their African territories and subject cities and all their moveable possessions (meaning no more Roman plundering). There would be no occupying garrison.

Predictably, though less palatably, they would have to pay reparations for the damages done during the armistice, along with handing back the transports and their contents (in fact the value of these, since it turned out that the Carthaginians had used up the contents). Of course, prisoners of war and deserters must be handed over too. They must pay an indemnity twice as much as in the aborted earlier treaty, 10,000 talents, but at a remarkably reasonable rate in the circumstances: two hundred a year over fifty years – something Carthage would have no trouble with once some prosperity returned. The amount was actually less than the yearly indemnity, 220 talents, that Carthage had had to pay for a decade after the previous war. Scipio would select a hundred Carthaginians aged from fourteen to thirty, evidently young aristocrats, to take to Rome as hostages (in practice, they would be replaced every decade or so).

But other provisos must have appalled even the Barcids' enemies. Carthage had to surrender all its warships save ten triremes, and all elephants. (Scipio had captured eleven after the battle, but others perhaps were stabled in the city.) It was banned from waging war outside Africa, and within Africa should wage no war without first consulting – in other words, getting permission from – the Romans. Furthermore, the Carthaginians must restore to Masinissa all the properties, lands and cities 'belonging to him or his forebears', once his kingdom's boundaries were determined.

This was a clause loaded with potential future trouble. Scipio imposed it perhaps partly to satisfy Masinissa. The king's immediate profits from peace were limited. He had been recognized by Scipio as ruler of Numidia and the Senate in Rome would soon confirm this, but he still had to impose his rule over much of it (Vermina was holding out in the west). He owned plunder from the Zama campaign plus the expensive gifts lavished on him by his Roman friend, and would soon be sent others conferred by the Senate. All the same, most of these were personal gains. Making the Carthaginians recognize his kingship and his territorial claims would add to his security, especially as the peace effectively put him under Rome's protection.[16]

This implicit protection was no doubt another reason of Scipio's for the clause. With a united Numidian kingdom under Roman patronage, the Carthaginians would always have a counterweight on their borders should they ever harbour dangerous thoughts about relations with the war's winner. One of the wiliest men of his (and any other) age, Masinissa would take exploiting the clause to extremes that even Scipio may not have foreseen.

When the thirty envoys returned to Carthage, Hannibal had to quell vociferous opposition to a diktat that cut the republic down to becoming more or less Rome's client. This was a fate that, among once prime Mediterranean powers, had as yet befallen only Syracuse. A senator named Gisco – was he the father of the late general Hasdrubal? – called on his fellow senators (or on citizens in the people's assembly, in Livy's version) to reject the terms. Hannibal, also present, angrily rose to drag him from the podium. He then apologized to the offended audience for acting like a military man rather than a civilian, and carefully expounded why Carthage had no choice but to accept.

With that, opposition collapsed. Spokesmen went back to Tunes to confirm that Carthage would send an embassy to Rome to ratify his terms. In return the proconsul granted an armistice – again on his terms. It would last three months; the Carthaginians must report any foreign envoys who arrived and send out no envoys other than to Rome. They meantime had to pay 25,000 pounds of silver (11.5 tonnes; about 350 talents) as compensation for the goods, private and public, from the looted supply fleet. That episode plainly rankled with Scipio, laden though he was with massive plunder from all over Libya.

The peace embassy to Rome would be chaperoned by Scipio's friend Veturius Philo; M. Marcius Ralla, another senior officer; and his own brother Lucius. Carthage's chief spokesman was again, it seems, Hasdrubal the Kid (the aged Hanno did not take part). The group did not leave for Rome at once. Winter months were not good for sea travel – storms could be fatal, and risking the lives of Carthage's envoys, not to mention Scipio's brother and friends, was out of the question. The journey was no doubt made only in a safer season, late February 201 or even March. Scipio must have had to extend the armistice, since its original three months would have expired soon after.

This fits Livy's report that bitter winter weather had so held up the elections for 201 that the new consular year opened on the Ides of March with no consuls at all. The actual date seems to have been 3 February or so, the Roman calendar being what it was. It was just before elections finally took place, under a dictator specially appointed, that the envoys arrived in Rome: thus later in March by Rome's calendar, in real time probably late February.[17]

Scipio meanwhile was busy during the winter preparing for peace and departure. The Carthaginians had not only to pay the required quantity of silver bullion to meet the value of the looted transports, but find and free the crews who had been seized. They must have been enslaved by opportune citizens, not all of them happy to hand the sailors back. He also spent time working out where Masinissa's and Carthage's territories met, a border Appian opaquely and uniquely calls 'the Phoenician trenches'. Where Masinissa was at this time, and whether he had any say in the work, we are not told. He may not have got the borders he would have most liked. The demarcation left important places like Sicca, Theveste and their prosperous regions to Carthage – prizes that decades later he would shamelessly try to annex as 'ancestral lands'.

To receive the Carthaginians' payments, and tell the Carthaginian authorities his decisions about their borders, Scipio no doubt met, once or more often, with *sufetes* and senators. Roman and Carthaginian aristocrats were no strangers to one another (as Hannibal would be reminded some years later). It is a teasing thought that just possibly another Carthaginian representative the proconsul happened to meet was Hannibal, still the city's military chief as well as a senator.

The delay over ratifying the peace treaty lasted longer than it should have. Not only did the election of the year's consuls take place sometime after the Ides of March, but one of the new pair was the already mentioned Cn. Cornelius Lentulus, who promptly caused trouble for everyone. Like Ti. Nero and Servilius Caepio before him, he wanted the glory of fighting, or at any rate pacifying, Carthage. He insisted so stubbornly, even defying reminders that Scipio had been appointed by overwhelming vote of the Roman people, that a compromise had to be worked out. The Senate decreed that he could sail to Africa and command at sea while Scipio continued on land, if the war went on. But if not, then not. To make doubly sure, Scipio was again reconfirmed as proconsul.

Lentulus was not placated. After the envoys from Carthage had been heard (sympathetically, Livy claims) – Hasdrubal the Kid apologizing on his city's behalf for the war and blaming it on 'a few greedy individuals' who never listened to him or Hanno, the other envoys pleading for compassion for a helpless homeland – the frustrated consul blocked the Senate from further discussion. Two tribunes of the *plebs* had to have the citizen assembly in effect order the Senate to authorize Scipio to conclude the treaty and bring his army home. Fortunately, after this was done Lentulus subsided, contenting himself with commanding his fleet in Sicilian waters.

Two of Rome's fetials were authorized to bear their sacral herbs and flint knives – the rites were very old – to conduct the peace ceremony in Africa. Sailing with them were ten senators formally delegated to supervise the procedure with Scipio and then assist him in implementing the peace terms. Other passengers included the thirty Carthaginian envoys and two hundred eminent prisoners of war, freed without ransom as a mark of goodwill. Possibly one of these was an aristocrat whose name we do not know but whose descendant Himilco, nicknamed Phameas, half a century later was Carthage's best cavalry general in its final war with Rome. Phameas would rely on his ancestor's friendship with Scipio when he deserted his doomed city to join the Romans led by Scipio's grandson. There were not many times when Scipio had the opportunity to form such a friendship with a former enemy. It could have happened if, for instance, Phameas' forebear had been lodged, when a captive, in Scipio's house at Rome under Aemilia's supervision (other examples are known of such lodgements), then met Scipio himself when sent home.

Or he might have been an official in the city whom the proconsul met during this winter.[18]

The closing stages of the expedition to Africa were measures marked with ceremony and severity. Once the fetials had met representatives from Carthage, no doubt priests too, to exchange ritual oaths, the peace treaty came into force. The Carthaginians handed over no fewer than 4,000 prisoners of war, together with the Roman deserters and fugitives in the city, plus its fleet and elephants. One notable released prisoner was a senator named Q. Terentius Culleo, who a while later would show how grateful he was in overstated fashion – walking in Scipio's triumph at Rome and wearing a liberty cap like a freed slave. Like Laelius, he would be Scipio's devoted admirer all his life.

Then, on an appointed day, the entire navy of Carthage – five hundred oared ships of all sizes, said some of Livy's sources – was gathered under Roman supervision on the waters some distance offshore. Filled with pitch, resin or other flammable materials, they were on a signal set afire. For the citizens of Carthage, 'it was as painful as if it were Carthage itself going up in flames': they were watching their long era of greatness come to a pathetic close. Scipio probably felt few pangs. A day later it was the turn of the surrendered deserters and fugitive slaves. The fugitives were handed to slave merchants for markets in Sicily or Italy. The deserters had no such relative reprieve. In public view, those who were Romans were crucified, the rest beheaded.[19]

Once the Carthaginians paid over the reparations for Scipio's looted transport goods, he was ready to leave. (Livy thought it was the first instalment of the war indemnity, but that was paid two years later.) At a final parade of his army, he again acclaimed Masinissa as king and declared that his kingdom would include Cirta and the rest of Syphax's dominions. Earlier, the proconsul had stressed to him that all Syphax's lands and people were Rome's rightful booty, so making a gift of them now put the king under a perpetual obligation to the republic. Masinissa may have been nearly as relieved as the Carthaginians to see him go.

At Rome the Senate had voted that the victorious proconsul should have the honour of a triumph. He and the army crossed to Lilybaeum, then parted. Most of the soldiery was sent on to Rome by sea to await him, but Scipio himself with a small escort (probably his elite *extraordinarii*) travelled across Sicily, then crossed to Italy to make their way north by land. They were greeted by huge and happy demonstrations in cities and the countryside, many of them in genuine joy at the plain proof that the war was over, some no doubt by ex-rebel communities in Bruttium, Lucania and Campania anxious to show renewed loyalty.

Scipio's return to Rome reunited him with Aemilia and their boys, now teenagers, after three years away. Some while later he celebrated his triumph, the religious and military celebration of victory that started outside the city walls with the general at the head of his soldiers, captives and booty, and wound through Rome's streets to reach the Temple of Jupiter on the Capitoline Hill – a shrine especially familiar to Scipio – to lay before the god his divine share of the spoils. This triumph was, Livy writes, the most splendid ever seen. As with every Roman leader who earned the honour, it was the grandest day of Scipio's life.

In the throng of soldiers and captives that followed him through Rome, two men stood out: Syphax, fallen king of the Masaesyli, and Terentius Culleo in his freedman's cap. Scipio brought 56 tonnes (123,000 lb) of silver into the Roman treasury as the state's quota of military booty, and he gave each soldier a gift of 400 *asses*, equivalent to about six weeks' pay (an ordinary soldier would possess a share of the plunder of Libya, too), while centurions and other higher-ranking men would receive more. Citizens in Rome then enjoyed days of public games and festivities – races, gladiators, even plays – all paid for by the *triumphator*. The good cheer did not extend to Syphax. He died soon after at Tibur, still interned despite Scipio's earlier sympathy.[20]

At some stage (Livy was not sure when) Scipio gained an admiring nickname, Africanus: 'the man of Africa'. Not as a joke about sunburn or his long absence there, but to recognize his achievement as the man who for the first time in Rome's history extended the republic's power to that continent. The term was not a formal name and was not in common use until a later era; Livy thought it may have been used only by his friends and admirers. By the time his grandson and namesake destroyed Carthage half a century later, though, honorific addenda to some victorious proconsuls' names were coming into use. The younger Scipio would take on 'Africanus' too, but for all time to come the epithet was reserved by custom for the victor of Zama.

9
Scipio in Peacetime

After more than a decade and a half at war, Scipio Africanus now had to live as a civilian. He was still only 34, younger than most Romans who reached the highest magistracies. His history-making successes had made him both admirers and enemies, a reality that would affect the rest of his life.

A leading Roman (later times used the term *princeps vir*, 'foremost man') had a wide circle of kinsmen, friends, supporters and social dependents – their *propinqui*, *amici*, *fautores* and *clientes*. Scipio's after the war with Carthage must have been one of the widest, though not even all its main members can be traced. His wife's brother, like their father who died at Cannae, was L. Aemilius Paullus (one day to be the conqueror of Macedon). A first cousin was P. Scipio, nicknamed Nasica, son of the uncle Gnaeus Scipio who had perished in Spain ten years before; another cousin was M. Pomponius Matho, who when praetor had helped deflect the scandal over Pleminius. Among Scipio's friends (besides Laelius) were P. Crassus, the *pontifex maximus*, L. Veturius Philo, who had served under him in Africa, and Q. Metellus – all recent ex-consuls. Two other likely *amici* are worth mentioning: Q. Minucius Thermus, one of his officers in Africa, and M'. Acilius Glabrio, who may have been another officer there, both then becoming plebeian tribunes in 201. These two thwarted Lentulus the consul's effort that year to make Scipio share the African command and the peacemaking.

Every eminent Roman also had enemies. Scipio, however charming and charismatic personally, faced many. Nor, it seems, did he put much effort into conciliation. Though his most persevering critic, the former dictator and Delayer Fabius Maximus, had died in 203 unimpressed to the end by Scipio's victories, there was a ready successor. Scipio's former quaestor M. Porcius Cato was a newcomer in Rome's politics, a substantial landowner and entrepreneur from the nearby city of Tusculum (Frascati). His career in public life was backed by his lifelong friend (some might say patron) L. Valerius Flaccus, a member of one of the patrician *gentes maiores*, and he had gained the blessing of Fabius Maximus.

Cato was an assertive – not to mention aggressive – personality, a powerful orator and author, and notoriously a traditionalist with strong though not absolute scepticism about importing Greek ideas and habits. From early on, things about Scipio Africanus and his kin irritated him, notably their greater openness to foreign – that is, non-Italian – cultures and persons. His criticisms had begun early, after his quaestorship (he had been scandalized by Scipio's easy Greek ways in Syracuse), and they would become open attacks in time.[1]

Who shared Cato's animus towards Scipio is not explicitly recorded. The recent consuls Ti. Nero, Servilius Geminus, Servilius Caepio and Cn. Cornelius Lentulus, perhaps: all had wanted to get a share of peace-making glory at his expense. But that they went on being hostile after 201 does not have to be assumed. Lentulus and Nero took no known part in any diatribes against him. One man whom Livy and others do report as a personal foe is Ti. Sempronius Gracchus, son of a leading Hannibalic War general, but he took no known part in later attacks on Scipio or his brother, and the personal *inimicitia*, we shall see, is open to question.

Another view sees various grandees as unfriendly members of a so-called Fulvian group, because in 205 the eminent Q. Fulvius Flaccus had seconded Fabius the Delayer in resisting Scipio's plan of invading Africa. Fulvius, though, was dead before Scipio's return, and no further Fulvius was highly prominent before a distant relative, M. Fulvius Nobilior, became consul in 189. Then it was another decade before two Fulvii Flacci did. Other political foes might be surmised: possibly Cn. Lentulus' brother Lucius (though, not long after Scipio came home, as consul in 199 he supervised the election that chose Scipio as one of the censors), their kinsman P. Lentulus Caudinus (but he had been helpful to Scipio a year earlier with supplies from Sardinia) and maybe M. Valerius Laevinus, who in 205, according to Livy, had seconded Fabius in opposing the expedition to Africa (but Laevinus could play little part in 201, for he was sent on a naval mission to Greece and soon died).[2]

P. Sulpicius Galba, one of the new consuls in 200, is yet another suggested political foe. As soon as he entered office, he browbeat the harassed voters in the *comitia centuriata* into reversing their recent disapproval of a new war – this one versus Macedon – and thereby, some infer, rebuffed Scipio because Scipio supposedly was against the war. The argument is convoluted. The *comitia*'s disapproval was prompted by a plebeian tribune named Q. Baebius, a kinsman of the L. Baebius who had been one of Scipio's officers in Africa. And Scipio may have been friends (like his brother-in-law Aemilius Paullus) with several Baebii, a family fairly notable in magistracies in these years. On the other hand, Q. Baebius' key objection was that fresh war meant fresh troop levies when the exhausting war with Carthage was barely over. The Senate promptly dealt with the matter: it forbade Galba from conscripting any men who had served in Spain or Africa – under Scipio, in other words – though he could accept any who volunteered (and many did). That done, Q. Baebius sank out of sight. Further hostility by Galba towards Scipio is not recorded.

What Scipio did think about Rome fighting Macedon, directly after fighting Carthage, no informant mentions. Possibly he judged it risky, maybe even unnecessary. Equally possibly he thought the opposite. Macedon had allied with Carthage in 215 and now was busy reasserting dominance in the Aegean Sea and Greece with not only a strong army but a powerful navy. But exempting his veterans from unwanted further service (especially the men of Cannae, already sixteen years or more under arms) must have pleased Scipio. Equally so the land grants in Samnium and Apulia decreed for them later that year: two *iugera* per man (2.5 hectares/6 acres) for each year served. The ten-man commission to make the grants included his friend Q. Metellus; one of the current consuls, P. Aelius Paetus; the ex-consul Geminus, who had once wanted to join or displace Scipio in Africa; Geminus' brother (also an ex-consul); and half a dozen middle-ranking past magistrates, one soon to be elected consul for 199. That it was a body largely rigged against Scipio, as sometimes urged, should not be inferred. Neither he nor Metellus is known to have made any complaint, and the grants (it seems) were made efficiently.[3]

Scipio's recorded activities in the new year of 200 were few and quite different. At his own expense he put on splendid celebratory games, which he had vowed while in Africa, and then offered himself for election as censor for 199–198. Livy writes that 'many eminent men' sought the office, without mentioning who lost. The election was held early in 199, supervised by one of that year's consuls, L. Lentulus, brother of the Gnaeus who had wanted to displace Scipio in 202. But even if L. Lentulus was unenthused by him, as is sometimes theorized, Africanus was successful. So was the most recent ex-consul, P. Aelius Paetus; and over the next eighteen months, Livy assures us, the two censors carried out their duties 'in great harmony'.

Censors' wide-ranging duties included inspecting, and if necessary emending, membership of the Senate and of the *equester ordo*, the citizens officially registered as Roman cavalrymen entitled to a war horse at state expense. They decided what public works and projects needed to be started, updated or overhauled, such as temples and other public buildings, roads, fortifications, contracts for military supplies and tax collections, and leases of state lands. The five-yearly census of Roman adult citizens and their allocation to the voting assemblies' *centuriae* and *tribus* according to property status – or lack of property – or to domicile was another crucial task. Scipio and Paetus may have been especially careful to collaborate, because in 204 their predecessors Livius and Claudius, joint victors at the battle of the Metaurus but intemperate personal enemies, had ended their term with farcical and unseemly wrangling.

The new pair revised Senate membership without disgracing anybody, let out contracts for customs dues at Capua and elsewhere, sold land confiscated from the same ex-rebel city and – probably, though it is not recorded – carried out the citizen census. If they did census the citizenry, the figure resulting should have been around 230,000, about halfway between the total recorded in 204 and the one in 194. Scipio and Paetus would have been heartened. A few years before Hannibal's war, the total had been 273,000, but the war's ravages and defections had pared citizens' numbers drastically.

Paetus performed another task, one particularly pleasing to his colleague. He appointed Scipio *princeps senatus*, as mentioned earlier: honorary first senator. It made Scipio literally *primus inter pares*. In any

Senate debate, he would be the first to be called on to speak and propose motions. The position had been empty since the death of Fabius the Delayer; replacing him must have given Africanus a sense of quiet satisfaction. Not even Cato criticized the appointment.[4]

In the post-war years, as a leading senator Scipio must have taken part in debates, given support to friends and kinsmen standing for office and perhaps (it was normal for aristocrats) acted on behalf of plaintiffs or defendants in court cases. No doubt he again paid night visits to Jupiter's temple on the Capitol. When in 200 a delegation came to Rome from Syphax's son Vermina, whose territory in western Numidia remained outside Masinissa's power, Scipio surely had something to say. Vermina asked for forgiveness and a formal treaty. The Senate sent an embassy to set the terms for this, a decision Scipio may well have recommended in memory of his and Syphax's one-time association – and perhaps too with an eye to keeping Masinissa within bounds.

Yet his role in public life was less than he would probably have liked. After the multiple consulships and extended proconsulships of the Second Punic War (Fabius the Delayer's and Q. Fulvius Flaccus' three, Marcellus' four and so on), the republic went back to the convention of replacing consuls in military commands yearly, with few exceptions. But though the new war with Macedon ran into stalemate – neither Galba in 200 nor his successor Villius, consul in 199, achieved much – there was no public demand for Scipio to seek a consulship again (it would have needed a special exemption) or be given a special grant of *imperium pro consule* to take over command, as in 210. Instead, a new and charismatic personality emerged to take charge and revolutionize Rome's dealings with the Hellenistic world.

T. Quinctius Flamininus, youngest of the land commissioners for Scipio's veterans, was elected consul for 198 along with Sex. Paetus, brother of Scipio's fellow censor. The allocation of consular *provinciae* then gave him charge of the war. Scipio may well have seen possibilities in him and backed him for election. It was against some opposition, for Flamininus was not yet thirty and was only a quaestor in 199. But he had drive and ideas, like Scipio himself at a similar age. The recent war's veterans were among his enthusiastic supporters, and Flamininus was then able to recruit 3,000 of them for his army. The commander he replaced,

Villius, already had among his troops another 2,000 veterans – who had frustrated his military efforts by mutinying over their unrewarding conditions in Greece. But it seems they served uncomplainingly with their comrades under his successor. Goodwill to Flamininus from Africanus can have helped.

Flamininus was affable, charismatic and unscrupulous, again rather like Africanus. In Greece he was as brutal to unfriendly cities as Scipio had been in Libya. His military successes pressed Philip v into making overtures for a compromise peace – but Flamininus primed his friends at Rome to support peace only if the Macedonian command was to be assigned to one of the incoming consuls for 197. If it was, then he would seize the glory of concluding the war at once. But as soon as the Senate decided to keep both consuls at home – and therefore prolong Flamininus as proconsul – Philip's hopeful ambassadors were denied a fair hearing, and the war went on.[5]

Scipio is not reported as one of the friends in this devious affair, though it would be worth knowing his view of these proceedings. An observer might recall how he had carefully misled Hasdrubal and Syphax outside Utica, until it was time to ambush them.

The Second Macedonian War was not a long-drawn-out agony like the recent Punic War. In June 197 Flamininus, now proconsul, destroyed the Macedonian army at Cynoscephalae in Thessaly. Philip v was forced to a peace that ended his predominance over Greece – it passed to Rome, hardly a surprise to Flamininus, Scipio and other informed Romans – and that undermined his position in the rest of the Hellenistic world. The booty was huge: it took three days to parade it all through the city when Flamininus finally came home with his troops in 194.

As proconsul over the intervening three years, he settled (or so he thought) the affairs of the always quarrelsome Greek states. He backed pro-Roman politicians in the mainland cities, was coolly prepared to overlook the occasional murder of their opponents and issued the momentous proclamation at Corinth in July 196 that from then on – so 'the Roman Senate and T. Quinctius commanded' – all Greeks were to be free. To complete this grand principle, after settling Greek affairs he prevailed on the Senate to have him bring all Roman forces home. Scipio was not at all happy about this aspect.

In the years following his censorship, the conqueror of Carthage was still an honoured figure. Kinsmen and friends won elections to magistracies, no doubt with his backing: Laelius became a praetor in 196, then in 194 cousin P. Nasica and the obscure Sex. Digitius (last heard of storming New Carthage fifteen years before), followed by L. Scipio in 193 – though this was an oddly lengthy wait for a brother who had been Africanus' trusted and busy lieutenant for years – and two years later Africanus' brother-in-law L. Aemilius Paullus in 191.[6]

Several Cornelii held consulships during the 190s: L. Lentulus in 199, a Cethegus during Scipio's censorship, Scipio himself in 194; then came a Merula in 193, and after him Nasica and brother Lucius. The clan of the Cornelii no doubt thought this not only right and proper, but normal. Yet only Lucius' consulship did much for Africanus (and that would prove less satisfactory than he would like). Most of the other consuls and Scipio himself had their hands full fighting the resilient peoples of Cisalpine Gaul. Success there was limited.

As the years passed, Scipio found his once unique pre-eminence gradually ebbing. On some noteworthy issues, in spite of *dignitas*, *auctoritas* and *gloria* that no one else could match, he failed to get his way. In 195 he suffered a rude rebuff when he tried to defend his and Rome's old enemy Hannibal from the Barcid leader's foes at home. Elected *sufete* at Carthage a year earlier, and enacting progressive political and economic reforms, Hannibal enraged his aristocratic foes enough for them to complain to *principes viri* at Rome who were their personal friends. Who these were Livy does not say, but three can be surmised: the ex-consuls Cn. Servilius Caepio and M. Claudius Marcellus (whose famous warrior father Hannibal had fought and respected) and Q. Terentius Culleo, the war captive brought home by Scipio. The three would afterwards be sent as envoys to Carthage – Culleo included, perhaps, because he could speak Punic. The current consuls, none other than the *novus homo* M. Cato and his patrician friend Valerius Flaccus, probably wanted action too on the complaints, but they were away on military campaigns (Cato in Spain, Valerius in Cisalpina fighting Gauls).

The Carthaginian grandees complained that Hannibal was conniving with Rome's newest eastern Mediterranean problem, the Great King Antiochus III of the Seleucid dynasty, to start a fresh war. Scipio had his own friends in Carthage and easily saw through the allegations. He strenuously opposed taking any notice of them, arguing that doing so was at odds with the *dignitas* of the Roman people. It was a case of factional hatreds against Hannibal, and Romans should be satisfied with beating him in war and not condone lies about him. For some time during 195 his opinion prevailed, but with more pressure from Carthage the Senate finally decreed the embassy of Caepio, Marcellus and Culleo. It used a diplomatic pretext: the envoys were to mediate (unasked) in a dispute between Carthage and Masinissa.[7]

The rebuff to Scipio was striking. Not only was he *princeps senatus*, but by now his intention to seek a consulship for 194 must have been known and he had good voter support. Yet he lost the argument over Hannibal. Terentius Culleo's appointment to the embassy was a small and meaningless concession – a minor senator alongside two ex-consuls. When they reached Carthage, Hannibal realized their true mission and at once left his homeland for life in exile.

Nonetheless, the consular elections later in the year did return Scipio and Ti. Sempronius Longus for 194. Their fathers had likewise been consuls together 24 years earlier (though the elder Ti. Longus had fought Hannibal at the river Trebia against the elder P. Scipio's advice, with a bad result). Africanus and his colleague were on good though not perhaps close terms, but neither would make a major mark on events in 194. Cicero does declare that in the city Scipio ordered the aediles to provide separate benches for senators in front of other spectators at public events: a divide obviously meant to enhance senatorial *dignitas*. It may be seen as typical of Scipio's aristocratic arrogance. All the same, Cicero averred, Scipio afterwards blamed himself for it, as did all his wisest contemporaries – and we know too that Valerius Antias earlier had put the measure down to the censors of 194.[8]

Scipio's real concern was the eastern Mediterranean. By now he held strong suspicions about the Great King. Antiochus' realm was the largest surviving from the break-up of Alexander's empire over a century earlier. It stretched (rather uneasily) from the Aegean side of Asia Minor to the edges of India, and every so often it fought a war with Egypt's Ptolemaic dynasty over disputed territories. At the same time, the Seleucid king had ancestral ambitions over lands in eastern Europe too. These were a danger to Flamininus' arrangements in Greece and the Aegean, especially as those arrangements had left several Greek states feeling wronged – notably the pugnacious Aetolian League in western Greece, because it had not won satisfying territorial rewards for supporting Rome against Macedon.

Scipio forecast war with Antiochus. His worries must have grown when word came that Hannibal had joined the royal court at Ephesus in Asia Minor and was being treated with honour. Diplomatic tensions mounted. News came that Antiochus had renewed military activities in Thrace (the northeastern region of the Balkans, adjoining Macedon and the Aegean) and in western Asia Minor. He was subduing recalcitrant cities and regions and founding new settlements. Worse still, he gave ear to the aggrieved Aetolians. Scipio demanded pre-emptive action to forestall any threat from them or the king, and more precisely, that Macedonia (the region) be made one of the year's consular *provinciae* in anticipation of war, not with Philip v but with Antiochus. Naturally, he would expect to be the consul sent out. Nor, of course, did he want Roman troops withdrawn from Greece.

He failed to move the Senate. Instead, Italy was assigned to both him and his colleague Ti. Sempronius Longus as their *provincia*. They were instructed to levy two new legions to strengthen military operations – against the Gauls. Then the Senate accepted Flamininus' request to bring his forces home.[9]

This rebuff to Africanus was more serious, and no doubt more humiliating, than the one over Hannibal and Carthage the previous year. It stamped him (in effect) as less important in the new age of Hellenistic geopolitics than leaders like Flamininus – this in spite of his past achievements and his eminence. In spite, too, of the fact that in this year other men of the *gens Cornelia* were in important offices: C. Cethegus was censor (so was Sex. Paetus, the brother of Africanus' agreeable censorial colleague); three of the six praetors were Cn. Blasio, Cn. Merenda and P. Scipio Nasica. But voters' favour was one thing, support from other leading men another. Nor did kinship (which could be remote, like Blasio's and Merenda's) guarantee political alliance or warmth. If any of the other Cornelii spoke up to second Scipio, they must have done it with little enthusiasm. Flamininus' friends carried the day.

Flamininus made an impressive return to Italy, leaving the Greek world ringing with his praises and adding his name to those of the gods in festive rites. He landed at Brundisium (Brindisi) to lead his troops, laden with plunder and prisoners, and with them 1,200 released Roman war captives across the peninsula to Rome. This quasi-triumphal cavalcade recalled, perhaps deliberately, the one from Africa that Scipio had led through Italy to the city seven years before. At Rome the new victor celebrated a triumph even grander than Scipio's. It took three days to show off the spoils gathered from defeated Macedon and its allies. At least temporarily, Africanus was outshone.

His year as consul for the second time made an unmemorable contrast with his first, eleven years earlier. The censors, his kinsman Cethegus and Sex. Paetus, did nominate him once more as *princeps senatus*, and later some of Livy's sources tried to devise something military for him to have done. All they could concoct, though, was a short foray into part of Cisalpine Gaul (his colleague Sempronius was busier). It is better to believe Livy's other sources, who, he says, reported Scipio doing nothing of note on campaign.

He probably kept an eye on the foundation of a number of small Roman colonies (*coloniae*) at strategic sites along Italy's Tyrrhenian and Ionian coasts, but they were not his idea or planned to be coastal defences against Antiochus. Five had been legislated in 198, long before any prospect of a Seleucid war and while the war with Macedon – which had a strong fleet – was being waged. One of the three appointed colonial commissioners was not Scipio but his colleague Sempronius: he only because he had been nominated back in 198. Commissioners for three others in the south did include his brother-in-law Aemilius Paullus and friend Baebius Tamphilus; if Scipio exerted himself to get them appointed, it was a small success. The best he could do politically was to help his brother Lucius win election as one of the six praetors for the coming year.[10]

An anecdote survives, undated but probably from this second consulship, that appealed to Scipio's admirers and critics alike. One day – it may have been when readying for Cisalpine Gaul – he was in a hurry to draw funds from the treasury, the *aerarium Saturni* stored in the Temple of Saturn below the Capitoline Hill. But the quaestor in charge refused to let him go in, because it was legally a day when no business was allowed.

The irate Scipio took the keys from him and said he would open it himself, because it was thanks to him that it was closed. In other words, that it was well stocked with the wealth he had brought to Rome.

The story is told, by Polybius and many others, as an example of Scipio's high-minded pride in his achievements. That went back, no doubt, to the family or Laelius. The punctilious quaestor at the treasury and Africanus' critics, in and outside the Senate, could see it instead as high-handed arrogance. Possibly too as impious presumption, if the temple was shut because it was a sacred day (of which there were plenty at Rome). In any case, if true the anecdote gives a glimpse of a man who by now could be thought of as one almost too towering to fit a free state.[11]

Cato's biographer Plutarch oddly has Scipio take the newly annexed territories in Spain as his consular *provincia*, replacing his old foe Cato, who had been warring there since his previous year's consulship. There is a simple explanation: Plutarch, or whomever he was copying, confused Africanus with his cousin P. Scipio Nasica. As praetor in 194, Nasica did receive one of the new territories, Hispania Ulterior (Further Spain, the south and west of the peninsula), as his *provincia*. There, Nasica bitterly criticized Cato for executing six hundred recaptured deserters (earning a typical sneer from that departing proconsul), a reproof that Africanus may have repeated in the Senate. But no amount of censure could thwart Cato being awarded his own triumph. The distinction was no doubt especially satisfying to him because Africanus while still consul would have to watch.

As Scipio had forecast, relations with Antiochus III grew worse. Antiochus wanted to stay at peace with Rome but to have a free hand in the European and Asiatic territories he claimed. When his envoys Menippus and Hegesianax arrived in Rome in winter 194, Flamininus, along with the ten senators who with him had recently organized Greek affairs, was assigned to discuss matters privately with them. Flamininus at first insisted on universal Greek freedom. Then, delicately and cynically, he hinted that if the king would guarantee to stay out of Europe, Rome might not worry about the Greeks of Asia after all. The envoys did not take the bait.[12]

Scipio was consul until mid-March 193; Antiochus' envoys reached Rome in late 194 or early 193. Scipio too was in Rome, for he had to supervise the elections for 193. Yet he played no part in the talks, which were run by Flamininus and Sulpicius Galba. It is a measure of how sidelined Scipio was on eastern affairs, even though he was intently concerned about them. Flamininus and his friends among the *principes viri* apparently felt they could do quite well without his input.

Next, a high-powered Roman embassy – the three recent consuls Galba, Villius and P. Paetus – was sent to Ephesus in Asia Minor during 193 to discuss matters with the king himself. Scipio, now ex-consul, very probably supported this. But again no agreement was reached with Antiochus. The envoys did manage, though, to plant doubts in the royal mind about his prize guest from Carthage, by paying Hannibal much friendly attention during their stay at Ephesus.

In one of the authors he used – Livy cites him as 'Claudius', pretty certainly his recent predecessor Claudius Quadrigarius – Livy found a pleasing story about this embassy. It makes Africanus one of its members and he too has conversations with Hannibal. On one occasion, he asks which commanders his old opponent judges the greatest. Hannibal names Alexander as the greatest, Pyrrhus the next greatest and himself as the third. Scipio laughs, and asks: 'So what would you say if you had defeated me?' Hannibal urbanely replies, 'That I was ahead of Alexander and Pyrrhus and all other commanders.' Scipio is impressed by the Carthaginian's ready response and delighted by the implicit praise. Livy, though, takes care to hint that he does not necessarily believe the story (Plutarch is happier with it later). Nor does it fit well with what else kept Scipio busy that year, including heading a separate embassy to Carthage.

A theory with some defenders is that after this embassy to Carthage, Scipio sailed east from there to make an offering on Apollo's sacred Aegean isle of Delos – and, still more speculatively, that he went on from Delos to Ephesus. Zonaras, channelling Cassius Dio, has him leave Africa for 'Asia', where he receives Hannibal's oblique praise. A surviving inscribed list of gifts to Delos' shrine of Apollo mentions a gold laurel crown dedicated by 'Publius, [son] of Publius, Cornelius consul of the Romans', which – by a rather forced inference – would show him donating the crown while, or just after, being consul. As he did not leave Italy or Cisalpine Gaul when consul in 194, it would follow that he was at

Delos the year after. From there it was (arguably) a fairly short summer sail across to Ephesus.

This further trip is unlikely, all the same, even if Scipio did deliver his gift at Delos in 193. Livy's careful citation implies he found the story only in Claudius, who in turn cited an earlier writer, Acilius' 'Greek books'. For the supposed Ephesus visit to be told by only one early writer – and that writer not Polybius, a close friend of Scipio's family – makes it sadly suspect. There are two other possibilities. If Hannibal's neat praise was delivered, more likely he said it to the envoys Galba and Villius, and they told of it after returning home. It could then tempt a later writer, on purpose or carelessly, to make the questioner Africanus himself by declaring him one of the envoys. Or, as mentioned earlier, just possibly Scipio had met with Hannibal outside Carthage during the winter of 202–201, amid the final peace embassies, and the exchange happened then only to be mislocated, perhaps in family members' vague recall. The writer Acilius, known as a senator in the 150s, could have got it from them.[13]

While the real envoys to Antiochus were on mission – with the king deliberately making himself hard to find – Scipio was part of the different trio sent to Carthage in summer 193. Masinissa had seized parts of Byzacium, the region on Libya's east coast that Scipio in 201 had left within Carthage's borders. In response to complaints from both sides, the Senate authorized him, his kinsman Cethegus and an ex-praetor, Minucius Rufus, to investigate. Neither Cethegus nor Minucius had served in the North African campaigns; no doubt they deferred to Scipio.

Given Rome's friendship with the Numidian king, the territory decision might have been expected – and probably Masinissa did expect it – to go in his favour. Instead (Livy claims), the issue was left open. The reality is rather different. Twenty-one years later, Masinissa's renewed land-grabbing, taking over not only the region disputed in 193 but others, elicited a firm rebuke from Rome: that the Senate did not wish to see any changes in the old borders or the territories left to Carthage after its defeat. In other words, Scipio and his fellow envoys in 193 did not give the king what he wanted. They left the borders as he had drawn them in 201. Writers later on would choose to see this as a non-decision.[14]

The elections for 192 showed how ambivalent Scipio's position in the post-war republic was – honoured public hero and diminished political force, both together. We have unusually full details. His cousin P. Nasica was one patrician candidate, just back from two years' vigorous and victorious campaigning in Spain. One rival to him was Flamininus' brother L. Quinctius, undistinguished in his own recent praetorship, and a third was Cn. Manlius Vulso, who had been almost as unnoteworthy earlier as praetor. One of the three plebeians seeking consular election was Laelius, Scipio's oldest friend and partner in all his victories.

Africanus and (writes Livy) the entire *gens Cornelia* strongly supported his cousin's bid. Nasica not only was a successful general but had religious distinction: in 205 he had been named the finest of Rome's moral men and was deputed to welcome into the city a sacred offering from Asia Minor's most hallowed shrine, that of the Great Mother. Laelius too had Scipio's and other family members' backing. T. Flamininus, and surely other Quinctii of the time, were as emphatic for L. Flamininus. The result was a sad surprise for Africanus' side. Even though the consul presiding at the vote was another Cornelius, L. Merula – and consuls often could influence voters – neither Nasica nor Laelius was elected for 192. The new consuls were L. Flamininus and one Cn. Domitius Ahenobarbus, the first Domitius elected to the office in 91 years and only the second in history. It cannot have been much consolation to Scipio that a Baebius Tamphilus (perhaps brother to his friend Q. Baebius) gained a praetorship, or that the new consuls then spent most of their year fighting in the north against the indomitable Gauls, even though war was looming with the Seleucid Empire.

Livy draws on a perceptive source, Polybius or another, to comment. Scipio Africanus was the most eminent man of the day, but his fame was already ten years old. Flamininus' glory was newer: he had just celebrated his brilliant triumph over Macedon and Philip v. But much always depended on who, among the republic's 250,000 citizens, could actually attend an election held in autumn or winter and wished to do that. Skilful oratory and (sometimes) artful promises played their part, too. Scipio and his family, beaten in 193 for 192, did much better within a year.

In the consular elections for 191, held in autumn rather than winter 192 because war now did break out, P. Nasica was finally successful. The plebeian consul elected was the family friend M'. Acilius Glabrio. Like Cato in 195, he was a *novus homo* (not that this endeared him to Cato). It did mean that Scipio's brother Lucius, also a patrician candidate, was not elected, but he would soon try again. Of the six new praetors, one was Scipio's brother-in-law Aemilius Paullus. On how friendly or unfriendly the others were, modern views vary.[15]

War could pause rivalries and enmities. Given Greece as his *provincia*, where Antiochus had arrived with small forces late in 192 apparently expecting an enthusiastic welcome, Glabrio took with him L. Flamininus and the irascible but experienced Cato, both ex-consuls, among his military *legati*. It was Cato who then scored a stunning success. He outmanoeuvred Antiochus' forces at the fated pass of Thermopylae and so shattered the ill-conceived Seleucid expedition to Greece. The Great King, like Xerxes three hundred years earlier after his own defeat in Greece, hurriedly sailed for Ephesus. By the end of the year, preparations could begin for a Roman invasion of Asia. Now Africanus was wanted again.

10
Scipio's Last War

The Seleucid Empire was vast but rickety. Antiochus III, becoming king at twenty in 222 BC, had had to spend years reconquering breakaway territories and pretenders in its far east, the north and Asia Minor, as well as fighting from time to time the still powerful Egypt of the Ptolemies. Asia Minor, Thrace and the Aegean Greeks, with their medium-sized kingdoms and plentiful small city-states, had been parts too of the empire or under its dominance: hence Antiochus' drive to redominate as many as he could. Rome's unprecedented entry into mainland Greek affairs, overthrowing a century and a half of Macedonian supremacy there, must have made him the more determined. He had not been anxious for war, all the same. In fact, during the 190s he had been officially declared an 'ally and friend of the Roman people'. But when four years of unproductive negotiating failed, he welcomed the call of the restive Aetolians to come to Greece and free it from Roman tyranny (a call their congress made, literally in the face of an ambassadorial Flamininus himself). Disaster duly followed.[1]

Once Antiochus and his forces were thrown out of Greece, the question arose of who should command the expedition into his Asian dominions. Acilius Glabrio could have been left in charge as proconsul, like Scipio and Flamininus after their year of office. But opinion had turned against lengthy proconsulships. Not only did they give single commanders too much opportunity for extra victories and *gloria*, but – as Scipio had found in Libya a decade before – while a war was being waged, every incoming consul coveted his opportunity for these valuables. At the consular elections in 191 for the coming year, Africanus' brother Lucius and their friend Laelius stood again, and this time both were successful.

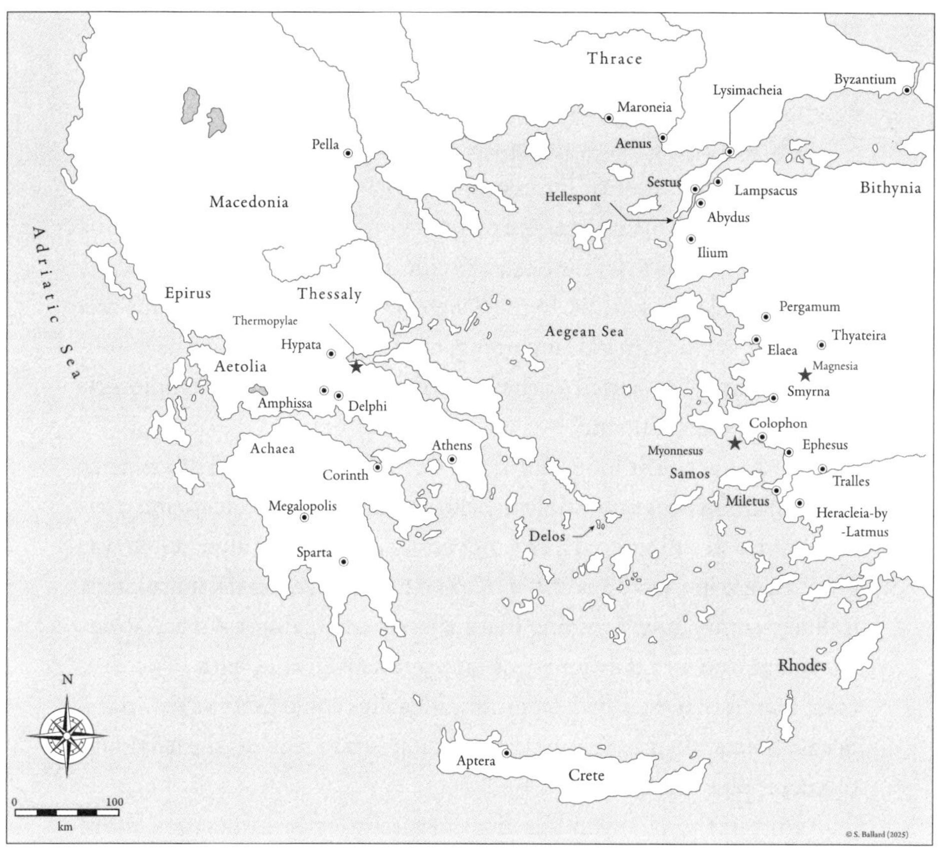

Scipio in the east, 190–189 BC.

It was a certainty that one or other would be sent to take over from Glabrio. Rather surprisingly it was not Laelius, the more than able soldier and commander. Lucius Scipio – solid but less experienced – received the *provincia* of Greece from the Senate. There was no move to make both consuls joint commanders, even though that had been done as recently as 206 against Hannibal in Italy and the new pair knew each other's military capacities. Instead, Laelius was left to supervise Italy and, inevitably, keep an eye on Cisalpine Gaul.

Conflicting accounts exist about the decision. Cicero in a speech in 43 BC claimed that L. Scipio had been assigned the eastern expedition by lot (the normal process) but, judged too lacking in vigour and valour, was then denied it by the Senate and the expedition was transferred to Laelius. Whereupon Africanus rose to fulminate against this insult to his family, vouch for his brother's qualities and pledge to serve under him as deputy (*legatus*) despite his own age. So emphatic was he that Lucius' appointment was confirmed.

Livy writes practically the opposite. The Senate bade Laelius – who, we are assured, had great influence there – and L. Scipio either to cast lots for their *provinciae* or agree on these between themselves. Laelius urged his colleague to let the Senate decide instead. Africanus, when consulted, agreed with Laelius. In the Senate he then said that, if Lucius was assigned *provincia Graecia* (including, implicitly, Asia Minor), he would be his *legatus*. This averted a debate and the Senate, almost unanimously, give Lucius the command.

Neither account looks accurate. For Africanus to treat Laelius as Cicero has him do is impossible to believe. Laelius was his oldest and closest friend, and still revered him (as Polybius attests) long after Scipio was gone. Cicero in 43 had a point of his own to push against altering eastern military commands. Bringing in a – not closely relevant – story about the one in 190 was only a part of his argument. Just as hard to accept, from Livy, is that the *novus homo* consul Laelius could exert a sway in the Senate greater than L. Scipio's consular *auctoritas*, still less the *auctoritas* of Lucius plus Africanus.

Quite likely, Lucius and Laelius did agree to refer the decision about military commands to the Senate, whether or not Africanus was consulted about it. It was an unusual procedure, as Livy also comments – but it had been done in 205 to put Africanus in charge of invading Africa. Now he let the senators know that he was ready to serve as subordinate to his brother, 'despite my age and great achievements', as Cicero makes him say. The remark could be genuine, even if not the exact words: a small touch of age pathos (Africanus was 46 and could already have begun to suffer in health) blended with predictable personal pride. Lucius in fact would need several *legati* for so crucial an enterprise, but clearly his brother was to be the chief one.[2]

There were other notable officers. One of the other *legati*, named by Appian, was Cn. Domitius Ahenobarbus, consul two years before. Africanus' old friend Sex. Digitius was another, one of three sent by Lucius to gather shipping along the Adriatic coast to carry his troops over to Greece. One of the army's military tribunes was the Ti. Sempronius

Gracchus mentioned earlier. Another was a quite young M. Aemilius Lepidus, whose father was to be consul three years later. Finally, and worth notice though not mentioned until 189 under a post-war commander, there was the cavalryman M. Valerius Mottones, once a North African officer in Carthaginian armies who, twenty years earlier, had requited insults from his aristocratic superior in Sicily by defecting to Rome, eventually to become a Roman citizen. He and his eldest son (he had four) were put in command of a body of Numidian cavalry sent by Masinissa.[3]

Africanus had a personal worry at this time. His younger son, another L. Scipio, now in his early twenties like Lepidus, had been captured in Greece by Antiochus' forces at the start of the war. He may have been serving in Glabrio's army or with the Roman fleet in Greek waters. (Scipio's older son, also named Publius, was too unhealthy all his life to have a military or political career; instead he wrote history.) Antiochus treated his prisoner with honour, not only out of respect for Africanus but because, Livy says, the king had a bond of guest friendship with the Scipio family. When that bond was formed it would be interesting to know.[4]

Just before the brothers and their entourage left Rome, Africanus dedicated an arch near the Temple of Jupiter Optimus Maximus on the Capitoline Hill, beside the pathway that led up from the Forum. The arch does not survive but Livy describes it: seven gilded human statues and two of horses adorned it, with two marble basins in front. A costly and complex structure – plainly to honour Scipio's cherished god – must have been planned and begun some time before he departed. The statues perhaps were of gods and heroes associated with Jupiter, or figures from Roman history – maybe even eminent ancestral Scipios, buried in the family vault outside the city wall. With the arch being constructed in full view of citizens, Scipio was asserting family pride (not for the first time) and reminding Romans that there was one family, above all, fit to lead them against yet another menacing foreign power. If building it had been well under way when the consular elections took place, the project may even have helped L. Scipio and Laelius as candidates. At the same time, a visible statement of Scipionic pride would add to some other Romans' irritation.[5]

For Lucius' eastern *provincia* the Scipios had to organize forces. There were already troops in Greece under ex-consul Glabrio, some 37,000 by modern estimate. But to face the army of the Great King, larger forces were needed. Lucius levied 3,000 Roman infantry and 100 cavalry, along with 5,000 Italian allied foot and 200 horse. Then came in 5,000 of his brother's veterans as volunteers, eager and still full of vigour. Some were probably men of the old Cannae legions with 26 years' experience. Enthusiasm for their old leaders no doubt brought the veterans in, along with the equally enthusing prospect of plundering the wealthy east. Many of the veterans who had enlisted under Flamininus were very likely volunteering again. In Greece, contingents from the Achaean League and volunteers from Philip v's kingdom were ready too. The land expedition was complemented in turn by large Roman and allied fleets in the Aegean.

Rome had a range of allies, especially the Achaeans in the Peloponnese, the island state of Rhodes with its powerful navy, and the small kingdom of Pergamum near the Hellespont and the site of Troy, ruled by the subtle Eumenes II, an old target of Antiochus and his bitter enemy. Meanwhile Prusias, since 230 the durable king of small but strategic Bithynia beside the Hellespont and sea of Marmara, was wavering. The two other leading states in the east, Macedon and Egypt, were formally neutral and in practice friendly. Apart from allowing or encouraging volunteers, Philip v's amiable neutrality would make possible a secure march for the Scipios across Macedon and Thrace to the Hellespont. For Philip this brought rewards: his elder son Demetrius, a hostage at Rome, was released and the outstanding balance of Macedon's war indemnity cancelled.[6]

Antiochus, chased out of Greece, had little appetite for warring on. His best hope for peace was to offer concessions while preventing the Roman expedition from crossing to Asia Minor. To block a crossing he concentrated his existing fleet at Ephesus, while calling on his Phoenician vassals for more ships. Strangely, the 'admiral' he sent to gather these Phoenician reinforcements was not a naval man but the greatest non-Roman land commander since Alexander. That Antiochus put no faith in Hannibal's bold if not very realistic proposal to invade Italy with 10,000 troops is (and even then was) clear. That he would not even keep his exiled friend as a prime military adviser, as L. Scipio was doing with his brother, is harder to explain. But it was an open secret that the king's generals and councillors resented the newcomer and feared his influence on the king. Antiochus needed them more than he needed Hannibal, so he found work for the ex-general on the seas. It would not be a success.

The Scipios mustered their Roman and Italian troops at Brundisium for the crossing to Greece. Livy gives the Roman calendar date: the Ides of Quinctilis, meaning 15 July (Quinctilis was later so renamed). In reality it was 18 March, for the eclipse of the Sun he puts on '11 Quinctilis' had occurred four days before (without raising any religious alarms). Rome's official calendar, already in disarray at the time of Zama as noted earlier, was now even less correlated with real reckoning. No one seems to have worried.[7]

Crossing from Brundisium over to Epirus, the brothers found Glabrio, now proconsul, still busy against the stubborn, and frightened, Aetolians. They had tried to come to terms much earlier but – so they claimed – had not understood that in Roman terms surrender, *deditio*, meant unconditional capitulation. This they refused, which left Glabrio attacking one toughly defended Aetolian centre after another. This was a nuisance to the Scipios, who were focused on marching for the Hellespont. Glabrio was fruitlessly besieging Amphissa, an important city near Delphi. After a brief push against the Aetolians' chief city Hypata, to the north near Thermopylae, Lucius sent his brother ahead to Amphissa and Glabrio to size up the position, while he followed with his troops. A rather unusual contretemps followed.

First there arrived on the scene an embassy from Athens – one of several goodwill gestures during the war. Athens, now neutral, was a long-standing friend of the Aetolian League and likewise of Rome. (One Roman argument for fighting Philip V in 200 had been to protect Athens from him.) The embassy's chief, Echedemus, met Africanus and readily persuaded him that milder terms should be offered to the Aetolians. Told to inform their leaders in Hypata, the Athenian at once set off. At this point the consul himself reached the siege camp.

When Echedemus returned with spokesmen from Hypata, Africanus was again approached. He received from the Aetolians a lengthy speech about the Aetolian League's past friendship and good deeds towards

Rome – not perhaps the most tactful way to seek concessions. They were treated, in return, to one of his trademark homilies: about his achievements in Spain and Africa, how he had dealt with the peoples there who had put their trust in him, and why the league should do the same now. His tone was mild and his manner benign.

But then his brother the consul took over. Lucius told the Aetolians they had just two choices: either surrender unconditionally or pay 1,000 talents at once and become allies (in practice, subject allies) of Rome. These were the alternatives that the Senate had decreed the year before. Learning of this appalled the Aetolian leaders in Hypata, unable to find a thousand talents – 6 million *drachmae* – and terrified of what surrendering might lead to. They sent a new embassy to beg Lucius to lower the sum or else exempt their leaders and womenfolk from *deditio*. He replied that he could not vary the Senate's terms.

For Lucius to override his elder brother (and supposed mentor) so firmly was remarkable. As consul, of course, he had the final say. Even so, there must have been some tense arguments in his military council, with Lucius quite likely feeling that Publius was stepping beyond his proper role. In the end, though, he agreed to make a concession. Echedemus had gone back to Hypata and convinced the Aetolian leadership to ask for a six-month armistice, during which they would send an embassy to Rome to put their case. When he and the current envoys returned, Africanus put enough pressure on his brother to get Lucius to agree.

Suggesting an armistice had probably been Africanus' idea, which Echedemus then took to Hypata. Polybius stresses that Scipio viewed the Aetolian business as a sideshow holding up the thrust into Asia. By now it was sometime in May by the actual calendar. A six-month pause in Greece would free the expedition to march to the Hellespont and cross into Asia, where Antiochus was already operating against Eumenes' kingdom. The Scipios could aim to bring him to battle before Lucius' consulship ran out. In Greece, if the Aetolians chose to renew fighting it would be winter, and by the time of the next campaigning season Antiochus would arguably be out of the war and Aetolia left to Roman mercy. This made sense to Lucius. The armistice was signed, Amphissa was freed from siege and Lucius formally took command of Glabrio's army. The march north could start.[8]

Of course, they had to be sure that they could pass through Macedon without interference. This was all but certain, as Philip v had regained his son from Rome and had been promised remission of his war indemnity. Nonetheless, formal agreement was needed, and so the military tribune Ti. Gracchus was sent off to Philip's capital, Pella. He made the ride in three days using relays of horses, was genially received and the next day was shown ample preparations made by the king to help the march: provisions readied, bridges built or repaired, roads tended. Riding back as swiftly as before, he informed the Scipios, now advancing beyond Hypata, and the army headed for the Hellespont. Both brothers, separately it seems, wrote ahead to L. Aemilius Regillus, the praetor commanding Rome's fleet at Samos in the Aegean, to let him know. The upshot was that Regillus, Eumenes and their Rhodian allies turned down an offer from Antiochus of immediate peace talks. He would have to wait until the consul came to Asia.

It was now late summer. On the journey through Macedon and into Thrace they were joined by Philip himself, anxious to show gratitude for the concessions made to him. No doubt too he showed proper admiration for the conqueror of Spain and Africa: Africanus, Livy stresses, found him a regal and congenial personality. The meeting led to Scipio later writing for the king, at Philip's request maybe, an account of his capture of New Carthage two decades before (a letter that Polybius would one day use).

The advance took time. Sick soldiers were left at forts along the route, guarded by detached units. Antiochus still had strong garrisons at Maroneia and Aenus on the Thracian coast; the army was able to bypass them but had to move with care. The Thracian Chersonese (the Gallipoli peninsula) was another problem. Antiochus' powerful fortress city there, Lysimacheia, blocked the crossing points to Asia. His naval forces posed an equal problem. Unless they could be put out of action, they could make crossing from Europe to Asia risky if not impossible. The Scipios had to look to events at sea.[9]

The Bithynian king Prusias' attitude was another uncertainty, for Antiochus was making a strong effort to win him over. Prusias, though, proved not hard to conciliate. The brothers sent a letter assuring him that Rome had no intention of deposing foreign kings like him. Africanus' many royal friendships and confirmations in Spain and Africa (Masinissa figuring notably) were soothingly listed, as was Rome's now amicable treatment of Philip v. The letter worked, especially after a confirmatory visit by Livius Salinator, Rome's recent fleet commander in the Aegean. Prusias rebuffed Antiochus' latest overture and declared neutrality.[10]

In September, as the army skirted Maronea and Aenus on the Thracian coast, the Scipios at last learned that the combined Roman and Rhodian fleets had heavily defeated Antiochus' fleet off the isle of Myonnesus, near Ephesus – so heavily that the king had, all too rashly, sent orders to his garrison at Lysimacheia to withdraw. The Romans quickly took over the city, still stocked with copious munitions. There they stayed for some days to ready for the crossing. The sick and other troops left back in forts along the way were gathered in. Eumenes, unobstructed by Prusias, was assembling transport ships lower down the peninsula: probably around Sestus, 60 kilometres (37 mi.) southwest of Lysimacheia and directly opposite Abydus on the Asian side, or 20 kilometres (12 mi.) further south at the even narrower sector facing modern Çanakkale. The Romans left Lysimacheia, reached the crossing point – and stopped there for a month.

The explanation given was that the rites of the *sodales Salii* were taking place at Rome. Scipio was still a Salian priest and therefore, even though far from Rome, was required to stay in one place, not only during the actual days of the ritual but for their entire month. Neither his brother nor the rest of the expedition was equally bound to be immobile, but that they were emphasizes Scipio's importance to the venture.[11]

Oddly enough, over Scipio's ten campaign years from 210 to 201 the Salian rituals are never mentioned by any source. Nor, more generally, is the claimed rule that a Salius away from Rome must stay rooted to one place during the ceremonial month. Until 190, then, the rituals never seem to have got in Scipio's way. The contrast with his delay at the Hellespont is surprising. Had he been lucky in the war with Carthage that none of his actions had needed doing during a March or October? But the Battle of Zama had. Or perhaps, as he reached middle age, Scipio became more punctilious. A third possibility is that he had fallen ill (as he soon would again in Asia), but the brothers feared harming army morale by announcing it at so critical a stage of the expedition and instead put out the Salian immobility story – a sacred need that their soldiers could understand and accept.

The Salian spring rituals fell on five separate March days in the Roman calendar, but – the calendar being so disjointed in the early second century – the rituals of Roman March 189 were actually performed in chilly autumn, November 190. Ten months later, Roman January 188 (a supposed winter month) would really open in mid-August 189 (summertime). The disparities had to be obvious to every Roman but, as with the earlier eclipse, no one appears to have been troubled.

In the Scipios' case, they had now reached the moment (Roman 15 March 189) when Lucius' term as consul expired. At Rome, in fact, the Asian command would soon be transferred to the new patrician consul, Cn. Manlius Vulso. Fortunately it would take some time for details to reach the Hellespont. Meanwhile the Senate in Rome was content for Lucius to continue until Vulso came.

The Great King was now anxious to secure peace if he could get bearable terms. As L. Scipio and his army waited by the Hellespont, a royal friend, Heracleides of Byzantium, arrived as a new ambassador. His instructions included making a personal approach to Africanus, so he had to wait a few days until the Salian month ended. But when Africanus did appear, Heracleides was told to put Antiochus' proposals to the entire military council. The king offered to give up several key cities in the eastern Aegean coastlands, notably Lampsacus and Smyrna and others that had taken Rome's side. He also promised he would pay half of Rome's costs in the war.

Heracleides made the elementary error of speaking for too long and lecturing his hearers. The Romans should remember they were but men, and avoid testing Fortune too severely. They should put limits on their dominion, for it was already the largest in history, and indeed they should restrict it to Europe. Or if they did want to take over parts of Asia too, let them say which precisely and Antiochus would strive to comply if he could. This style of address did not improve the temper of the council or the consul. Yet their reply would not have been very different had Heracleides' discourse been more obsequious. Rome required that Antiochus must pay all the Roman costs of the war, as he had been the one to start it – and must give up everything he ruled west of the Taurus mountain range, 1,000 kilometres (620 mi.) to the southeast.

This would strike a shattering blow to Antiochus' territorial ambitions and imperial prestige, and at the same time hugely extend Rome's influence in the eastern Mediterranean. Heracleides had no instructions for dealing with such demands. Instead, invoking the Scipio family's guest friendship with the king, he asked for and got a private interview with Africanus.

First, he gave Scipio the pleasing news that the king would send back his son ransom-free. Next, he made an offer that Antiochus obviously hoped Scipio could not refuse: the king would gift him at once whatever sum he cared to name, and afterwards would share the Seleucid Empire's revenues with him, if Scipio helped secure the terms Antiochus sought.

Scipio turned down the colossal bribe but gave his thanks for his son's promised release. He also gave Antiochus, through his envoy, a frank lecture. Had the king put forward his proposals while still holding Lysimacheia and the approaches to the Hellespont – or even, Scipio added, had he moved afterwards to threaten the Roman crossing with his army – he would have been successful. Now it was too late. So the best advice Scipio would give, as a return for his son's promised freedom, was that Antiochus should face up to reality and, above all, should avoid battle.

So at least Scipio afterwards reported (he is the only likely source for what was said). That he was quite so frank with stern advice is possible, but it may well have been more diplomatically phrased. Scipio was a masterful diplomat, and Antiochus had not yet sent young Lucius back. In any case, Heracleides departed to relay to the king that his mission had failed.

As soon as Scipio's Salian pause was over, the Romans made the crossing to Asia Minor and encamped outside Ilium, beside the site of ancient Troy. There, L. Scipio and no doubt his brother paused to pay pious respect with sacrifices to Troy's tutelary goddess, Athena. Alexander the Great had done the same after he too had first set foot in Asia, a parallel both brothers must have known – and if not, the welcoming citizens of Ilium certainly told them.[12]

Heracleides was not the only envoy to approach the Romans. According to a later historical epitome on the Greek city of Heracleia (today Eregli), by the Black Sea 600 kilometres (370 mi.) east of the Hellespont, the Heracleians thought it wise to offer to be Rome's friends – they had little love for the predatory Antiochus – and, as a start, earned a cordial response from a 'Publius Aemilius', who may in fact have been L. Aemilius Regillus, the fleet commander. If so, their letter probably preceded the Scipios' arrival at the Hellespont, for Heracleia then sent not one embassy but two in succession to the brothers, the first to confirm their new friendship, the second to offer to help negotiate peace. Both Africanus and L. Scipio replied amiably (says the epitome). No doubt encouraged, the Heracleians sent off a decree to Antiochus bidding him to cease being Rome's enemy. No doubt again, Antiochus ignored them.[13]

We happen to know of Heracleia's friendship-seeking messages from a Byzantine résumé of a history by a second-century AD son of the city, Memnon. It was surely not the only city now paying careful court to Asia's new and armed arrivals. The Romans' ability to bring down powerful and imperial enemies had been firmly proved over the last eighty years. But cities like Heracleia counted for little in the military scale of things. Polybius and then Livy found no room for them in their narratives.

Antiochus now felt that even if he lost, he could not expect harsher terms. Battle was the only way forward. He had positioned himself with his army at Thyateira, about 100 kilometres (62 mi.) inland from Smyrna and three times that distance from the Scipios. With him were his son Seleucus as second in command and his nephew Antipater as another senior commander. He was not going to move closer. The Scipios would have to move against him.

Camp was duly struck and the army began a southward march. Six days later, what looked like a disaster happened. As the Romans advanced past Pergamum, to be joined by King Eumenes, Africanus fell seriously ill. It may not have been as life-threatening as his collapse in Spain sixteen years before – this time no one feared he would die – but it laid him so low that he could not go on. Instead he rested at Elaea, Eumenes' naval base 30 kilometres south of Pergamum. Receiving this news, Antiochus was as good as his word. He freed Scipio's son and sent him to Elaea. Scipio was grateful, gracious and enigmatic: he sent his thanks to the king and warned him 'not to come down to fight until he learns that I have returned to camp'.[14]

No one knows what he meant. Obviously not that if Antiochus took his advice, he would let the king win. But perhaps a hint that he would not let him be defeated too badly? Realistically, that could not be guaranteed. Rather more likely, Scipio wanted to convey that once back in camp, he would influence his brother to offer more acceptable terms; no battle would be needed. Of course he could not guarantee that, either.

Antiochus did not take the advice. On a winter's day in December 190 or perhaps January 189, on the plain by the city of Magnesia across the mountains northeast of Smyrna, he deployed an army said to be 72,000 strong and was utterly defeated.

With Africanus absent and Polybius' account likewise, the ancient sources surviving could not believe that his brother was capable of such a victory. Livy names no Roman officer during the battle except young M. Aemilius, the tribune in charge of the camp, who rallied the Roman left as it retreated under Antiochus' personal attack. He then rather grudgingly credits Eumenes' cavalry charge from the victorious allied right wing with completing the enemy's rout. Appian offers the victor's credit to Cn. Domitius, one of the other legates. In fact there is no real reason to deny the laurel to L. Scipio for a success that for a time came near to a defeat.[15]

Antiochus retreated, minus most of his grand army, first to Sardes (the one-time capital of Croesus), then further inland to Apameia in Phrygia. Lucius Scipio marched to Sardes, occupied it peacefully but decided against chasing after the king. His brother Publius, only just recovered, joined him and the army there. One city after another across western Asia Minor – Sardes, Ephesus, Tralles and more – was now offering congratulations and declaring devotion to Rome. Antiochus' power still stretched from eastern Asia Minor to India, but his wish to end the ruinous war was more powerful. He sent envoys to Sardes, first a herald to ask for an armistice, then a high official named Zeuxis and his own nephew Antipater.

The Roman they dealt with was Scipio Africanus. For negotiating, Lucius was clearly content to defer to his brother's judgement. Scipio, loftily assuring Antipater and Zeuxis that victory never made Romans harsher or defeat milder, reiterated the terms put to Heracleides a few weeks earlier. The king must withdraw beyond the Taurus range and pay Rome's full war costs – now specified for the first time as 15,000 talents. He had to pay 500 at once, then 2,500 when peace was ratified and the rest in twelve yearly instalments. It was a far heavier indemnity than Scipio had put on Carthage only a dozen years before. The 400-talent debt the king must also repay to his old foe Eumenes was trifling by comparison.

Next came a more sinister demand. Antiochus was to hand over Hannibal to the Romans, as well as four of his own counsellors whom Rome saw as warmongers. Would Africanus, who had defended him against his enemies five years before, have wanted him dead at Roman hands? The decision, though, would not have been his. Of the four counsellors, at least one was soon pardoned by the Romans, and maybe all were; but Hannibal would surely not have been as lucky. The exile, who had spent the war being an unsuccessful commodore in the waters of southern Asia Minor, was able – very likely forewarned – to flee from Seleucid territory to Armenia and later to Prusias of Bithynia, who would protect him for years.[16]

A final demand was for twenty named hostages, one of them the king's younger son – later Antiochus IV – as guarantees of good faith. The fight had gone out of the Great King; his ambassadors agreed to everything. The victors then left Sardes for Ephesus, no longer Antiochus' western capital. There arrangements were made for a large company to sail to Rome for the ratification of peace: officers from the Scipios, King Eumenes in person, ambassadors from Antiochus and the hostages. Inevitably too, a swarm of envoys from states all over the Greek world set forth in their wake to bring congratulations – and petitions – to the Mediterranean world's now unchallengeable hegemon.

Africanus and his brother met several such spokesmen as the Scipios readied their own return home. Requests to them were plentiful. An inscription survives with the text of a letter they wrote to the small city of Heracleia-by-Latmus, just east of Miletus. They thank the city for its honorific decree, stress their goodwill to all Greeks and welcome the city into Rome's good faith (*pistis*, in Latin *fides*, the ideal of trust and loyalty always claimed by Rome as its special virtue). More practically, 'We grant you your liberty, just as to other cities which have entrusted themselves to us.' A Roman official named Orbius will be sent to look after Heracleia's interests (the brothers do not say for how long).

A fragment of another Scipionic letter, to Colophon near Ephesus, shows them guaranteeing the security of its sacred oracle of Apollo. Cities in Crete too looked for favour from the new world power – Rome had fleets in the Aegean – and its agents. A partly preserved inscription from Aptera, a small west Cretan place, honours the brothers, their cousin Cn. Scipio Hispallus, who was probably a *legatus* like Africanus, and the admiral Aemilius Regillus. Not that Africanus and Lucius went to Crete (they had little time for that); Regillus may have put in there when taking the fleet home and delivered the Scipios' replies to missives they had received. Such guarantees, promises and interventions must have been on a sizeable scale after Magnesia. All were subject to confirmation at Rome, of course, but with both brothers returning home in triumph the beneficiaries could rest easy that they would arrange it.[17]

Only a dozen years earlier, as for millennia past, the eastern Mediterranean's peoples and states large, medium and small were still being driven by their own rivalries and friendships. Romans in the Hellenistic world were well known as traders, donors to Delphi and Delos and (in small numbers) hired mercenaries. Abruptly, thanks to two major eastern wars, Rome now was their dominant power. Scipio Africanus and his brother were the latest in a lengthening series of Roman leaders who dispensed rewards and penalties to cities and rulers in the east, received pleas, petitions, complaints and lavish praise from them, and earned huge dividends in booty and prestige that marked these *principes viri* out ever more sharply from less fortunate Romans, even fellow aristocrats. The brothers' own fame as the men who had taken Roman arms and hegemony to two continents was higher than ever.

11
Scipio under Siege

On the day before the Kalends of March 188 – it was, in real terms, 6 November 189 BC – L. Scipio as proconsul celebrated the most magnificent triumph so far seen in Rome. It outdid not only recent ones by Acilius Glabrio and Aemilius Regillus but even his brother Africanus' a dozen years earlier. The riches of plundered Asia Minor were on show, itemized in turn by Livy. For instance, 234 gold laurel crowns, silver bullion weighing 137,420 pounds (62,330 kg), silver vases 1,423 pounds (645 kg) in weight, gold vases (1,023 pounds/464 kg), 545,070 silver coins and 140,000 gold staters. The procession featured, too, 134 models of captured cities and no fewer than 1,231 elephant tusks (these no doubt from a royal storehouse). More grimly, 32 of Antiochus' leading generals and councillors walked through the city in front of their conqueror's bedecked chariot.

Lucius had reached Rome a few days before this resplendent event. His brother probably arrived with him, though Publius is not mentioned by Livy. A triumphal proconsul could not re-enter the city until the great day, so on arriving Lucius reported to the Senate in the Temple of Bellona, outside the walls by the Campus Martius. His sense of his own importance as a Cornelius, consul, commander and conqueror was always as firm as his brother's. In Greece he had insisted on a sharper response than Publius' to the Aetolians' pleas at Amphissa. And he had chosen not to wait for Publius' return (as Publius plainly would have preferred) before committing to battle at Magnesia. He now made it clear to his fellow senators that he wished to take 'Asiagenus' as a further name: in his own view at least, his achievements in war were on the same level as his brother's.[1]

A portent of trouble ahead for both Asiagenus and Africanus had already occurred. After Acilius Glabrio celebrated his own gaudy and popular triumph in 189, some months before L. Scipio's, he was attacked – with M. Cato in the lead – for not displaying in the parade, or placing in the state treasury, large amounts of the royal money and booty he had brought back. The motive for this attack was fairly certainly to discomfit Glabrio's candidacy at the upcoming censorship election (like consuls, it was common for one censor to be plebeian and the other a patrician).

Cato's testimony was particularly hurtful. He had served in Glabrio's army and had helped win the fight at Thermopylae, as he never tired of mentioning in speeches. Not everyone was impressed: he was a candidate for censor too. Still, Glabrio was then threatened with prosecution by two plebeian tribunes named Sempronius – one of them a P. Sempronius Gracchus, probably elder brother or else cousin to the Scipios' energetic young officer Ti. Gracchus. If Ti. Gracchus was already at odds with Africanus, his kinsman must have been still more unenchanted by Glabrio (Tiberius later refused to back efforts to humiliate L. Scipio).

Livy offers another motive for attacking Glabrio: snobbishness. Many *nobiles* – men who had consuls for ancestors – disliked the idea of a *novus homo*, Glabrio, beating a *nobilis* candidate, the namesake son of Rome's Hannibalic War hero M. Claudius Marcellus. But with Cato no less a 'new man' than Glabrio – as the latter promptly pointed out – snobbishness cannot have been the chief motive. Glabrio was a friend of the Scipios. Cato was far from being the only Roman of rank who had little time for the brothers, in spite of Publius' past and Lucius' present glory, or indeed because of that. Humiliating a leading friend of theirs, despite his very Roman achievements in war, would be only a rehearsal for what was planned for them.[2]

The double upshot in 189 was that the disgruntled *triumphator* withdrew his candidacy and the two Sempronii their threat. Instead of Glabrio (the people's favourite), his rival M. Marcellus was elected censor along with the illustrious T. Flamininus – who defeated the Scipios' cousin P. Nasica, another patrician candidate. The Glabrio affair perhaps played a part in Nasica's failure too, for in Cato's eyes, whatever his moral and military qualities, Nasica was a Scipio. The family's continuing difficulties in relating to many of their fellow aristocrats, even amid the splendour of their latest victory, was plain. Even so, there was no move – yet – to bring down Africanus. Flamininus and Marcellus readily reappointed Hannibal's conqueror as *princeps senatus* for a further five years.

After that, things started to change. Within a year of the most opulent triumph yet in Rome's history, L. Scipio Asiagenus began to be asked questions about some of the funds extracted from Antiochus III. Almost at once his brother became involved too. The conquerors of the east found themselves embroiled in controversies, courts and even convictions that left them and their contemporaries stunned and later ages baffled.

The details of what happened are not easy to work out. All surviving accounts – save for a very short Polybian excerpt – date from centuries later. Livy's is fullest, but equally is full of confusions: mainly because he chose to follow not Polybius for the events but the more recent, and idiosyncratic, annalist Valerius Antias (who himself was confused about details and probably invented some). Repeated debates in modern times are the result.[3]

Livy's Antiate account has P. Africanus prosecuted first in 187, after bitter criticisms by two tribunes – cousins each named Q. Petillius – but he aborts the trial in the Forum by leading the gathered crowd up to the Temple of Jupiter on the Capitol to celebrate the anniversary of Zama. He then retires to his country estate at Liternum in Campania. Another tribune of 187, none other than Ti. Gracchus, forbids further proceedings, and Africanus soon dies.

Still in Livy's relay from Antias, the two Petillii, pushed by an undeterred Cato, next turn their attack on his brother L. Asiagenus. They allege peculation of both the indemnity from Antiochus and the war booty owed to the treasury, and carry a law setting up a special investigation (a *quaestio*). This is headed by, of all people, the praetor Q. Terentius Culleo – a detail that puzzled Livy – and Lucius is convicted along with two of his former subordinates. But he insists he is innocent and has no means to pay the resulting fine, so refuses to name guarantors for the payment. For this he is imprisoned, but then is freed by the tribune Ti. Gracchus, Gracchus paradoxically insisting that he himself remains a personal foe (*inimicus*) of Lucius' brother yet will not let Antiochus' conqueror languish in chains. Gracchus does let the authorities seize and sell off Lucius' possessions (though no illicit funds are found), leaving Antiochus' conqueror to subsist on the support of kinsmen.

Problems infest this dramatic scenario. Scipio Africanus in reality died years later. Ti. Gracchus' double rescues, first of one brother and then of the other, look oddly repetitive – worse, duplicated. Livy, meantime, knew other accounts with variant details, such as one that reported Africanus being prosecuted by a tribune called M. Naevius, who was in that office in 184. Another told how Scipio, goaded in the Senate over his and his brother's alleged misuse of the Seleucid funds, took their account book from Lucius and tore it to pieces in fury before the senators' eyes. Livy alerts readers to these reports only later on.[4]

The same details turn up in various entries by Aulus Gellius in his compilation *Noctes Atticae*, written in the second century AD. He offers first the story of Scipio stymieing his trial by leading the crowd up to Jupiter's temple, but with M. Naevius as his nonplussed prosecutor, not the Petillii cousins. But then the cousins do come on the scene, as the critics who goad Scipio into tearing up the account book in the Senate. These items, writes Gellius, come from *veteres annales*, 'old annals', meaning one or more of the earlier Latin histories of Rome that preceded Valerius Antias, Claudius Quadrigarius and other historians of the generation before Livy.

Another story in Gellius is about L. Scipio's trial, likewise taken from 'old annals'. It tells of Africanus appealing, without success, to the tribunes after his brother is convicted, but then Ti. Gracchus steps in to veto Lucius' imprisonment – a version (Gellius emphasizes) contrary to Antias' account, which put these events after Africanus' death. In this 'old annals' version, the official who fined L. Scipio was a tribune, C. Minucius Augurinus, not the praetor Terentius Culleo as Antias had it.[5]

If Polybius gave a detailed version of all these proceedings (it is not clear that he did), Livy decided against following it. Finding so many contradictions in his predecessors, he plainly thought that Valerius Antias had sorted everything out, so opted for his version of events. Choosing some other version – by Claudius Quadrigarius, or by a second-century BC annalist – would almost certainly have brought no better result.

The conflicts over trials, dates, charges (was Lucius fined for misusing Antiochus' payments or for taking royal bribes? was Africanus attacked on similar grounds or for arrogance and pride? was he put on trial at all, and if so when?), over accusers and judges and over outcomes have no clear-cut solution. But plainly Antias had faced the same problems and opted for too many wrong answers.

It is clear that Africanus did not incur trial ahead of Lucius; he did not die before Lucius' trial, either. It is close to certain, too, that the two Petillii did not initiate prosecutions of both Scipios. Nor did Ti. Gracchus spring to the rescue of one Scipio after the other. Livy's reproduction of Antias' topsy-turvy account recalls his aberrant version of how Scipio's original peace terms in 203 had been received at Rome: Laelius undermining them, the Senate rejecting them, Carthage's ambassadors denounced as spies and expelled. Antias, conceivably, was his source there too.

A cautious and basic reconstruction of what happened to the brothers in 187 and after can be tried. First: in that year, L. Asiagenus was accused by the two Petillii tribunes of mishandling funds from the war against Antiochus – whether the initial 500 talents of indemnity, or other booty proceeds. Behind the tribunes was Cato, eager to take down personal enemies and punish what he saw as wrongdoing. There was also trouble over the further 2,500 paid after peace had been ratified; as ratification had come when Lucius' successor in the east, Manlius Vulso, was in command, he was in trouble too. Not only Antias was confused about this. Polybius was too, to judge by his one short excerpt on the dispute, making Africanus complain to the Senate that he and Lucius were being hounded for '3,000' talents when they had brought 15,000 into the treasury. With Lucius the likely issue was whether he had used the 500 talents to supply the bonuses to his troops, or had paid the bonuses out of his share of war booty and deposited the king's payment into the treasury as law required.

Lucius' defence was either on the one hand that he had paid into the treasury all sums due and paid his men from his own booty, or on the other hand that paying them bonuses out of the 500-talent indemnity was acceptable. The legalities were probably as arguable in 187 as they certainly are now. At a Senate session one Petillius demanded he produce his accounts, in other words the relevant papyrus roll, to back his case. Lucius had expected this and had brought the account book with him. But in a towering rage the *princeps senatus*, his brother Africanus, stood up, took hold of the book and tore it to shreds. Throwing the pieces to the floor, he told their questioner to collect the evidence himself and berated his nonplussed peers for demanding proof of innocence from brothers who had made Rome ruler of Asia, Africa and Spain, and rich with the treasure from Antiochus.

Supposedly his fellow senators took his side (so Polybius' excerpt reports) and the questioner was too abashed to persist. Yet it was far from the end of the affair. On the likeliest reconstruction, the inquisition was taken up by another tribune, C. Minucius Augurinus, who charged Lucius before the people's assembly with mishandling Antiochus' 500 talents. It seems a surprise: the Minucius family had traditional friendships with the *gens Cornelia*. But Augurinus may have been an exception or, like Ti. Gracchus, a citizen who felt strongly about law and propriety.

Cato, too, may have intervened again: the title preserved of one of his orations was 'On King Antiochus' money', though its date is unknown and nothing survives of the speech itself. The Petillius cousins took a back seat, but when Minucius called for a large fine on L. Scipio they – and six of the seven other tribunes – supported it. Then Minucius demanded that Lucius provide guarantors for the payment. If not, he would be imprisoned until he did.[6]

The spectacle was again too much for his brother. Scipio Africanus appealed to the tribunes as a body to protect Lucius, an ex-consul and *triumphator*, 'from the violence of their colleague'. Eight still backed the verdict and rejected the plea from the conqueror of Hannibal and Carthage. But Lucius was saved nonetheless. The tenth tribune was Ti. Gracchus, and though (in all the accounts) he was a bitter personal enemy of Africanus, he would not let Africanus' brother be humiliated. Gracchus exercised his tribunician veto to keep Lucius free, although at least some of Asiagenus' property was seized for the fine (unless that was remitted, in practice).

After that, it looks as though Lucius' tormentors, their political points made, let the case drop. If his goods at Rome were sold off, it did not leave him utterly impoverished. Not only does his case disappear from the record, but a year later he was able to put on ten days of public games in the city. He said the cost was paid by the grateful kings and cities of Asia, but he himself was probably not as destitute as later ages fancied.

Ti. Gracchus' bitter *inimicitia* towards Africanus is strange. He had been a trusted officer in the war only three years before. More striking still, after Africanus' death he was chosen by the family to marry Scipio's younger daughter Cornelia (a marriage to be famous in its own right). If there had been a falling out after 190 and before 187 we are not told why, any more than when and why reconciliation happened so that he could marry Cornelia. In the story, Gracchus swears that his action on Lucius' behalf will not affect his ongoing enmity to Africanus. Even if the *inimicitia* really existed around 187 – it cannot be positively ruled out – it cannot have lasted long.[7]

L. Scipio's problems with war indemnities, plunder and accounts were not unique. The unheard-of riches in money and moveable goods that Rome won from the struggles with Carthage and then in the east were drawing concern as well as awe, and not only from the pugnaciously righteous M. Cato. The impressive loot hauled from sacked Syracuse as far back as 212 seems to have troubled some Romans (as it did Livy later) because they saw it encouraging luxury and greed. The campaigns in Spain, from Scipio's onwards, poured gold and silver bullion, coins and plundered goods into the city. Less profuse but not unattractive was booty, human captives included, from still unconquered Cisalpine Gaul and Liguria in the north.

Along with material gains, victorious warfare brought the intangibly vital prize of *gloria*, especially if crowned by a triumph – and these were becoming frequent. In just the decade between 197 and 187, the official triumphal lists, the *Fasti Triumphales*, along with written sources record ten of them, plus four ovations. One colourful triumph, in 189, was Acilius Glabrio's, as mentioned earlier, but the four greatest hauls and triumphs in the decade and half after Zama were Scipio's in 201, Flamininus' in 194, then L. Scipio's in 188 and – in 187, not long before Minucius Augurinus prosecuted Lucius – the scandalous spoils delivered by his successor in the east, Manlius Vulso.

The furore over L. Scipio, and implicitly over his brother too, was not a one-off event either. Triumph requests by returning consuls and proconsuls after 201 were often criticized – including a request by their cousin P. Nasica in 191 after he came back victorious from Spain – though most went through. In 190 Cato had helped block another consular claimant, Africanus' former officer Q. Minucius Thermus, because (Cato insisted) the victories he claimed in Liguria were fiction but Thermus' vicious treatment of both the natives and his own troops had been all too real. And a year later came the already mentioned allegations against Acilius Glabrio, much like those that would be thrown at the Scipios.[8]

Irritation and suspicion were plainly rife over the behaviour, too often self-serving and arrogant, of the republic's chief annual magistrates. And in fact the whole of the next century and a half of Roman politics would be distracted by efforts, increasingly stressful and decreasingly successful, to keep wayward *principes viri* from bypassing laws, responsibility and public control – until control was imposed by a new regime of autocrats called the Caesars. Cato and other critics, even if they sometimes pushed their efforts out of political calculation, were aiming at enforcing responsibility on magistrates. Self-confident and ambitious aristocrats – like Africanus and his brother – saw things differently.

In 187 itself, one controversy after another had erupted even before L. Scipio's own ordeal. M. Fulvius Nobilior, consul two years before, had wantonly battered the Greeks of Ambracia and plundered them. On returning home he had to push hard, against Cato among others, to be granted his triumph. Even more furious opposition boiled up when Manlius Vulso came back from the east and he asked for a triumph, too. Unable to keep the war with Antiochus going in 189, he had settled instead for a ruthless – and unauthorized – invasion and looting of Galatia, the central region of Asia Minor where Gallic migrants had settled a century before. Their accumulated wealth, itself the product of generations of pillage, was systematically seized by Manlius, who also brought back the first major instalment, 2,500 talents, of Antiochus' indemnity. His request to triumph was resisted even by most of the ten senatorial commissioners sent out with him in 189 to ratify the peace, notably Scipio's brother-in-law Aemilius Paullus. Yet Manlius prevailed, holding his triumph on 5 March 186. The vast quantities of booty he delivered, from Galatia and other unfortunate parts of Asia Minor, would trouble Livy even more than the loot from Syracuse had: he saw luxury, greed, corruption and moral decay resulting. Very likely, the Asian treasure equally troubled many of Manlius' contemporaries besides Cato.[9]

Aulus Gellius' 'old annals' made Cato the man prompting the Petillii to badger the brothers in the Senate. Certainly, if he stayed aloof this time it would have been as surprising then as it would be now. Other *principes viri* with an interest in humbling Africanus and Asiagenus can only be surmised: Cato's best friend and virtual shadow L. Valerius Flaccus, Ti. Nero, Cn. Caepio, M. Marcellus, even Manlius Vulso. The initiative would not have come from lesser political lights like Minucius Augurinus or the Petillius pair. And taking the matter as far as a heavy fine – even possible jailing – points to deeper acrimony against the Scipios than against even a delinquent like Manlius. More than moral outrage was in play: Scipionic eminence and arrogance also goaded their attackers.

Even so, Lucius' effective reprieve ended the furore, for some time anyway. He was able to put on his ten-day entertainments in Rome the following year – he said he had vowed them during the war. Nor did he give up political ambitions. In 184 he would be a candidate in another busy censorial election, though beaten by Cato's friend Valerius Flaccus and Cato himself. It was perhaps an unwise effort by Lucius, as will be seen.

Africanus, except for his fruitless intervention when Lucius was fined, lived more quietly once back from the east and after Lucius' resplendent triumph. He took little recorded part in public affairs even though he must have attended the Senate's meetings. He had a gentleman secretary, C. Cicereius, but little is known about the man except that he later became a praetor. In 189 while Scipio was still abroad, his admirer Terentius Culleo, then a plebeian tribune, had carried a law requiring future censors to allocate citizen sons of freedmen to all 35 *tribus* in the *comitia tributa*, not just the four city ones as before. Supposedly this was a dig at the aristocracy, though why so is not obvious: spreading out such citizens' votes might well weaken, not improve, those men's already modest influence in affairs. Africanus is not known to have prompted Culleo to it. Then in 187, as already mentioned, his friend moved up one more step in political ranking by reaching the praetorship. The Senate was receiving complaints from the Latin cities about too many of their residents migrating to Rome, so Culleo was authorized to order all 12,000 Latin males in the city to go home.

Scipio may have agreed with both measures or at least the later one. He knew the sterling contribution the Latin cities always made to Rome's armies and would hardly want to see their manpower shrink. All the same, he is nowhere recorded taking an actual interest in either measure. And he certainly did not exert himself over Culleo's failed effort to win the plebeian consulship for 184 (he did have other things on his mind, as we shall see), nor over the parallel effort by a competitor from the Baebius clan.

Scipio did take time off from public affairs to holiday on the coast; it was a diversion he had probably started years before. A family reminiscence, handed down from Laelius' son-in-law Q. Mucius Scaevola and then Scaevola's own son-in-law, L. Licinius Crassus, told of the hero of Zama and his best friend wandering along the seashore at Caieta and Laurentum, south of Ostia, picking up oysters and mussels as they went. Scipio had another estate at Liternum, close to the Campanian Greek city of Cumae just west of Naples: a comfortable but unpretentious coastal retreat, built like a small fortress. The philosopher Seneca later visited and described it (he was amazed at its tiny bathroom). There, wrote Seneca, Scipio kept himself healthy with physical work in the fields.

It may have been his way of life at Liternum that prompted his most famous saying: he never felt less leisured than when he had leisure, never less alone than when he was alone. That could have been a reply at Rome to friends who probed why he was so fond of his out-of-the-way retreat – or to a query from senators, because the man who told of Scipio's retort was none other than his old scourge Cato.

A different story in Valerius Maximus, but rather less believable, tells of a group of pirate chiefs once coming ashore near the Liternum estate, hoping to view the great man – who naturally expected robbery and readied himself and his household for a fight. But the chiefs sent away their armed followers, made it clear they were peaceful and were invited in. There they venerated him almost like a god, then departed, leaving gifts at his threshold.[10]

He shared other Romans' steadily widening interest in Greek culture and newly developing Latin literary forms. It would be pleasant to think that in Rome he went to performances of the comic poet Plautus' plays, very popular during the later years of the Punic War and after, which were largely free and funny borrowings from Greek comedy. That Scipio was more philhellenic than most, though, is a modern rather than ancient view. Even Cato, pugnacious defender of old ways, took an interest in some things Greek (and in old age could tease Polybius with an allusion to the *Odyssey*). Scipio's and his brother's friendly assurances of regard and protection to Heracleia-by-Latmus and other places did not mark them out as particular philhellenes. It was conventional – and not always sincere – for Roman generals and officers in the Greek East to assure cities and kings of their own and Rome's high regard, and promise to do them all the good they could. More telling was how easily Scipio had adopted Greek dress and interests when in Sicily – and as consul at that – and the excellent education he made sure all his children, the girls and the boys, were given.[11]

One of his friends was the poet Q. Ennius, originally from southern Italy. Ennius was an ardent adopter and adapter of Greek literary forms, including the hexameter verse and the genre of tragedy. Ironically, he had first been patronized by none other than Cato, who had met him in Sardinia and brought him to Rome. Ennius wrote a poetic panegyric on Scipio, according him heroic status together with a self-confident pride that rings true on other evidence too. Ennius had him say:

> If it be lawful for any man to rise to the regions of the heavenly ones,
> to me alone stands wide their greatest portal.

And in another surviving couplet:

> from the sun arising to beyond Maeotis' marshlands,
> there is no man able to equal my deeds.[12]

These enthusiastic praises may date to the 190s. By 189 Ennius had been embraced by the contentious M. Fulvius Nobilior, accompanied him on campaign to Greece, and afterwards wrote encomia and even a play about Fulvian exploits. In 184 Nobilior gained Roman citizenship for him.

Scipio, meanwhile, had a still growing family. Neither son would have a glittering public career, but Lucius (Antiochus' one-time prisoner) would eventually be praetor in 174. The anaemic Publius was well regarded enough to be chosen an augur in 180 – by then his father was dead – and win praise for his learned writings. As well as these sons, Scipio and Aemilia were parents of two daughters, Cornelia the elder and younger. The age gap between the two sets of siblings was wide, for the girls were born in Scipio's later years. Their mother Aemilia was (by Roman standards) rather old to have children again, a quarter-century or more after the sons. Nevertheless, Polybius remembered her as a lively and rather loud lady in her widowhood, always keen to show off her finery and fine-looking servants. She was probably little less outgoing while her husband was alive. We may suspect she spent more time in Rome than at Liternum.

She was also tolerant of his ongoing sexual misbehaviour, if another of Valerius Maximus' anecdotes is sound. He was having an affair with one of her slave maids and Aemilia found out. Instead of protesting or punishing, she put up with it. Later, when Scipio died she freed the girl and gave her in marriage to one of her freedmen.[13]

Scipio at some date arranged for Cornelia the elder to marry his cousin Nasica's son and namesake (a young man with the extra nickname Corculum). The younger Cornelia after her father's death wedded the outspoken Ti. Gracchus, who would be consul twice in 177 and 163. Gracchus was much older, but that was common enough in Rome. How much choice either girl had in these arrangements is unknown; very probably not much.

In 184 L. Scipio Asiagenus stood for election to be one of the next censors. Candidates were plentiful and some of them controversial. Scipio Nasica his cousin, Manlius Vulso and Fulvius Nobilior competed too, but the winners were Cato and his inevitable ally Valerius Flaccus. Lucius' defeat was not enough for Cato. When the censors came to review the roster of the senators and other wealthy men (*equites Romani*) who were entitled to a cavalry horse for military service, the first man to be struck off was the ex-consul L. Scipio Asiagenus.

Charitable excuses for Cato – that Lucius was too old (probably late forties) or too unwell – might be offered. But there is no evidence that L. Scipio was an improper holder of his public horse. Another senator, expelled from not only the public horse roster but the Senate itself, was one L. Veturius, fairly certainly a kinsman (maybe the son) of Africanus' old friend the ex-consul L. Veturius Philo. With him, Cato's argument, or one of them, was that he was too fat to sit on a horse, which hardly justified expelling him from the Senate as well as the *equester ordo*. The only insult Cato seems to have refrained from was removing Africanus himself as *princeps senatus*. Had he done that, we would certainly have heard of it from Livy, Plutarch and others.[14]

Certainly the two censors had come to office promising unprecedented strictness in matters moral and administrative, and they pursued their goals firmly. Some of their public measures, like firmer control of finances and proper attention to building works, were admirable. But the treatment of L. Scipio went down badly with other Romans, then and later. Lucius would never figure in public life again.

Even so, his double humiliation, in 187 and now again, was not enough for Cato and other foes of the family. A new storm, as nasty as the trial three years before, broke: this time directly over his brother Africanus.

The date and details are thoroughly disputed, again mainly thanks to Livy choosing Valerius Antias as his source and so putting everything back into 187. As noted above, that was Antias' date for Africanus' trial as well as Lucius'; he not only reversed the two prosecutions but had Africanus die before Lucius' case was heard, had the Petillius cousins conduct both attacks and had them frustrated in each. Fortunately, enough evidence survives elsewhere, especially from plausible items in Aulus Gellius, for a likelier account of what befell Scipio.

The accusation this time came from a tribune named M. Naevius. Livy knew this version too. But he was puzzled: having put both assaults in 187, he afterwards found that Naevius had been tribune only in 184. He also found that not only Polybius but a respected Roman author, P. Rutilius Rufus (writing in the 80s BC), dated Scipio's passing to 183, the same year when both Hannibal and the Greek leader Philopoemen died. All the same, Livy rejected this year too on rather complex grounds and argued for the year before. In fact, Naevius' prosecution of Scipio should date to 184, and the death of Africanus most likely to the year after as Polybius reported.[15]

Why attack him at all? He was 51, was playing little part now in affairs and may have been in bad health. The commotions over proconsuls misbehaving abroad were in the past. His sons were politically unimpressive. They posed no challenge (or stimulus) to their ambitious young contemporaries, nor carried on old rivalries or feuds. The one constant in the ageing *triumphator*'s life was the animosity of M. Cato. Partly this festered for purely personal reasons: Cato was a persistent hater. Probably a further factor was at play too. With a censorial programme of returning Rome to strict morality after years of corruption, Cato looked for suitable examples to chastise. Some were justified, like Flamininus' sleazy brother who had killed a Gallic prisoner at a party to excite his boyfriend. Cato expelled him from the Senate. Humiliating L. Scipio and fat Veturius satisfyingly combined moralizing with vendetta. To bring down Scipio Africanus, other charges had to be raised.

The tribune Naevius summoned Scipio to an assembly in the Comitium, just outside the Senate house. A large crowd gathered, likely enough with the two censors Cato and Flaccus and the consuls – one a Claudius Pulcher, the other a distant relative of Cato named Porcius Licinus – looking on too. Naevius claimed that Africanus had dealt corruptly with King Antiochus. To free his son, he had promised the king easy peace terms and had in turn pocketed a huge bribe to bring it about.

One or both of the Petillius cousins may have chimed in, a few days earlier perhaps, to raise their own accusations in the Senate – but only if Valerius Antias got that detail right, despite displacing it three years earlier. Or else similar vituperation could have come from Naevius with his denunciations. Certainly there is a Cato-esque ring to some of what Antias, via Livy, had the Petillii say – when consul, Africanus had lived in Greek-style luxury at Syracuse; he had let Pleminius run riot at Locri; in the eastern war he had behaved like a dictator, not a subordinate, to his brother the consul; and he wanted to be seen in the east, as already he was in the west, as the master and mainstay of Rome's empire.

Next it was Scipio's turn to speak from the Rostra, the speakers' platform in the Comitium. No doubt his chastened brother Lucius, their cousin P. Nasica, P. Crassus the *pontifex maximus*, and other friends and kinsmen were with him in support. Expectations must have run high about what he would say in his defence.

Scipio made no defence. Instead, with a strategic deftness recalling how he won his many victories, he outflanked his accuser. First he spoke a few words about his own and his family's *dignitas*, his pride in having served the republic and the eminence he had won through doing it. Then (writes Aulus Gellius, quoting a much older account) he went on:

> I remember, men of Rome, that today is the one on which I conquered Hannibal the Carthaginian, your empire's bitterest enemy, in a great battle in Africa and won for you a peace and victory of splendour. So let us not be thankless to the gods but, I propose, let us leave this nonentity and go at once from here to offer our thanks to Jupiter Greatest and Best.

The enthralled crowd followed the victor of Zama from the Comitium up to the great Temple of Jupiter on the Capitoline above them, leaving behind Naevius and a few attendant slaves. (Livy over-imagines the drama, as Antias doubtless did, making Africanus and his fellow citizens enthusiastically visit every temple in the city.)[16]

Was it really the anniversary of Zama? Quite possibly, or, if not, it was probably the right month. Zama had been fought and won only eighteen years before. Many Romans, including Scipio's plentiful critics, were well acquainted with their religiously and festivally full calendar. If he was making it up, they could have called him out and ruined his gesture. Scipio's own lifelong devotion to Capitoline Jupiter suggests his act was genuine as well as resourceful.

The attack on him – there was no actual trial – lapsed. Nothing more is heard of Naevius, but one of the Petillius cousins did prosper for a time, becoming praetor three years later and consul in 176, to be killed on campaign in Liguria. Before long Scipio left Rome, this time forever. He went to live at Liternum. We are not told whether Aemilia and the girls joined him.

Less than a year later, he died at Liternum. Polybius placed the death in the second year of the 184th Olympiad in Greek chronology: this ran from summer 183 to summer 182. Cato and Flaccus were still in censorial office (censors held office for eighteen months, and they had started in March 184), for Cato now named his colleague as the new *princeps senatus*. The passing of Scipio, then, should probably date to late summer in 183 BC. In that same year his great friend P. Crassus, the *pontifex maximus*, also died, to be given a splendid funeral – and so too, far away in Bithynia, his greatest foreign foe, Hannibal, driven to suicide by a pursuing Roman embassy headed by Flamininus.[17]

Scipio was barely 52. He had refused to be buried at Rome, in the great family tomb that stood (as its remains still do) outside the old city wall. Instead he directed that he be interred at Liternum. A century and a half later, Livy saw his monument and statue there. On the other hand, the historian adds, there were three statues at the family tomb in Rome, which people declared were of Africanus, his brother Lucius and Ennius the poet.

In his will, Scipio left fifty talents – in Roman terms, 300,000 *denarii*, a large fortune for the time – to each of his daughters, with the stipulation that this should be the dowry when they married. Aemilia, meantime, looked after these sums. Their sons must have received a share in his property and funds too. In an era when an eligible Roman could be a senator if he possessed at least a million *asses* (100,000 *denarii*) and an ordinary legionary was paid 180 *denarii* a year, Scipio – whatever his later admirers said about his modest lifestyle – was plainly as wealthy as indeed befitted a consular and conqueror.[18]

His wife and four children all survived him. Aemilia lived to old age, showy and supremely self-assured. She and her brother-in-law L. Asiagenus both had descendants, all with mixed fortunes. Africanus' younger son Lucius, Antiochus' one-time prisoner (something Roman writers never wearied of mentioning), reached a praetorship in 174, as noted earlier. It was supposedly thanks to the electoral efforts of his father's quondam secretary Cicereius. But in that same year the censors expelled him and two other praetors from the Senate, reasons unstated. (Valerius Maximus accuses him of moral turpitude but does not offer evidence.) Nothing is heard of him after that. Asiagenus had a son named Lucius too, but a sad epitaph in the tomb of the Scipios records his short career – quaestor, military tribune and then death at 33. With no great achievement to record for him, the epitaph offers a plaintive extra: 'His father defeated King Antiochus.'[19]

Africanus' infirm elder son Publius possibly had a son whom he outlived, as a namesake's epitaph in the Tomb of the Scipios may be that youth. Instead, he took a historic step. His uncle L. Aemilius Paullus, who later overthrew the Macedonian monarchy, had four sons. Some years after Africanus died, the childless P. Scipio adopted one. In standard Roman usage this boy, born in 185 or 184, took the names P. Cornelius Scipio Aemilianus.[20]

Scipio Aemilianus would reach a height of *dignitas* and *auctoritas* at Rome to match his adoptive grandfather's. He would be consul twice, and censor, would sack and raze Carthage in 146 to end a three-year siege, then repeat the treatment on the recalcitrant northern Spanish town of Numantia in 133. His victories brought him the added *cognomina* Africanus and Numantinus; his hereditary patronage of peoples, cities and kingdoms ranged across the Mediterranean world. He would be all but idolized by Polybius, who became his friend, and later by Cicero, as a model of all the Roman virtues.

Aemilianus married Sempronia, daughter of the younger Cornelia and Ti. Gracchus (and thus his aunt Aemilia's granddaughter and his own cousin – Roman families could be intricate). They had no children. But he was not the sole adoptee from Aemilius Paullus' house: an older son went to the equally childless grandson of Fabius the Delayer, to become Q. Fabius Maximus Aemilianus. (Tragically for their father, Paullus, both his other sons later died young.) Fabius Aemilianus would be the ancestor of two grandees of the Augustan age and intimates of that emperor. To recall their illustrious ancestry they were grandiosely named Paullus and Africanus Fabius Maximus, the younger brother neatly combining in his names the memory of his venerated collateral forebear with the memory of Scipio's bitter enemy the Delayer. Scipio would probably not have appreciated the historical irony.[21]

Cornelia the younger lived to old age like her mother. Famously cultured, friendly with intellectuals, she supposedly refused a marriage proposal from King Ptolemy VIII of Egypt when a widow. Tragedy marred her old age. First her older son Tiberius in 133, then in 121 the younger, Gaius, would be murdered in political upheavals, signals of corrosion in Rome's republican norms. The former's violent death was even grimmer because the senator who instigated the fatal riot was the ex-consul and current *pontifex maximus* P. Scipio Nasica, nicknamed Serapio – Cornelia's sister's son, and he too, therefore, a grandson of Scipio Africanus – and her other nephew, the new Scipio Africanus, applauded the killing.

Scipio Aemilianus Africanus Numantinus, as he came to be called, would die abruptly too, a few years after (no one was sure why), and would leave no children. There would be descendants of L. Scipio Asiagenus for another century, but the dominant future line of Cornelii Scipiones, lasting into the time of the emperors, would stem from Africanus' elder daughter and her husband Scipio Nasica. The name Scipio would be remembered, all the same and for all time, as the name of the man who crushed the Carthaginians and their general Hannibal.

12
Evaluating Scipio

Livy's judgement of Scipio Africanus is sound, though one might admit a little sad.

> He was a remarkable man, but more for his military than his peacetime activities. The early part of his life was more remarkable than his final years because in his youth there was incessant warfare, whereas with old age his career also lost its bloom, and no scope was offered to his talents. How could his second consulship stand comparison with his first, even if one adds the censorship? And what about his position as legate in Asia, made insignificant by ill health and sullied by the mishap of his son? . . . But no war fought by the Romans was greater and more fraught with danger than the Punic war, and he alone earned the paramount glory of bringing it to an end.[1]

The Roman Republic had a knack for picking young military talent. Scipio was not the first. Tradition recorded M. Valerius Corvus, another famous soldier, at 23 holding the first of six consulships (in 348, the sixth in 299). Nor was he the last: Flamininus and Pompey would be others. But Scipio was the ablest general – young or old – in Rome's history. Pompey and Caesar, his only rivals, mixed occasional defeats with their victories; Africanus, intuitively responsive to strategic and tactical challenges, won every battle and siege. He was charismatic not only to his own troops and allies but to his foreign foes, and an agile – at times over-agile – diplomat. Outside the theatre of war, by contrast, he was less sure-footed.

Controversy, bitter in his last years, disappeared once he was dead. Writers and poets, Roman and Greek, from Ennius on are unanimous on Scipio's eminence, excellence and exalted place in history. Polybius, the Achaean notable who, in exile at Rome in the 160s, became a close friend of young Scipio Aemilianus, praises Africanus' achievements, leadership and virtues, with few reservations: his Scipio is charismatic, generous, shrewd, far-sighted, brave – and calculating. Even Cato, so Cicero imagined or knew, in old age came to value Scipio's worth. In Cicero's famous essay 'On Old Age' ('De senectute'), the veteran critic is on good terms with Scipio Aemilianus. Cicero apparently tried to get the facts about Cato's life and career right, but how accurately he portrays the ex-censor's view of his old target cannot be known. At the same time, it must be noted how even the friendly narratives of Polybius, Livy and others let intermittently contrary items in; just enough of them to allow some balance in assessing Scipio's personality and achievements.[2]

The Roman political system of his time was flexible and could innovate. In 210 Romans chose a middle-level ex-magistrate, in other words a private citizen, in his mid-twenties, to take command in a war theatre that had suddenly become a disaster, although more senior and proven generals could have been sent. Later, he was elected consul at only thirty, without holding a praetorship as convention would have expected. The Senate backed him on invading Africa, and Scipio was confident that the people would too: this in the face of opposition from experienced fellow generals, even the revered Fabius Maximus, who all thought it madness for him to leave Hannibal at large in Italy. The series of consuls who insisted on their claim to supersede him in Africa were refused support from Senate and people. In every case, Scipio proved these decisions right.

His strategic and tactical prowess was unmatched. The lightning pounce to seize New Carthage was a triumph of planned risk-taking. He regularly thrust deep into enemy territory, risking attack – to take New Carthage, find Hannibal's brother Hasdrubal at Baecula and then again the other Hasdrubal at Ilipa. (When his father and uncle had tried a similar dangerous thrust, they had been destroyed.) At Ilipa, he boldly divided his army into three separating units while his opponents looked on. In Africa, with bold calculation again he left his coastal bridgehead

Castra Cornelia twice, first to push well inland to the Great Plains and then, still further away, to the Naraggara battlefield.

He repeatedly exploited his opponents' insouciance, a gift they never wearied of giving. Their forces' dispersal far from New Carthage enabled his pounce. Hasdrubal, son of Gisco, and Mago left Mago's brother to fight alone at Baecula. In 206 the same Hasdrubal, rather than seize the initiative and seek out Scipio in the northeast, stolidly chose to wait in the Carthaginian south, no doubt hoping defeat there would leave the Romans marooned and doomed like in 211. Then, in the battle itself, Hasdrubal hesitated and was lost. At home in Africa, Carthage's authorities left themselves and the state unready – ample advance warning ignored – to waylay Scipio's invasion at sea or confront it in strength as it landed. Hasdrubal and Syphax let themselves relax into deceptive peace talks that winter, then paid the terrible price. A decade later, Antiochus the Great would do no better in dealing with Scipio.

Scipio learned from the disasters that Hannibal's invasion wrought in Italy. He trained his troops to levels of skill in manoeuvre and coordination not seen before in Roman warfare and not renewed for generations. His outflanking tactics at Baecula and Ilipa and the strenuous ordering and reordering of his heavy infantry at Zama in the face of the enemy would have been beyond the armies of the Trebia or Cannae, not to mention any in the previous Punic War. His veterans were so valued that they were recruited for fresh wars for another dozen years at least. Flamininus probably would not have won Cynoscephalae without them.

Scipio achieved such soldierly expertness partly through strict drilling and exercises like those Polybius describes after the fall of New Carthage, partly thanks to the ample plunder he won for his troops and partly with personal charisma. The charisma worked equally on allies like Masinissa, on city-states from Saguntum to Heracleia, and on foreign foes – Syphax, Hasdrubal, son of Gisco, Antiochus III, perhaps Philip V and maybe Hannibal. The Ilergetans Indibilis and Mandonius also gave in to it, for a time, until they realized Scipio meant not to liberate Spaniards from Carthage but to replace Carthage with Rome.

Skill, calculation and daring were (and are) not the only methods of warfare. Cruelty and fraud also figure. Scipio used either or both when he thought them necessary or useful. Deviousness along with severity ended the mutiny at Sucro; at Ilugo, the indiscriminate massacre – women and children as well as men – was deliberate vengeance for the local men's treachery to his elders years before. Outside Utica, careful deception – it could be called plain fraud – engineered the obliteration of Hasdrubal's and Syphax's armies. He was frankly indifferent to Pleminius' atrocities at Locri, even against Roman officers, until the scandal forced him to act. Then his action, abetted by his friends at Rome and a compliant Senate, was minimal: he knew, in sum, that he would get away with it.

Scipio combined leadership and personal magnetism with an immovable self-confidence. The visits from early adulthood to the temple of Capitoline Jupiter rested on both piety and realist calculation, as Livy hints: he knew the practice would add to the mild air of mystery he always bore. If the story of him cowing would-be deserters after Cannae has any basis, it shows him asserting at a mere nineteen years of age a force of personality that lasted all his life. To offer himself as commander in the disaster-struck Spanish theatre – no matter who his sponsors, secret or open, were – was perhaps the most daring act of self-confidence in all his risk-taking career. Daring again, after Ilipa he chose to put himself into the Numidian Syphax's power by sailing to Siga. When he found that the king's other guest was Hasdrubal, son of Gisco, his skill in charming both men relieved the peril. To Antiochus through his envoy Heracleides, Scipio's advice – though he was formally only his brother's *legatus* – was to wait until he should arrive on the scene: the plain implication being that he, rather than Lucius, would resolve the issue of war and peace.

Self-confidence could become open arrogance – even towards other *principes viri*. In 205, as consul and bent on taking the Punic War to Africa, he made it plain (without actually saying it) that if the Senate did not support him he would put the question directly to the people. Two decades on, tearing up his brother's expedition accounts in front of their fellow senators was the most famously brazen example of the same trait; facing down the Cato-abetted attack from Naevius the tribune, near the end of his life, still another. This assertiveness attracted many perceptive and able men to be his friends, from Laelius and P. Crassus early on to Ti. Gracchus much later. Equally strongly they put others off, some like Cato into long-lasting enmity.

Scipio's personal beliefs and spiritual life are elusive. Devotion to Jupiter is well documented; he was, one way or another, an active Salian priest; and he invoked Neptune to his men at the storming of New Carthage. He no doubt took part in the secret rites of the *gens Cornelia*, whatever they were. He made an offering, along with his brother, at Apollo's temple on the isle of Delos. One of his closest friends was P. Crassus, who was *pontifex maximus* for 29 years. These were all normal activities for a third- and second-century Roman aristocrat. His one strikingly individual religious trait was the early morning visits to the Temple of Capitoline Jupiter. It was obviously a habit well known at the time and – as Livy saw – carefully cultivated by the young Scipio. We do not know if he continued it in later life, or worshipped Jupiter in a different way when far from Rome.

Overall, Scipio plainly kept his personal religious life strictly private. He may have venerated some or all of the other gods of the Roman pantheon, but we do not hear of this. His cousin P. Scipio Nasica was chosen in 204 as Rome's most virtuous citizen to bring the sacred stone of the eastern great goddess Cybele into the city, but Africanus is not known to have paid it special attention once he came back to Rome. Any individualistic belief of his lacks mention; maybe there was none. Nor is he recorded as interested in philosophy, although his literary friend Ennius was, and his adoptive grandson Aemilianus would be.

It was as a general in a military theatre that Scipio could give his leadership, organizing skills and fighting abilities full scope. There he was the peak authority, his orders obeyed unchallenged. Civil life was different. Here he was one, even if the most distinguished, of many *principes viri*. Problems needing debate and decision were not limited to war or diplomacy. Competing to sway senators or voters, or both, to one's point of view was intense and unremitting. Criticism from opponents, sometimes legal attacks, were unavoidable. On the evidence, Scipio was uncomfortable with much of this.

Nor did his wishes always prevail. Even as *princeps senatus* he could not prevent the vengeful embassy to Carthage in 195 that pushed Hannibal into exile, or later persuade voters to elect to the consulship either his outstanding friend Laelius or Scipio Nasica, his competent cousin, on their first try. His happiest period in civilian life may have been the eighteen months in 199–198 when he and Aelius Paetus were censors and made administrative decisions that everyone accepted.

The war with Antiochus III reinvigorated Scipionic military renown, more thanks now to L. Scipio than his brother. It added both, too, to the select group of Romans (Flamininus was the most obvious other) who attained near-princely prestige in states and kingdoms across the eastern Mediterranean – and Africanus, with like prestige in North Africa and Spain, outdid even Flamininus. An unstoppable trend had begun. Mediterranean states, large and small, more and more focused their fears, complaints, needs, demands and admiration on Rome as the new world hegemon, and honoured the Roman consuls and proconsuls they encountered as their patrons. It is not clear whether Scipio (or his brother) made much of this – a contrast to Flamininus' ongoing years of busy involvement with Greece, Macedon and Aegean states, and a contrast as well to Scipio's adoptive grandson Scipio Aemilianus, who by 140 would find much of the Mediterranean world looking up to him as their great and powerful friend. But the Scipio brothers, Africanus and Asiagenus, played crucial roles in the momentous process by which their republic, only one among the leading states in the Mediterranean in 218, just thirty years later was potentially dominant over all. By 168, when a Senate decree ordered the Seleucid Great King Antiochus IV to quit his invasion of Egypt and he instantly obeyed, the dominance was patent. That continuing process made the *imperium populi Romani* – the 'commanding power of the Roman people' – into what we call the Roman Empire.[3]

Empire brought exploitative riches to the Roman state, Roman aristocrats and the Roman economy. The trend had already made a start in Scipio's lifetime. That there need be no end to it Scipio, and all his fellow *principes*, surely realized. There would always be territories outside the ones Rome ruled or controlled, always be challenges to Rome's power and always be ambitious or avaricious consuls like Manlius Vulso. Neither Scipio nor any other Roman (certainly not Cato) had a formula for halting it.[4]

The plunder and profits from victories and from empire over subject nations were already beginning to eat away at old societal conventions. Eventually, time-honoured competition for *dignitas*, *auctoritas* and *gloria*, and contention over how – or whether – the proceeds of empire should trickle down to ordinary Romans and Italians, would sharpen more and more often into violence. Harassed and denounced by his opponents, Scipio did not call in some of his loyal veterans to assault or kill Naevius and Cato; he retired to Liternum to die. Ninety-six years later, another Cornelius put in the same position, the able general and consul L. Sulla, left Rome to call up his loyal legions in Campania, return in arms and slaughter every political foe who could not flee. Republican politics and enmities on this scale culminated in a long series of civil wars and the monarchic regime of the Caesars. It was the grimmest of the many outcomes – and one he would not have foreseen or welcomed – of the stellar achievements and military genius of Scipio Africanus.

ROMAN TERMS

aedile One of four middle-level yearly magistrates, responsible for maintaining city amenities, structures and temples and for funding and putting on some public festivals. Two were termed plebeian aediles (only plebeians could be elected) and two were curule aediles (both patricians and, eventually, plebeians were eligible). Like all other Roman officials, aediles were not salaried and were expected to contribute as necessary from their own resources.

aerarium The treasury of the state, stored in the Temple of Saturn diagonally opposite the Senate house in the Forum.

ager Romanus The territory of the Roman state, which grew as other regions in Italy were incorporated; subdivided from 241 BC into 35 *tribus*. Areas incorporated after 241 were added to one of the more distant *tribus*. Towns and communities in the *ager R.* remained self-administering, but to vote and participate in the republic's affairs their male citizens had to travel to Rome.

amicitia Friendship; not solely an emotional bond, but sometimes an almost formal one between families, and it could even be treated as hereditary. Guest friendships between Romans and foreigners were quite common; the tie was termed *hospitium*.

asses The *as* was the basic bronze coin in Scipio's time; an ordinary legionary soldier was paid 5 *asses* a day, equivalent to half a *denarius*. A senator was expected to own more than a million *asses* in landed property.

auctoritas Moral weight and influence in Roman society, accrued from political and military successes, personal qualities and family background.

augur Member of one of Rome's principal priestly colleges. The nine augurs interpreted signs and omens, prescribed correct ritual and carried out other priestly duties. Vacancy was filled by co-option and tenure was lifelong. In practice only leading men were selected.

ballista A catapult that fired iron bolts or shaped stones.

censor One of two officials, usually ex-consuls, elected every five years by the *comitia centuriata* to hold office for eighteen months. Normally one was a patrician and one a plebeian. Their duties were complex: holding a census of adult citizens (sixteen years and older); allocating these to *centuriae* and *tribus* according to economic and social status; regulating membership of the Senate and *equester ordo* (delinquent senators, *equites* and citizens could be punished); letting out contracts in public administration (including for collecting taxes); and building and maintaining public infrastructure of all kinds. An overall superintendance of public morals was a major censorial obligation. At the end of their term, they formally 'closed the *lustrum*' in a complex ceremony to signify that they had cleansed the state of impurities.

centuria In civic life, one of 193 units in the *comitia centuriata*. In the army, one of the infantry units in a legion; normally sixty strong.

clientes Romans of lesser social status who held personal ties, hereditary or acquired, to Romans of higher rank. The number and usefulness of a leading Roman's *clientes* was always variable.

cognomen The third name of a Roman man, for example Scipio. It was not the family surname (the *nomen* was) and might vary over generations or be added to (as with Scipio Africanus and his cousin Scipio Nasica). Not every Roman bore one.

cohort A term first used for the infantry contingents that Latin colonies and Italian allies contributed to Roman armies; later – perhaps starting with Scipio – a new grouping of a legion's thirty maniples into ten *cohortes*, one from each line of the *hastati–principes–triarii* array but all three manoeuvring as one unit. Where needed, this gave a further type of flexibility to a Roman army that enemy forces found hard to match.

coloniae Towns founded (or sometimes enlarged) by Rome outside Roman territory, originally as military outposts. A colony of Roman citizens alone was quite small, one of Romans and Latins usually larger.

comitia A formal assembly of citizens; in Latin a plural noun. *Comitia* always met at Rome or just outside. Several existed, some from very early times. The two main *comitia* were:

(1) The *c. centuriata*, assembling on the Campus Martius beside the Tiber river: comprising 193 *centuriae* organized in several groups or *classes*, whose membership was assigned by the censors according to citizens' economic status. Each *centuria* had one vote, determined by members present. The *centuriae* were unequally distributed in the *classes*. The *centuriae* of senators, *equites* and other affluent citizens formed a majority of unit votes; an adjustment, circa 230 BC, to the distribution of the wealthier voting *classes* did not change this. All landless – that is, poor – Romans were assigned to a single *centuria* at the bottom of the rankings, and it was seldom or never called on to vote.

The *c. centuriata* was presided over by a consul or praetor. It elected magistrates (including, very occasionally, a dictator) and enacted or rejected legislation put to it by the presiding magistrate. It could try persons prosecuted by a senior magistrate; it alone could declare war and ratify peace.

(2) The *c. tributa*, originally based on the *concilium plebis*, was composed of the territorial districts, *tribus*, of the Roman state. Again, each *tribus* had one unit vote. Within each 'tribe', citizens who attended were equal. Tribes close to Rome were older and smaller and the city itself was distributed into four tribes. The *c. tributa* elected quaestors and curule aediles, and could also enact or reject laws proposed by a presiding magistrate.

concilium plebis The assembly of plebeian citizens, based on the territorial *tribus* into which the *ager Romanus* was divided. It met at Rome too and voted by *tribus*. Patricians were, naturally, excluded. After 287, resolutions (*plebiscita*) of the *concilium p.* had the force of law and were termed *leges*. The *concilium p.* was convened by one or more plebeian tribunes, to elect tribunes and plebeian aediles, and to vote on proposals put to it.

consul The chief magistrate of the Roman state. Two were elected annually, to take office (from the 220s on) on the Ides (15th) of March. One had to be a plebeian, the other was always a patrician. Normally but not always, a consul had held previous magistracies up to the praetorship. The consuls' *imperium* was superior to all other regular magistrates' authority; they were the prime convenors of the Senate, unless away at war, and of the various *comitia*. Re-election within ten years was prohibited by law. Ex-consuls were called *consulares*; a consul whose *imperium* was extended for a further year (or years) became a proconsul.

deditio Capitulation; in Roman terms, total surrender by a defeated body, which then was subject to whatever decision Rome made about its future. A fuller phrase was *deditio in fidem*, 'capitulation to the good faith' of Rome.

denarius Silver coin introduced around 211, worth ten bronze *asses*. An ordinary legionary was paid about 180 *denarii* a year in Scipio's time, while a senator was expected to own property worth at least 100,000 *denarii*.

dictator Appointed only in a military emergency, such as after Hannibal's victory at Lake Trasimene in 217; or else for single specific tasks, some involving ancient rituals. His *imperium* outranked all other magistrates' authority. He was nominated by a consul, or exceptionally (as in 217) was elected by the *comitia centuriata*; once the necessary task was done he had to abdicate. He chose his own deputy, the *magister equitum*.

dignitas Social eminence, partly inherited (by men of eminent families) but chiefly gained through success in public life and moral respectability.

equester ordo, equites Romani Formally, the 1,800 cavalrymen, senators included, whom the censors registered as entitled to state-supplied horses for war. In the *comitia centuriata* they formed eighteen *centuriae*, and these always voted first. Informally, all Roman men financially able to afford cavalry service were called *equites Romani*. In 225 some 23,000 Romans (out of a total of 273,000) ranked as *equites*. The minimum financial level in Scipio's time for being registered as an *eques* is not known but would have been at least half the amount a senator would have needed.

extraordinarii, delecti extraordinarii A bodyguard corps a few hundred strong, chosen by a Roman general from Latin and Italian allied soldiers.

fetiales Priests whose task was to announce war and peace ritually to an enemy state, or to a symbol of the enemy state. The fetial rituals were very old, involving for instance sacred herbs and flintstone knives.

fides Good faith, trust: a prime Roman virtue, stressed by the state as much as by private citizens.

gens A family group sharing a common, if often legendary or mythical, ancestor. Patrician *gentes* usually shared and practised strict rituals, not now known. The six most eminent patrician *gentes*, like the Cornelii and Fabii, were called the *gentes maiores* (greater *g.*); the other patrician *gentes* were *g. minores*. Patricians only very reluctantly conceded that eminent plebeian families could be termed *gentes* too.

gloria Renown, especially military; the ideal of every Roman in public and military life.

imperator The unofficial title given to a victorious general by his soldiers' acclaim, first heard of for Scipio. It was the action noun from the verb *imperare*, 'to command'. Much later it could be used as a semi-formal title for such a general (e.g. 'imperator Caesar') and so evolved into the title of Roman emperors.

imperium The legal power to command, the highest level of *potestas*, power. Only higher magistrates and promagistrates held it, with the dictator's *imperium* being superior to the consuls', and the consuls' *imperium* to the praetors'. Over time, it also came to mean the regions over which Rome formally or informally exercised control, leading to the phrase *imperium populi Romani*, the Roman Empire.

inimicitia Enmity, the opposite of *amicitia*. In public life, both could be more or less formally announced and acted on, and even inherited.

iugera, singular *iugerum* A measurement of arable land, about 0.25 hectares (0.6 ac).

Kalends, Ides Two of the three nodal points in a Roman month: *Kalendae*, the first day and, for most months, *Idus*, the thirteenth – though this was the fifteenth in March, May, July and October. The third point, the Nones, fell on the fifth of most months, but the seventh in the months just mentioned.

Latins, *nomen Latinum* (1) The peoples of Latium, the region east of Rome; most had become incorporated into the Roman state by 300 BC. (2) The inhabitants of *coloniae Latinae*, cities founded by Rome in Italy (and later abroad) with the privileges once held by the original Latins; for instance, a Latin who moved to Rome could become registered as a Roman citizen and hold office there. Founding colonists were mostly Romans transplanted to the new colony.

legatus (1) The deputy to a military commander; always a senator. The position developed only from Scipio's time onward. (2) An ambassador or special envoy, again always a senator.

legion The main infantry unit in a Roman army, notionally 4,200 strong on recruitment though sometimes larger. Deployed for battle in three lines (a *triplex acies*), its front-line soldiers were called *hastati* – 1,200 men in ten maniples; the second line, *principes*, in similar numbers and maniples; and the third, the *triarii*, had six hundred older and experienced men in ten smaller maniples. Another 1,200 light-armed *velites* and three hundred cavalry troopers completed the *legio*. Legions never fought alone: roughly equal numbers of similarly equipped Latin and Italian allied infantry as well as six hundred cavalry were the other element of every army, with infantry bodies termed *cohortes* (a name later adopted for other purposes by Roman commanders, perhaps starting with Scipio). Contingents from foreign allied states often played important roles, too, in campaigns and battles.

magister equitum Master of horse; the deputy to a dictator, chosen by him; always a senator.

magistrate Term used for an elected Roman official with *potestas* or *imperium*. Magistrates, like senators and priests, were unpaid. Immediate re-election to the same magistracy was firmly against convention; consuls legally could not be re-elected for at least ten years.

maniple A legion's infantry unit (*manipulus*, handful), consisting of two *centuriae*.

'new man' A consul with no consular ancestors, like M. Cato in 195, was called (unofficially) a 'new man', *novus homo*, but his sons and descendants were accepted as *nobiles*.

nobiles 'Notables', the unofficial term for men who had held a senior magistracy. The designation became increasingly restricted to ex-consuls and, by extension, to their descendants. The collective term was *nobilitas* (also an unofficial appellation).

nomen A Roman's family surname, such as Cornelius; this always second after the *praenomen*. Some Romans bore only a *praenomen* and *nomen*, like C. Flaminius, consul in 217.

patricians The small but high-ranking body of Roman families who claimed ancient and sacred ancestry, and retained some special privileges: e.g. only a patrician could be *princeps senatus* or a Salian priest, and every year one consul was a patrician. Patrician *gentes* shrank in number over the centuries; in Scipio's time fewer than twenty remained active in public life.

pietas Sense of duty and religious devotion; prized by Romans as a cardinal private and public virtue.

plebeians, *plebs* A Roman who was not of patrician status was a plebeian, one of the *plebs Romana*. Plebeians thus included Romans of every economic and social status, including families that later reached the consulship and so counted as *nobiles*.

pomerium The sacred boundary of the city of Rome, alongside but religiously distinct from the city walls. A proconsul or propraetor could not cross it into the city without forfeiting his *imperium*, unless the Senate granted exemption for a triumph.

pontifex The prime priesthood of the Roman state, headed by the *pontifex maximus*. Pontiffs held office for life and had responsibility for the religious health of the state and community: organizing or supervising major ceremonies, public games and festivals, and deciding issues of religious import (including *gentes*' rituals and relationships). When death removed a pontiff, the others would select his replacement by co-optation, but from the mid-third century BC the *p. maximus* was elected by the people in a procedure involving seventeen *tribus* of the *comitia tributa* (these would be chosen by lot). The pontifical college also included the priests (*flamines*) of particular gods and also the Vestal virgins. All these persons were expected to be aristocrats; at least three had always to be patricians.

praenomen A Roman man's first name. There were only twenty or so and were regularly abbreviated (see Roman First Names, before the Preface).

praetor One of several annually elected magistrates with *imperium* lower than a consul's, but able to command military or naval forces in lesser expeditions. At Rome, praetors were responsible for conducting major trials before the people, and they carried out the consuls' tasks when these were away. A consul could instruct a praetor to act, or prohibit him from acting, on any matter. To meet Rome's growing administrative and military needs, praetors increased in number from an original one in 367 to four by the 220s, six from 198 on. A praetor whose *imperium* was extended for a year or more after his term was called a propraetor.

princeps senatus The senator whom the presiding consul or praetor first requested to give his views on a matter; an honorary position limited to ex-consuls, it was conferred by the censors and normally renewed for life.

princeps vir, principes viri The unofficial term for leading men in the body politic.

proconsul, propraetor If a consul or praetor had not completed his tasks away from Rome when his year ended, the Senate (sometimes the people) could extend his *imperium* for one more year or until the tasks were finished. He was then termed a proconsul or propraetor. A consul in office could issue orders to such promagistrates. On returning to Rome, a proconsul or propraetor could not enter the city without losing his *imperium*, unless given permission to celebrate a triumph or (if a propraetor) a lesser celebration called an ovation.

provincia Originally the range of tasks assigned to a consul or praetor. Then the term also came to mean the region where tasks were to be carried out; later it could further mean the region itself.

quaestor A junior magistrate, annually elected; the numbers grew over time. Quaestors' duties were largely financial, for example as finance officers to the consuls or to magistrates and promagistrates operating outside Rome. Quaestors were usually young men starting a career in public life. They did have permanent, more or less professional staff, *scribae*.

quinquereme The standard battleship of the third and second centuries BC, much larger but more unwieldy than the trireme (which was still used too). Crewed by three hundred rowers grouped in fives on benches along either hull; like other warships, equipped with a massive bronze ram below the waterline under the prow.

scorpion One type of torsion catapult, hurling iron bolts or iron-tipped arrows.

Senate, senator The three hundred or so leading men who formed Rome's formal advisory council; appointed for life by censors, who every five years updated the membership. Ex-magistrates expected to be appointed senators at the next census, but other deserving men could be appointed too (this was rare). Senators were called on to speak in order of seniority, but those below ex-praetor status rarely had the opportunity though they could then vote on a motion.

A Senate decree was termed a *senatus consultum*. The Senate had religious as well as political and governmental functions; its sessions ended at sunset; it could not meet on certain sacred days. It had no legislative or judicial powers, yet for a magistrate to ignore senatorial wishes or decrees was rare (and unwise). In Scipio's time a senator was expected to own at least 1 million *asses* in landed property; of course, many were much richer.

talent A unit of money value (not a coin) that was equivalent to 6,000 Greek drachmas or 6,000 Roman *denarii* (60,000 *asses* in Scipio's time).

tribunus militum A legion had six military tribunes as its senior officers, usually young men with military experience. Those in the first four legions levied for a campaign (the consuls' legions) were elected by the people; those for other legions were selected by the commander. Military tribunes were drawn from the *equester ordo* or sometimes were senators. As military distinction, *gloria*, was a requisite for a successful public career, there was no shortage of men ready to serve as military tribunes.

tribunus plebis One of ten annually elected plebeians, informally though not officially recognized as magistrates, who originally spoke for plebeians in struggles with early Rome's dominant patricians. Tribunes of the *plebs* were elected by the *concilium plebis*. In practice, candidates were mostly members of equestrian and senatorial families, but the tribunate always kept a tradition of independence, watchfulness against magistrates' arbitrary behaviour and readiness to intervene against what they perceived as wrongdoing or impropriety.

A plebeian tribune could intervene to protect anyone he viewed as being wronged. His person was sacrosanct while he held office: so if assaulted he could punish the offender directly. Any tribune could pronounce a veto (an *intercessio*) against the action or proposal of any other official – or even veto a proposed Senate decree. His veto lasted until he lifted it, usually after discussion with other tribunes. Unlike praetors and other lesser magistrates, tribunes could not be given orders by the consuls or Senate. They could put legislative proposals to the *concilium plebis* and could launch accusations there against a citizen or citizens they considered at fault, as happened to Scipio.

tribus (singular and plural) Rome's territory was divided into districts called tribes, *tribus* (from *tribuere*, to allocate): four within the city and the rest outside. Those near Rome were ancient and small, though populous; the others were much larger. The *comitia tributa* and *concilium plebis* voted in tribal units.

triumph The victory parade through Rome by a returned consul or proconsul with his army, captives and plunder, culminating in him delivering the gods' share of plunder to Jupiter's temple on the Capitoline Hill. A ceremony religious as well as military and communal, the *triumphus* could be authorized only by the Senate and people. The *triumphator*, dressed in a special toga to impersonate Jupiter – and constantly reminded by a slave attendant to remember he was a mortal – rode through the city in a four-horse chariot, preceded or followed by his sons, his officers and other persons, including eminent enemy captives on foot (some shortly to be executed), then by soldiers and wagons displaying the plunder. It was the greatest day in a Roman leader's life.

velites Light-armed and largely unarmoured foot soldiers in a legion; before the Second Punic War they were called *rorarii*. In a standard 4,200-strong legion, a little under one-third were *velites* (1,200 men), recruited from poor Romans. They fought and skirmished before a battle, then around the main fighting, using small round shields, javelins and swords or daggers; they also pursued fleeing enemy foot soldiers after a victory.

ABBREVIATIONS

App., *Hann.*, *Iber.*, *Lib.*, *Syr.*:	Appian, *Hannibalica*, *Iberica*, *Libyca*, *Syriaca*
CIL	*Corpus Inscriptionum Latinarum*
frg	fragment (of text or papyrus)
Gellius, *NA*	Aulus Gellius, *Noctes Atticae*
ILS	*Inscriptiones Latinae Selectae*, ed. H. Dessau
Philop., *Pyrrh.*, *Ti. Gr.*:	*Flamininus*, *Philopoemen*, *Pyrrhus*, *Tiberius Gracchus*
Plut., *Agesil.*, *Fab.*, *Flam.*,	Plutarch, *Agesilaus*, *Fabius Maximus*,
Pol.	Polybius
SIG^4	*Sylloge Inscriptionum Graecarum*, ed. W. Dittenberger, 4th edn
Val. Max.	Valerius Maximus, *Facta et dicta memorabilia*
Zon.	John Zonaras (epitomator of Cassius Dio)

SPECIAL NOTES

A SCIPIO'S PROVINCIA

Scipio's appointment in place of C. Nero is discussed by F. J. Vervaet and T. Ñaco del Hoyo in *Impact of the Roman Army*, ed. L. de Blois et al. (Leiden, 2007), pp. 23–6, holding that his and Silanus' *imperium* were equally proconsular, even though Silanus voluntarily gave his young colleague practical superiority in command. F. K. Drogula, *Commanders and Command in the Roman Republic and Early Empire* (Chapel Hill, NC, 2015), p. 161 n. 98, concurs, though Drogula thinks Scipio was superior because only he was appointed to the *provincia Hispania*. But whether Scipio's superiority depended on such technicalities may be doubted.

J. S. Richardson (*Hispaniae: Spain and the Development of Roman Imperialism, 218–82 BC* (Cambridge, 1986), pp. 41–9) followed by Drogula (*Commanders and Command*, p. 251 n. 53) think Scipio may have decided to operate in Spain with his army in two sections, with Silanus positioned at the Ebro much of the time, because of Spanish topography; and that this helps explain why after 206 the Senate had two commanders in Spain and then two provinces. But Scipio's forces were never very large, and the bodies he did occasionally send off to act separately (Silanus against a Hanno in Celtiberia, Marcius against Gades after Ilipa) were temporary and limited.

B THE LAGOON AT NEW CARTHAGE

Maps in H. H. Scullard, *Scipio Africanus: Soldier and Politician* (London, 1970), pp. 50–51, show how between 1500 and 1800 the lagoon dried out. On sea level rises and falls in Cartagena harbour, e.g., for mid-January 2024, see www.tideschart.com/Spain/Murcia/Murcia/Cartagena and www.tidetime.org/europe/spain/cartagena.htm. For other recent maps of this type: www.basilioparedes.com/en/blog/urban-evolution-cartagena (all accessed 16 January 2024).

Walbank's map of the capture (*A Historical Commentary on Polybius*, vol. II (Oxford, 1967), p. 206) shows the shoreline route as 'possible route of wading party', but the north-to-south crossing as the 'probable route'; so too Scullard, *Scipio Africanus*, p. 49; B. J. Lowe, 'Polybius 10.10.12 and the Existence of Salt-Flats at Carthago Nova', *Phoenix*, LIV/1–2 (2000), pp. 39–52 (p. 42). The lagoon's northern shoreline closest to the Punic city seems to have lain along the southern edge of the Parque de los Juncos, where there is a slope; this is about 800 metres (½ mi.) from the ancient city's northern edge. (The Molina de Truchao, cited in that area in earlier studies, seems no longer to exist even as a place name.) J. Seibert thinks the men waded through the middle of the Almarjal's waters from its eastern edge (*Hannibal* (Darmstadt, 1993), Karte 9b at end).

C THE SITE OF ILIPA

Ilipa identified with Alcalá del Río, a few kilometres north of Seville, is the standard view (set by G. De Sanctis, *Storia dei Romani*, vol. III, part 2 (Florence, 1968), p. 483 n. 86). Near Andújar by the upper Baetis/Guadalquivir: D. Hoyos, 'The Battle-Site of Ilipa', *Klio: Beiträge zur Alten Geschichte*, LXXXIV/1 (2002), pp. 101–13. Near Carmona (ancient Carmo, in Andalusia): R. Corzo Sánchez, 'La segunda guerra púnica en la Bética', *Habis*, 6 (1975), pp. 235–8 (as Appian, but see Chapter Four, note 2). J. S. Richardson (*Hispaniae: Spain and the Development of Roman Imperialism, 218–82 BC* (Cambridge, 1986), pp. 50–51) doubts Alcalá but leaves the question open. Neither Polybius' 'Ilinga' or 'Elinga' ('Ιλίγγα, or, in one manuscript, 'Ηλίγγα) nor Livy's 'Silpia', near which Hasdrubal camped, is a known Spanish site. 'Ilipa' is therefore a modern surmise.

In reality, 'Ιλίγγα/'Ηλίγγα could be a later copyist's distortion of what Polybius wrote. His manuscript will have been in Greek capitals: lowercase forms were not yet invented. The manuscripts that survive have ΙΛΙΓΓΑ or ΗΛΙΓΓΑ because, possibly, a scribe miswrote an original ΙΛΙΠΑ – or ΗΛΙΠΑ, as place spellings could vary. 'Silpia' in Livy could in turn have been due to him misreading Polybius' (or some other source's) spelling. Or if he in fact wrote ILIPA – his own text would have been in Roman capitals – 'Silpia' could have emerged thanks to later miscopying.

Noteworthily, if Alcalá del Río was the battle site, Scipio must have marched west for 250 kilometres (155 mi.) from Castulo's environs near modern Linares, along the Baetis' right (northern) bank. There, the often steep slopes of the Sierra Morena, edging the river, would be close to his army's right flank and offer opportunities – untaken by the enemy – for Trasimene-style ambushes. Large tributaries of the Baetis would need to be crossed too, as they flowed down from the north – notably the Rumblar, Jándula, Yeguas and Guadiato – all without being harassed by Mago and

Masinissa's cavalry, even though Hasdrubal knew he was coming and Masinissa, if no one else, knew what to do.

Polybius and Livy report no lengthy march and no river crossings. According to Polybius, once Scipio reached the neighbourhood of Castulo and Baecula he decided to move against the enemy (11.20.3–5; echoed by Livy 28.13.3–5). As soon as they were in sight, he pitched camp on low hills close to them. Clearly, for both writers the armies were somewhere near Castulo.

There were other places in Baetican Spain with the same or very similar Iberian names: Ilipa, Ilipula and Ilipla, even Iulipa – all known from inscriptions, coins and the Roman highway list called the *Antonine Itinerary*. Not all can be precisely located. Worth noting is that the encyclopedist Pliny the Elder, in his administrative survey of southern Spain, includes the town name 'Ipra', on the upper Baetis, sandwiched in a list of river towns between 'Iliturgi quod Forum Iulium' and 'Isturgi quod Triumphales' (*NH* 3.10). Iliturgi and Isturgi are known towns sited in the same region as Castulo. 'Ipra' might be a manuscript error for an Ilipa also near Castulo, and that could be the site of Scipio's victory in 206.

D DID SCIPIO TRIUMPH IN 205?

F. W. Walbank (*Historical Commentary on Polybius*, vol. II (Oxford, 1967), p. 311) and others speculate that Scipio may have held a private, that is, unofficial, triumph, or possibly was granted the lesser honour of an *ovatio*. Yet it is hard to see why either a triumph or an ovation should be ignored by Livy; his admiration for Scipio was nearly as enthusiastic as Polybius'. In fact, Polybius' wording is rather different: Scipio 'took back to his homeland a brilliant triumph and brilliant victory' (11.33.7). Almost certainly, 'triumph' (θρίαμβον) here is metaphorical. Appian, imaginative as usual, sends Scipio home with a large fleet, then has him loaded with honours at Rome and with a triumph too (*Iber.* 38.154–6). This is either a mere fancy (such things cannot be ruled out in Appian) or just possibly is a mistaken anticipation of Scipio's brilliant return from Africa four years later (lavishly recounted in *Lib.* 65.292–66.300). From some other earlier source, if not from Dio's own imagination, Dio (frg 57.54–56 = Zon. 9.11) strangely thinks Scipio was relieved of his Spanish command out of fear of his ambition; yet adds that he was then allowed to stand for a consulship – but not right away. This is confusion rivalling Appian's intermittent oddities.

E SCIPIO'S SICILIAN CAVALRY CORPS

The story is sometimes doubted (so H. H. Scullard, *Scipio Africanus: Soldier and Politician* (London, 1970), p. 266 n. 81) because it resembles one told of the Spartan king Agesilaus nearly two centuries earlier. Campaigning across the Aegean in 396, the king had levied a fully equipped cavalry force from wealthy locals in Asia Minor, requiring each to provide a fully fitted-out horse and rider or else serve as such themselves (Xenophon, *Hellenica* 3.4.15; Plut., *Agesil.* 9.3–4). But Agesilaus needed much larger cavalry numbers, and Scipio's procedure was the other way round – he conscripted Sicilian locals as cavalrymen, then granted exemption in exchange for their horses and arms, on condition they then trained the Roman replacements. At worst, we can suspect Scipio of having read Xenophon. Plutarch tells an anecdote of Scipio showing a visitor his three hundred riders and boasting that any of them would leap off a tower nearby if he ordered it (*Sayings of Romans: Moralia* 196 C). One hopes this is mere fiction.

F SCIPIO'S EXPEDITIONARY ARMY

See for example, De Sanctis, *Storia dei Romani*, vol. III, part 2, pp. 502, 562–4; J. F. Lazenby, *Hannibal's War: A Military History* (Warminster, 1978), pp. 202–3; A. Goldsworthy, *The Punic Wars* (London, 2000), pp. 287–8; M. J. Taylor, 'Reconstructing the Battle of Zama', *Classical Journal*, CXIV/3 (2019), pp. 310–29 (p. 316). By contrast, and like Coelius Antipater (cited by Livy 29.24.3), C. Bourgeon, 'Le Récit de Tite-Live sur la bataille de Zama', *L'Antiquité classique*, LXXXVII (2018), pp. 137–53 (pp. 138–9), declines an estimate. The general consensus is 25,000–30,000, excluding warships' marines (another 4,000?). P. A. Brunt, *Italian Manpower, 225 BC–AD 14* (Oxford, 1971), pp. 655–6, 672–4, holds that before the 170s no legion had over 5,000. Similarly Taylor, 'Reconstructing', p. 307, limiting Scipio's two legions to 4,200 foot each, with complementary Italian *socii*; plus 1,500 horse in all. If so, he would have left Sicily with about 18,400 troops, or maybe 20,000 if the Latin and Italian contingents were rather larger than the legions, as often happened.

It is not possible to be certain, but if the figure 6,200 per legion is false, where Livy got this from is hard to see (see J. Seibert, *Hannibal* (Darmstadt, 1993), p. 431). Worth mention too is that, if Scipio's legions were each only 4,200 strong at the outset, then by the time of Zama – two and a half years later, with no reinforcements recorded coming over in between – the losses inevitable in campaigns would have made them notably smaller; so too his other contingents. If so, even 15,000 horse and foot would be too large an estimate for his strength at Zama, apart from the Numidians that Masinissa brought. This low total looks very unlikely.

G THE PAPYRUS FRAGMENT *P. RYL.* III 491

Translation (where practicable; column I illegible)

COLUMN II

. . . (?) . . . sending(?) to the envoys, they gave (had given?) the oaths and (had) already freed the captive-group of the . . . . . . (They) having heard . . . . more amenable(?) (were?) the . . . . . ., envoys(?) about the oaths they sent out, with the men from Carthage and from themselves, to render the oaths and to take (oaths) from them. They then from Rome therefore sailed to Scipio's city, but the Phoenicians, when they reached Carthage and (announced) the agreements about the peace . . . .

COLUMN III

. . . . the(?) . . . . (??) sent men (??) to them, repudiating the oaths they sent out men bearing, instead of peace, war. On this therefore being announced to both the generals(?) . . . .

This papyrus (in the John Rylands Library, Manchester), a very short and very damaged Greek narrative of events in 203 around Carthage, was written down not long after Polybius wrote, as internal evidence shows, though its author cannot be identified (D. Hoyos, 'Polybius and the Papyrus: The Persuasiveness of "P. Rylands" III 491', *Zeitschrift für Papyrologie und Epigraphik*, CXXXIV (2001), pp. 71–9). Just possibly, though not probably, it is a fragment of the senator Fabius Pictor's history of Rome, written in Greek not long after 201. If so, the narrative would be virtually contemporary with its events. Even if not, the history to which the fragment belongs was earlier than any source except Polybius. What can be read in it starts (column II) with 'oaths' being given and taken, apparently at Castra Cornelia or Tunes, and prisoners released (from Carthage?); then oath-takers come from Rome to 'Scipio's city' (Castra Cornelia again) and to Carthage.

After a large gap, the text continues: (people) 'repudiating the oaths, sent out men bearing, instead of peace, war'. This most likely refers to the assaults threatened against Scipio's envoys and the looting of his wrecked supply fleet, both of which – at any rate in Scipio's eyes – amounted to resuming hostilities. The legible text then ends, 'On this therefore being announced to both the *stra* . . .' – probably *strategoi*, generals, thus Scipio and Hannibal; otherwise *stratopeda*, armies.

Less plausible is the interpretation that the author meant the Romans were the repudiators, or that he had in mind Scipio's new round (Pol. 15.4.1–2) of ravaging the countryside. Nor need column II's statement about men 'from Rome' sailing to Scipio's city, and 'the Phoenicians' reaching Carthage, conflict with Polybius' and others' report that the returning Carthaginian envoys reached Castra Cornelia too, whence Scipio sent them on to Carthage (15.4.5–10). That the text is a compressed narrative of events around Castra Cornelia and Carthage in the later part of 203 is plain. What may have preceded the surviving bits of narrative obviously cannot be known. But it is clear that the fragment is not a conflicting, and not a superior, rival account to Polybius' and Livy's.

H ZAMA: TIME AND PLACE

Explaining why Zama was not fought until well into 202 is a challenge, and so is determining where it happened.

1. *Chronology*

(i) Polybius' excerpts nowhere indicate a change of year or season (but there may have been an indication in his full text, between the excerpts 15.3.4 and 15.3.5). Scipio's raid inland, after his fleet was plundered, came before Carthage's envoys returned from Rome (15.4.1–5), so dates to 203. But next (15.5.1–3) Hannibal, now in Africa, finally obeys the Carthaginians' urgings and moves against him – so we have moved to 202 and Scipio's march westward to link up with Masinissa.

(ii) Livy writes (30.8.6; 8.10–12) that news of the renewed hostilities reached an alarmed Rome just as a massive flooding of the Tiber nearly forced the *ludi Apollinares* to be moved outside the city. This festival, instituted in 212, was held in mid-July by the Roman calendar (H. H. Scullard, *Festivals and Ceremonies of the Roman Republic* (London, 1981), pp. 159–60). In 202 that date was late June in modern terms (P. S. Derow, *Phoenix*, 'The Roman Calendar, 218–191 BC', XXX (1976), p. 273, as Roman 1 July 202 = real 13 June). This supports other items of evidence dating Zama to later in 202; but details of what happened in the weeks and months before the battle remain opaque. (For Appian's way of filling the time, see Chapter Eight, note 8.)

Astronomically, NASA's ancient solar eclipse website (https://eclipse.gsfc.nasa.gov/SEcat5/SEcatalog.html) gives access to a further webpage listing third-century BC occurrences. In the entry for the eclipse of 202, which for technical reasons is given the dating '–0201', the link '04284-0201 Oct 19' (accessing a map) shows that the eclipse was most visible diagonally across Africa from West Africa down to Tanzania, but (it seems) was noticeable further north, roughly from Tangier to the Horn of Africa. Not that it would really have made any participants in the battle panic, but if seen or learned of by savants, for instance at Alexandria, linking (and exaggerating) it with the battle might well appeal to later, portent-minded writers. P. Marchetti, 'La Marche du calendrier romain de 203 à 190 (années Varr. 551–564)', *L'Antiquité classique*, XLII (1973), pp. 481–6, puts Zama only some ten days before Vermina's defeat on (Roman) 17 December, which in turn he dates to 1 November (real time) because of the solar eclipse.

2. *Site*

Theories include: G. Veith in J. Kromayer and G. Veith, *Antike Schlachtfelder*, vol. III, part 2 (Berlin, 1912), pp. 598–638; F. W. Walbank, *Historical Commentary on Polybius*, vol. II (Oxford, 1967), pp. 446–9; H. H. Scullard, *Scipio Africanus: Soldier and Politician* (London, 1970), pp. 141, 271–4 n. 104; J. Seibert, *Forschungen zu Hannibal* (Darmstadt, 1993), pp. 311–14; M. J. Taylor, 'Reconstructing the Battle of Zama', *Classical Journal*, CXIV/3 (2019), pp. 310–29. Worth notice for comparison is that at Waterloo, the 1815 battlefield measured about 6.5 by 4 kilometres (4 by 2½ mi.); there, some 140,000 troops clashed before the Prussians came on the scene (D. Chandler, *Dictionary of the Napoleonic Wars* (New York, 1979), pp. 481–2 s.v.). This tract is not much larger than areas of open terrain around Naraggara/Sidi Youssef. In 202 the forces engaged were 80,000–85,000 in all.

Preferring Kbor Klib near Jama: D. Ross, *Kbor Klib and the Battle of Zama*, BAR International Series, S1399 (Oxford, 2005); M. Guirguis et al., 'Contribuzione alla localizzazione del campo della battaglia di Zama tra storia, epigrafia ed archeologia', *Hormos: ricerche di storia antica*, VIII (2016), pp. 102–39; see S. Lancel, *Hannibal* (Paris, 1995), pp. 278–80. On the Kbor Klib monument, E. Polito, 'Emblèmes macédoniens: une hypothèse sur une série de boucliers de Macédoine en Numidie', *Antiquités africaines*, XXXV (1999), pp. 39–70, gives a mid-second-century BC dating. For a mid-first-century BC date and Julius Caesar as possible author, see D. W. Roller, *The World of Juba II and Kleopatra Selene: Royal Scholarship on Rome's African Frontier* (New York and London, 2003), with a photograph of the plain below Kbor Klib (Roller, *World of Juba*, pp. 36 n., 37 fig. 2, 38 n.) – a plain not broader than at least one tract outside Sidi Youssef.

REFERENCES

PREFACE: SCIPIO AND HIS NARRATORS

1 Pol. 10.1.2 ('outstanding', *epiphanestaton*). Scipio brothers' letters: M. Austin, *The Hellenistic World from Alexander to the Roman Conquest*, 2nd edn (Cambridge, 2006), p. 362, no. 202; J. Ma, *Antiochos III and the Cities of Western Asia Minor* (Oxford, 1999), pp. 368–9, no. 46. On Polybius: F. W. Walbank, *A Historical Commentary on Polybius*, 3 vols (Oxford, 1957, 1967, 1979), and *Polybius* (Berkeley and Los Angeles, CA, and London, 1972); H. H. Scullard, *Scipio Africanus: Soldier and Politician* (London, 1970), pp. 11–25; C. B. Champion, *Cultural Politics in Polybius' 'Histories'* (Berkeley, CA, and London, 2004); B. McGing, *Polybius' 'Histories'* (Oxford, 2010); D. Baronowski, *Polybius and Roman Imperialism* (London, 2011); C. Smith and L. M. Yarrow, eds, *Imperialism, Cultural Politics, and Polybius* (Oxford, 2012); B. Gibson and T. Harrison, eds, *Polybius and His World: Essays in Memory of F. W. Walbank* (Oxford, 2013); F. Nicholson, 'Polybius', *Oxford Classical Dictionary* (Oxford, 2016).

2 On Livy's later books: J. Briscoe, *A Commentary on Livy, Books XXXI–XLIV*, 4 vols (Oxford, 1971–2012); T. J. Luce, *The Composition of Livy's 'History'* (Princeton, NJ, 1979); B. Mineo, ed., *A Companion to Livy* (Chichester, 2015). Livy notoriously evaluated Polybius in tepid-negative fashion: 'not at all a writer to be ignored' (30.45.5) and 'no unreliable author both on all matters Roman and especially on Greek events' (33.10.10). Livy and Polybius: e.g., P. G. Walsh, *Livy: His Historical Aims and Methods* (Cambridge, 1963), pp. 128–30, 138–46; H. Tränkle, *Livius und Polybios* (Basel and Stuttgart, 1977); Luce, *Livy's History*, pp. 141–3, 178–81; Champion, *Cultural Politics*, pp. 95–110.

3 Other ancient sources: Luce, *Livy's History*, pp. 92–104, 147–9, 159–68, 180–83; B. Mineo, in *A Companion to the Punic Wars*, ed. D. Hoyos (Chichester, 2011), pp. 111–27; D. Russell, 'Plutarch of Chaeronea', *Oxford Classical Dictionary*, 4th edn, online (2015–), *s.v.*; K. Brodersen, 'Appian

und seine Werk', in *Aufstieg und Niedergang der römischen Welt*, Part II, vol. XXXIV/1, ed. W. Haase (Berlin and New York, 1993), pp. 339–63. Silius Italicus and his epic-poetic Scipio: R. Marks, *From Republic to Empire: Scipio Africanus in the 'Punica' of Silius Italicus* (Frankfurt and New York, 2005).

4 Possible portraits of Scipio: Scullard, *Scipio Africanus*, pp. 249–51; H. Etcheto, *Les Scipions: famille et pouvoir à Rome à l'époque républicaine* (Bordeaux, 2012), pp. 261–78. The epitaphs of some other Scipios survived in the Tomb of the Scipios (but not his): J. Van Sickle, 'The Elogia of the Cornelii Scipiones and the Origin of Epigram at Rome', *American Journal of Philology*, CVIII/1 (1987), pp. 41–55.

1 THE CORNELII AND ROME

1 The early Scipios: H. Etcheto, *Les Scipions: famille et pouvoir à Rome à l'époque républicaine* (Bordeaux, 2012), pp. 25–40, 157–9.

2 How Rome's republican political system worked: A. E. Astin in *Cambridge Ancient History*, vol. VIII, ed. A. E. Astin et al., 2nd edn (Cambridge, 1989), pp. 163–91; A. Lintott, *The Constitution of the Roman Republic* (Oxford, 1999). Roman aristocratic values: N. Rosenstein in *A Companion to the Roman Republic*, ed. Rosenstein and R. Morstein-Marx (Malden, MA, and Oxford, 2006), pp. 365–82. The Pomponii Mathones: T. Schmitt, 'Die Marci Pomponii Mathones. Eine quellen- und sachkritische Analyse der Überlieferung', *Göttinger Forum für Altertumswissenschaft*, III (2000), pp. 83–110.

3 Rome's conquest of Italy and its first overseas wars: chapters in F. W. Walbank et al., eds, *Cambridge Ancient History*, 2nd edn, vol. VII, part 2 (Cambridge, 1989), pp. 309–574; W. V. Harris, *Roman Power: A Thousand Years of Empire* (Cambridge, 2016), pp. 1–23. Relations with its Latin and other Italian allies during the Second Punic War: K. Lomas, 'Rome, Latins, and Italians in the Second Punic War', in *A Companion to the Punic Wars*, ed. D. Hoyos (Chichester, 2011), pp. 339–56.

2 BOYHOOD, YOUTH AND WAR

1 Scipio's snake: Livy 26.19.7–9; Aulus Gellius, *Noctes Atticae* (hereafter *NA*) 6.1.1–4; [Victor], *de Viris Illustribus* 49. The epic poet Silius Italicus (late 1st century AD) has Pomponia herself, now a shade in the Underworld, confirm it to her visiting son (*Punica* 13.628–47; Silius alone of ancient authors records her name, 13.615).

2 Naevius on Scipio's escapade: Gellius, *NA* 7.8.5–6. 'Fond of women': Polybius 10.19.3.

3 Polybius on Scipio's supposed dream: 10.4.1–9; F. W. Walbank, *A Historical Commentary on Polybius*, vol. II (Oxford, 1967), pp. 199–200.

4 Scipio as a *sodalis Salius*: Livy 37.33.6–7. On the Salii: M. Patzelt, 'Chanting and Dancing into Dissociation: The Case of the Salian Priests at Rome', in *Cognitive Approaches to Ancient Religious Experience*, ed. E. Eidinow, A. W. Geertz and J. W. North, 2 vols (Cambridge, 2022), vol. I, pp. 118–42.

5 Aemilia (L. Paullus' third daughter, therefore called Aemilia Tertia): Pol. 31.26.1–5; Val. Max. 6.7.1; H. Etcheto, *Les Scipions: famille et pouvoir à Rome à l'époque républicaine* (Bordeaux, 2012), pp. 165–6.

6 On the Barcids, see, for example, G.-C. Picard, *Hannibal* (Paris, 1967); W. Huss, *Geschichte der Karthager* (Munich, 1985), pp. 252–424; S. Lancel, *Hannibal* (Paris, 1995); D. Hoyos, *Hannibal's Dynasty: Power and Politics in the Western Mediterranean, 247–183 BC* (London, 2003); P. Barceló, *Hannibal: Stratege und Staatsmann* (Stuttgart, 2004). Naravas figures, as 'Narr' Havas', in Gustave Flaubert's extravagant 1862 novel *Salammbô*.

7 The entry date to the consulship had changed from May to the Ides of March, probably in the 220s though first mentioned for 217: Livy 21.63.1, 22.1.4–7; T.R.S. Broughton, *The Magistrates of the Roman Republic*, 2 vols (Chico, CA, 1951), vol. II, pp. 638–9.

8 *Delecti extraordinarii:* Pol. 6.26.6–9; P. Connolly, *Greece and Rome at War* (London, 1981), pp. 134, 135–6; M. Dobson, *The Army of the Roman Republic: The Second Century BC, Polybius and the Camps at Numantia, Spain* (London, 2008), pp. 51–2, 95–6. Roman and allied armies of the period: P. Connolly, 'The Roman Army in the Age of Polybius', in *Warfare in the Ancient World*, ed. Sir J. Hackett (London, 1989), pp. 149–68; A. Goldsworthy, *The Punic Wars* (London, 2000), pp. 36–62; N. Rosenstein, *Rome and the Mediterranean, 290 to 146 BC: The Imperial Republic* (Edinburgh, 2012), pp. 71–118; M. Sage, 'The Rise of Rome', in *The Oxford Handbook of Warfare in the Classical World*, ed. D. B. Campbell and L. A. Tritle (Oxford and New York, 2013), pp. 216–35. Publius rescuing his father at the Ticinus: Pol. 10.3.3–7; Livy 21.46.7–10 (adding Coelius' variant version); Pliny, *Natural History* 16.14, has Publius declining the *corona civica* after the Trebia battle – either a Pliny error, or the consul may have been too injured to make the offer sooner.

9 The war in Italy in 218–216: for example, G. De Sanctis, *Storia dei Romani*, vol. III, part 2 [1916] (Florence, 1968), pp. 1–374; J. F. Lazenby, *Hannibal's War: A Military History* (Warminster, 1978), pp. 39–86; W. Huss, *Geschichte der Karthager* (Munich, 1985), pp. 294–334; Goldsworthy, *Punic Wars*, pp. 167–221; Hoyos, *Hannibal's Dynasty*, pp. 98–121.

10 Scipio at Canusium: Livy 22.53.1–13 ('fatalis dux huiusce belli', 53.6); Val. Max. 5.6.7; Broughton, *Magistrates of the Roman Republic*, vol. I, p. 251; H. H. Scullard, *Scipio Africanus: Soldier and Politician* (London, 1970), pp. 29–30; E. Cimolino, 'Scipion l'Africain chez Tite-Live: Remarques sur le portrait d'un jeune général exceptionnel', *Vita Latina*, CLXXXIX–CXC (2014), pp. 110–12. Some disbelieve the story of him preventing faint-hearts from fleeing abroad, e.g. R. T. Ridley, 'Was Scipio Africanus at Cannae?', *Latomus*, XXXIV/1 (1975), pp. 161–5; J. Seibert, *Hannibal* (Darmstadt, 1993), pp. 197–8.

11 On the elder Scipios' operations and ultimate disaster in Spain: D. Hoyos, 'Generals and Annalists: Geographic and Chronological Obscurities in the Scipios' Campaigns in Spain, 218–211 BC', *Klio: Beiträge zur Alten Geschichte*, LXXXIII/1 (2001), pp. 68–92. The plentiful Roman military debris, probably from Scipio's time, that has been found at Santo Tomé, 100 km (62 mi.) east of Jaén, accompanied by much less Carthaginian material, may be the site of one brother's last stand in 211, although its investigators see it as Baecula, where young Scipio defeated Hasdrubal the Barcid three years later (J. P. Bellón Ruiz et al., eds, *La Segunda Guerra Púnica en la península ibérica: Baecula, arqueología de una batalla* (Jaén, 2015); J. P. Bellón et al., 'An Archaeological Analysis of a Battlefield of the Second Punic War: The Camps of the Battle of Baecula', *Journal of Roman Archaeology*, XXIX (2016), pp. 73–104).

3 THE CAPTURE OF NEW CARTHAGE

1 Livy 26.18.1–19.2. Polybius' account does not survive but influenced Livy's: thus L. Beltramini and M. Rocco, 'Livy on Scipio Africanus: The Commander's Portrait at 26.19.3–9', *Classical Quarterly*, LXX/1 (2020), pp. 230–46. Livy and the literary theme of Scipio's young age: E. Cimolino, 'Scipion l'Africain chez Tite-Live: Remarques sur le portrait d'un jeune general exceptionnel', *Vita Latina*, CLXXXIX–CXC (2014), pp. 104–21.

2 Scipio's *imperium* and Silanus' status: see Special Note A. Scipio's vows: Livy 28.21.1, 10.

3 Livy 27.7.5–6 dates Scipio's capture of New Carthage to 210; refuted, G. De Sanctis, *Storia dei Romani*, vol. III, part 2 (Florence, 1968), pp. 453–4 n. 28; J. F. Lazenby, *Hannibal's War: A Military History* (Warminster, 1978), p. 132.

4 Scipio takes New Carthage: Pol. 10.6.1–20.8; Livy 26.41.1–51.14; App., *Iber.* 20.76–23.92 (full of errors); minor sources listed, T.R.S. Broughton, *The Magistrates of the Roman Republic*, 2 vols (Chico, CA, 1951), vol. I, p. 287. Polybius used, among other accounts, Scipio's letter to Philip V of Macedon, written about twenty years later (10.9.3), and Laelius was a personal

informant (10.3.2). Scipio's claimed seven-day advance from northern Spain is widely disbelieved (e.g. F. W. Walbank, *A Historical Commentary on Polybius*, vol. II (Oxford, 1967), pp. 204–5; H. H. Scullard, *Scipio Africanus: Soldier and Politician* (London, 1970), p. 254 n. 34; W. Huss, *Geschichte der Karthager* (Munich, 1985), p. 383 n. 42), but is defended variedly by J. Seibert, *Hannibal* (Darmstadt, 1993), p. 353 n. 68; J. M. Gallego Cañamero, '"Septimo die ab Hibero Carthaginem ventum est [...]" (Liv. xxvi.42.6). Virtus y strategemata en la conquista de *Qart-Hadasht* (209 ane)', *Ancient History Bulletin*, XXXVI/1–2 (2022), pp. 1–58. Another comparably fast move was the Achaean general Philopoemen's in 183, leading his cavalry from Argos through hill country to a threatened Megalopolis 400 *stadia* away, in one day (Pol. 23.12.1; Plut., *Philop.* 18.3); 400 *stadia* equate to 76.8 kilometres (47½ mi.; in fact, Argos is 85.8 km from modern Megalopolis).

5 New Carthage in the Second Punic War: S. F. Ramallo Asensio and M. Martín Camino, '*Qart-Hadast* en el marco de la Segunda Guerra Púnica', in *La Segunda Guerra Púnica en la península ibérica: Baecula, arqueología de una batalla*, ed. J. P. Bellón Ruiz et al. (Jaén, 2015), pp. 129–62. On the topography of New Carthage, see M. Martínez-Andreu, 'La topografía de Carthago Nova: estado de la cuestión', *Mastia*, III (2004), pp. 11–30 – noting the lagoon's changeable salinity due to influxes of fresh water (p. 18). Layout and structure of the Almarjal, including in Scipio's time: Josefina García-León, 'Historical Evolution of the "Almarjal" Lagoon, Cartagena (Spain)', *8th Int. gvSIG Conference*, www.youtube.com, accessed 16 January 2024. Rains could be heavy at Cartagena, like the 2.85 metres (112 in.) recorded in a 1919 downpour (Benedict J. Lowe, 'Polybius 10.10.12 and the Existence of Salt-Flats at Carthago Nova', *Phoenix*, LIV/1–2 (2000), pp. 39–52, on p. 41 n. 14). See Special Note B.

6 Livy puts Scipio's invocation of Neptune the next day – just before the commandos set out (26.45.9) – causing pain to some moderns, who, judging this a more likely occasion, then have to see Polybius as a dishonest narrator-manipulator (Walbank, *Commentary*, vol. II, pp. 194–6; Scullard, *Scipio Africanus*, pp. 58–60, discusses the issue). In fact, Livy too gives Scipio a speech where Polybius does (26.43.3–8) – but in the manuscripts it breaks off, incomplete. Mention of Neptune may have been lost there, even if Livy repeated it later on for effect. Gold crowns and other rewards promised: Pol. 10.11.6 and 9.

7 Livy 26.45.7; contrast Pol. 10.14.9–13 – Scipio sends his commandos on their way but plainly is not with them. Livy perhaps misunderstood Polybius' account, or on this point preferred a different, more dramatic source (Valerius Antias comes to mind).

8 Probably the most debated topic in Scipio's entire career, what happened at the New Carthage lagoon, is widely debated and even derided: e.g. J. Seibert, *Forschungen zu Hannibal* (Darmstadt, 1993), pp. 262–6; J. H. Richardson, 'P. Cornelius Scipio and the Capture of New Carthage: The Tide, the Wind and Other Fantasies', *Classical Quarterly*, LXVIII/2 (2018), pp. 458–74.

9 Pol. 10.14.8–9, mentioning 'the edges of the lagoon' (τὰ μὲν ἄκρα τῆς λίμνης); see Walbank, *Commentary*, vol. II, p. 215 ('the extremities'), though he thinks that the five hundred started from the northern shore of the lagoon, to cross southward via a narrow ridge still preserved (so H. H. Scullard, *Scipio Africanus in the Second Punic War* (Cambridge, 1930), p. 298) in Cartagena's topography.

10 Livy found typically varied statistics on booty and prisoners in his predecessors (26.49.1–3). Hannibal's friend and biographer Silenus of Sicily offered sixty scorpions large and small; the annalist Valerius Antias, overenthusiastically, 6,000 large scorpions plus 13,000 small (49.3; 'so much endless falsification', Livy sighs). Likewise the size of the garrison, though no sources' names are cited for these – 2,000 or 7,000 or 10,000 (49.2; but Polybius' figures come where it counts, at 44.2) – and the total of Spanish hostages (49.1): 300 (Polybius' figure, 10.18.3) or 3,724 (surely another Antias inflation). The number of city captives taken was 10,000 (this is Polybius' figure) – or was it 25,000 (quite possibly Antias')? Even the fleet commander on the day was Laelius in some accounts, Silanus in others, while Antias chose to call the city commandant Arines, not Mago (49.4–5). These contradictions illustrate vividly the pitfalls Livy, not to mention other ancients, faced in trying to compose historical narrative.

11 In 206, to launch an assault on the town of Ilugo, Scipio's officers 'distributed ladders to men hand-picked from the maniples' (Livy 28.19.9: *electis per manipulos viris*). At New Carthage, much the same process must have occurred, but with marines like Digitius selected too. Since Digitius was elected praetor in 194, he not only must have become a Roman citizen at some date (which points to him being a Latin in 209) but was from the start a man of some status: therefore a prefect of marines or the like at New Carthage.

12 Literary aspects of Polybius' narrative of the capture and aftermath: B. McGing, *Polybius' 'Histories'* (Oxford, 2010), pp. 7–11. Livy on Scipio, the wife of Mandonius and the beautiful Spanish captive: 26.49.9–50.14; see Gellius, *NA* 7.8.1–3; Plut., *Moralia* 196 B; Val. Max. 4.3.1 (confusing Mandonius with Indibilis). Valerius Antias waspishly claimed that Scipio did keep the girl for himself (Gellius 7.8.9); cynical too is Seibert, *Hannibal*, p. 355 n. 81. The episode in Livy an inverse response to the Lucretia

tragedy in his Book 1: J. D. Chaplin, 'Scipio the Matchmaker', in *Ancient Historiography and Its Contexts: Studies in Honour of A. J. Woodman*, ed. C. S. Kraus, J. Marincola and C. Pelling (Oxford, 2010), pp. 60–72. A fiction to imply Scipio's similarity to Alexander the Great and superiority to normal youthful temptations: Cimolino, 'Scipion l'Africain', pp. 112–14.

13 Italian allied infantry contingents were already termed *cohortes*, but Scipio used the word for the grouped *manipuli* of a legion (in Spain at any rate; not mentioned in his other campaigns): L. Keppie, *The Making of the Roman Army from Republic to Empire* (London, 1984), pp. 63–5; M. Dobson, *The Army of the Roman Republic: The Second Century BC, Polybius and the Camps at Numantia, Spain* (London, 2008), pp. 58–64; M. Sage, 'The Rise of Rome', in *The Oxford Handbook of Warfare in the Classical World*, ed. D. B. Campbell and L. A. Tritle (Oxford and New York, 2013), pp. 228–31; C. Petrocelli, 'Tactics: Republic', in *The Encyclopedia of the Roman Army*, ed. Y. Le Bohec, 3 vols (Malden, MA, and Oxford, 2015), vol. III, pp. 981–6.

4 BAECULA AND ILIPA

1 Santo Tomé the preferred site: J. P. Bellón Ruiz et al., eds, *La Segunda Guerra Púnica en la península ibérica: Baecula, arqueología de una batalla* (Jaén, 2015), pp. 195–232, 533–620; J. P. Bellón et al., 'An Archaeological Analysis of a Battlefield of the Second Punic War: The Camps of the Battle of Baecula', *Journal of Roman Archaeology*, XXIX (2016), pp. 73–104. Baecula sited near Bailén and Linares: J. Kromayer, *Antike Schlachtfelder: Bausteine zu einer antiken Kriegsgeschichte*, vol. IV (Berlin, 1931), pp. 501–10; so too, e.g., F. W. Walbank, *A Historical Commentary on Polybius*, vol. II (Oxford, 1967), pp. 248–50; H. H. Scullard, *Scipio Africanus: Soldier and Politician* (London, 1970), pp. 71–2; J. F. Lazenby, *Hannibal's War: A Military History* (Warminster, 1978), p. 141 and Map 16 at end; A. Goldsworthy, *The Punic Wars* (London, 2000), p. 277. R. Corzo Sánchez, 'La segunda guerra púnica en la Bética', *Habis*, VI (1975), pp. 231–4, argues for a rural area called Betela, about 50 kilometres (30 mi.) west-northwest of Jaén (he makes Scipio start out from New Carthage, not Tarraco); this looks implausible.

2 Battle of Baecula: Pol. 10.38.7–40.12; Livy 27.18.1–19.1. Polybius locates Baecula near 'Castalon' (Castulo), which stood near today's Bailén. Appian's version (*Iber.* 24.93–27.109) is ludicrously confused, terming Baetica (the Roman name for southern Spain) a city, putting the battle at 'Carmone' (modern Carmona, south of Seville) and, worst of all, blending it and the battle of Ilipa into one.

3 On the wily and very long-lived Masinissa: P. G. Walsh, 'Massinissa', *Journal of Roman Studies*, LV (1965), pp. 149–60; E. Storm, *Massinissa: Numidien*

im Aufbruch (Wiesbaden, 2001); B. Meissner, in *Brill's New Pauly Online* (2006), *s.v.* 'Massinissa'.

4 It may have been on his return march to Tarraco that Scipio arranged for Saguntine survivors of Hannibal's sack to be reinstated in their city, joining others restored in 212 by his father and uncle. So said a grateful Saguntine embassy to the Senate late in 206 (Livy 28.39.1–21).

5 Elinga, Silpia: Pol. 11.20.1; Livy 28.12.14; Special Note C. Diagrams of Scipio's battle manoeuvres: e.g. Scullard, *Scipio Africanus*, p. 97; Lazenby, *Hannibal's War*, Map 17 at end; P. Connolly, *Greece and Rome at War* (London, 1981), p. 200.

6 Cicero on a general's *felicitas: De imperio Cn. Pompei* 28, 47–48 (66 BC).

5 THE FALL OF CARTHAGINIAN SPAIN

1 Chronological difficulties: G. De Sanctis, *Storia dei Romani*, vol. III, part 2 (Florence, 1968), pp. 481–2 n. 84, and p. 669 (dating Ilipa to 207); J. Seibert, *Forschungen zu Hannibal* (Darmstadt, 1993), pp. 259–60. Silanus' and Marcius' roles reversed by Livy: H. H. Scullard, *Scipio Africanus: Soldier and Politician* (London, 1970), p. 96.

2 Livy 28.17.4–18.12; App., *Iber.* 29.114–30.119; Zon. 9.10. Siga was surely Scipio's and Hasdrubal's destination, though no source names it (F. W. Walbank, *A Historical Commentary on Polybius*, vol. II (Oxford, 1967), p. 306; J. F. Lazenby, *Hannibal's War: A Military History* (Warminster, 1978), pp. 151, 294 n. 63).

3 Ilugo: *Ilourgeia* in Polybius (11.24.10, 'Ιλούργεια), *Ilyrgia* in Appian (*Iber.* 32.128, Ἰλυργία); Livy's 'Iliturgi' is confusion with a different southern Spanish town (D. Hoyos, 'Generals and Annalists: Geographic and Chronological Obscurities in the Scipios' Campaigns in Spain, 218–211 BC', *Klio: Beiträge zur Alten Geschichte*, LXXXIII/1 (2001), pp. 79–80, 86–9). As mentioned, Ilugo was probably Santisteban del Puerto, a town 62 kilometres (38½ mi.) northeast of Bailén in the gap between the Sierra Morena on the west and the Sierras de Alcaraz and de Cazorla on the east. Livy's description of the deserters using iron spikes like crampons to scale the steep height (28.20.1–5) fits Santisteban's imposing rock. Santo Tomé, the possible site for one of the elder Scipios' end (Chapter Four, n. 1), lies 36 kilometres (22 mi.) to the south; this would fit too. That Ilugo was the later Ilorci – and this in turn modern Lorquí, 20 kilometres (12 mi.) north of Murcia and under 70 kilometres (42 mi.) from Cartagena (e.g. H. H. Scullard, *Scipio Africanus in the Second Punic War* (Cambridge, 1930), pp. 50–51, 142–4; *Soldier and Politician*, pp. 264–5 n. 70) – is not likely.

4 Marcius' movements: Livy 28.21.1, 22.1–23.8, 31.1–2. This outstanding officer is never heard of again after 206.

5 The Sucro mutiny: Pol. 11.25.1–30.5; Livy 28.24.1–29.8; App., *Iber.* 34.137–36.146 (vague on details). Livy at one point carelessly puts Sucro north of the Ebro (28.24.5), probably confusing its garrison with the forces left to hold the northeast. That the leaders' names, Albius and Atrius, look invented (Latin *albus*, white; *ater*, black) is not a sound reason for rejecting them (as does De Sanctis, vol. III/2, p. 625; see Lazenby, *Hannibal's War*, p. 153); other bearers of these *nomina* are known, including the Augustan poet Albius Tibullus.

6 Pol. 11.33.8 records Scipio leaving Silanus and Marcius in charge; for Livy (28.38.1) his successors, L. Cornelius Lentulus and L. Manlius Acidinus, were already present, but this is less likely (see Walbank, *Commentary*, vol. II, p. 312). Saguntum, which Scipio reconstituted now if not earlier, did not forget him: nearly four hundred years later, the city set up what must have been a statue of him to celebrate the restoration, with the inscription *P. Scipioni cos. | imp. ob restitu|tam Saguntum | ex s. c. bello Pu|nico secundo*, 'To P. Scipio, consul, *imperator*, for restoring Saguntum by decree of the Senate in the Second Punic War' (CIL, vol. II, no. 3836 = ILS 66).

6 CONSUL AND PROCONSUL

1 Livy 28.38.1–3; see Special Note D.

2 That Livy modelled his account of the debate (28.40.1–44.18) on Thucydides' narrative (6.9.1–18.7) of Nicias' and Alcibiades' confrontation over the proposed Sicilian expedition is propounded by B. S. Rodgers, 'Great Expeditions: Livy on Thucydides', *Transactions of the American Philological Association*, CXVI (1986), pp. 335–52. Of course, in Thucydides the issue was over starting a new war; in Livy it was how to end one. On the rhetoric of Livy's account: A. Tedeschi, 'Conflitto d'età e conflitto d'opinione. Q. Fabio Massimo, Scipione l'Africano e la spedizione anticartaginese in Africa', *Aufidus*, XXVI (1995), pp. 17–43. Upshot of the debate: Livy 28.45.1–46.1. Fabius' enduring hostility to Scipio: Plut. *Fab.* 25–26; R. Develin, *The Practice of Politics at Rome, 366–167 BC* (Brussels, 1985), pp. 231–7.

3 Gifts to Delphi, and the expedition's recruitment and preparations: Livy 28.45.12–46.1; J. Seibert, *Hannibal* (Dramstadt, 1993), pp. 418–19. By contrast P. A. Brunt, *Italian Manpower, 225 BC–AD 14* (Oxford, 1971), pp. 655–6, 695–6, suspects that Livy's details are inaccurate if not invented. But Livy may have drawn selectively from a fuller predecessor (Fabius or Cincius?). Warfare in Italy was almost completely confined to the south ever

since 215, so the north and centre had had ten years to work on regaining some prosperity. Some allies were keen to show their loyalty, now that the war was turning in Rome's favour (the Etruscans in particular had fallen under recent suspicion – and are listed as notable contributors in 205).

4 Livy 29.1.1–11; Seibert, *Hannibal*, p. 420; Special Note E.

5 Scipio in Sicily, and Laelius' African raid: Livy 29.1.1–18, 3.7–5.1.

6 Clash at Locri: Livy 29.6.1–7.10. Ancient Locri stood near the modern city, partly on two hills, the Abbadessa and the Mannella (thus its two citadels), separated by a steep valley (*The Princeton Encyclopedia of Classical Sites*, www.perseus.tufts.edu, *s.v.* 'Lokroi Epizephyrioi'). Where Hannibal was before marching there Livy does not say, but before returning to Africa in 203 he had been at Cape Lacinium 160 kilometres (99 mi.) to the north (Capo Colonna near Crotone) for three years (G. De Sanctis, *Storia dei Romani*, vol. III, part 2 (Florence, 1968), p. 527 n. 152). He probably took only some troops with him to Locri, as Crassus and Metellus with their armies were also in Bruttium; later that year, Crassus reported that Hannibal's forces and theirs were all stricken with plague (dysentery or malaria?): Livy 29.10.1.

7 Pleminius' criminal activities: Livy 29.8.1–9.12; Diodorus 27.4.1–8; brief other sources in T.R.S. Broughton, *The Magistrates of the Roman Republic*, 2 vols (Chico, CA, 1951), vol. I, p. 304. Polybius' report is lost.

8 Matho's investigative commission: Livy 29.19.1–22.12.

7 SCIPIO IN AFRICA: UTICA AND THE GREAT PLAINS

1 Scipio's embarkation forces: Livy 29.24.12–25.4; App., *Lib.* 13.51; Special Note F.

2 Scipio's departure: Livy 29.27.5–15. A. M. Eckstein, *Mediterranean Anarchy, Interstate War, and the Rise of Rome* (Berkeley and Los Angeles, CA, and London, 2006), pp. 223–4, views his prayer as a standard formula at the outset of a campaign (so standard that the comic playwright Plautus parodied it). Emporia as Scipio's destination: Livy 29.25.11–1. Only a piece of disinformation directed at the enemy: e.g. H. H. Scullard, *Scipio Africanus: Soldier and Politician* (London, 1970), pp. 120, 267 n. 85; J. F. Lazenby, *Hannibal's War: A Military History* (Warminster, 1978), pp. 204–5; S. Lancel, *Hannibal* (Paris, 1995), p. 265; A. Goldsworthy, *The Punic Wars* (London, 2000), p. 291. Against this theory: J. Seibert, *Hannibal* (Darmstadt, 1993), pp. 431–2 n. 38. – On the African campaigns, P. Edwell, 'War Abroad: Sicily, Macedon, Africa', in *A Companion to the Punic Wars*, ed. D. Hoyos (Chichester, 2011), pp. 330–37.

3 Uzalis was a privileged town in later times (Pliny, *Natural History* 5.29: an *oppidum Latinum*), then a Christian bishopric; today a titular Christian see.

4 Masinissa might have gathered 2,000 riders over the next weeks or months, prompting later the notion that he first arrived with that many. His many ups and downs before then are lengthily reported by Livy (29.29–33; quite likely from Polybius, who spoke with the still hale king fifty years later). They have to fit between his departure from Spain later in 206 after Ilipa, and Scipio's arrival in Africa in mid-204 – so within eighteen to twenty months at most. Appian (*Lib.* 13–14) quite unreliably has him then rejoin Syphax and Hasdrubal, despite them plotting to murder him, until the battle of Agathocles' Tower when he joins Scipio.

5 Scipio quoted: Livy 29.34.7. The two Hannos: 29.29.1, 29.34.1–17; Livy carefully but sceptically adds (35.2) that some of his sources held they were the same man. App., *Lib.* 14.56–9 knows only of the Hanno at the Tower of Agathocles (a site he alone names). Only one battle, mistakenly doubled by Livy: thus G. De Sanctis, *Storia dei Romani*, vol. III, part 2 (Florence, 1968), pp. 566–7; W. Huss, *Geschichte der Karthager* (Munich, 1985), p. 407; K. Geus, *Prosopographie der literarisch bezeugten Karthager* (Leuven, 1994), pp. 127–8. But the differences in Livy between the two battles refute a doublet; so too Scullard, *Soldier and Politician*, pp. 120–21, 207 n. 86; Lazenby, *Hannibal's War*, p. 205; see Goldsworthy, *Punic Wars*, pp. 291–2. Hanno was probably the commonest Carthaginian male name (33 in Geus, compared with eighteen Hamilcars and thirteen Hannibals) and Livy marks out the second Hanno as son of a Hamilcar.

6 Siege of Utica: Livy 29.35.3–15. App., *Lib.* 15.61–18.74 offers improbable battles and otherwise unknown towns (Locha and Tholous) that may be misnomers or inventions (Locha = Salaeca? Tholous = Theudalis, 25 km further inland?); see Huss, *Karthager*, pp. 407, 409 n. 39. Polybius' text starts again with the winter negotiations (14.1.1–4).

7 Truce: Pol. 14.2.13; Livy 30.4.8. Protville lies 9 kilometres (just over 5 mi.) from the Qa'lat al-Andaluus area. Just south of Protville, an area of rising ground is aligned roughly north–south but with a low and short east–west extension from its southern end. This fits Google Earth's images of the equestrian Protville Hippoclub 5.5 kilometres south of the town; these show a long low ridge in its background. About 4 kilometres west of the Hippoclub rises another low ridge, near the village of Mabtouh: clearly the Koudiat el Mabtouha on H. H. Scullard's map, taken to be Syphax's camp (Scullard, *Scipio Africanus*, p. 121 fig. 10; based on Map 8.4 in J. Kromayer and G. Veith, *Schlachten-Atlas zur antiken Kriegsgeschichte*, vol. II: *Von Cannae bis Numantia* (Leipzig, 1922). On those maps the rise behind the Protville Hippoclub is 'Koudiat Touba': that is, Hasdrubal's position.

8 De Sanctis (*Storia*, vol. III/2, pp. 568–9) and Scullard (*Scipio Africanus*, p. 124) estimate the Carthaginian and Numidian armies together at 33,000–35,000.

9 Cato sent to Sardinia as his quaestorship expired (Cornelius Nepos, *Cato* 1.4; T.R.S. Broughton, *The Magistrates of the Roman Republic*, 2 vols (Chico, CA, 1951), vol. I, p. 307), that is, in autumn as the office's expiry date was early December.

10 The three-way talks, and Scipio's and Masinissa's attack on the camps: Pol. 14.1.1–6.5; Livy 30.3.1–6.9; App., *Lib.* 18.73–24.98; Zon. 9.12; Broughton, *Magistrates of the Roman Republic*, vol. I, p. 212, for minor sources.

11 Anda: Appian, 24.97. Abba/Obba: Pol.14.6.12; Livy 30.7.10; F. W. Walbank, *A Historical Commentary on Polybius*, vol. II (Oxford, 1967), pp. 430–31. Thubba: *CIL* vol. VIII, *Supplementum*, Pt I, p. 1387; R. J. A. Talbert, ed., *Barrington Atlas of the Greek and Roman World* (Princeton, NJ, 2000), Map 32, square E2.

12 From the burning of the camps to the Great Plains: Pol. 14.6.6–8.14; Livy 30.7.1–8.9; Walbank, *Commentary*, vol. II, pp. 431–2; Scullard, *Scipio Africanus*, pp. 126–31, 268 nn. 95–6; Seibert, *Hannibal*, pp. 437–42; Y. Le Bohec, *Histoire militaire des guerres puniques 264–146 av. J.-C.* (Paris, 1996), pp. 245–6.

13 Ovid, *Fasti* 6.769–70, lauding 22 June as also the day when 'Hasdrubal died by his own weapons' (*cecidit telis ipse suis*). This should mean Hasdrubal the Barcid perishing at the Metaurus in 207, not Hasdrubal son of Gisco obscurely killing himself in Carthage; Ovid contrasts these 22 June events with Trasimene on 21 June (lines 765–8). That the Barcid Hasdrubal died 'by his own weapons' should be judged poetic licence – or a source different to Livy's.

14 Sophoniba: Livy 30.12.10–22, 13.11–15.8; App., *Lib.* 27.111–28.120; Diodorus 27.7 (forced suicide); Dio, frg 57.51; E. Lipiński, in *Dictionnaire de la civilisation phénicienne et punique*, ed. E. Lipiński et al. (Tournai, 1992), p. 421 *s.v.*; Geus, *Prosopographie*, pp. 200–201. Punic *Saponba'al* may mean 'Ba'al has judged' or 'my refuge is Ba'al', while 'Sophonisba' is a later misspelling. – On Livy's contrasting portrayals of young Scipio and the (supposedly) young Masinissa: E. Cimolino, 'Scipion l'Africain chez Tite-Live: remarques sur le portrait d'un jeune général exceptionnel', *Vita Latina*, CLXXXIX–CXC (2014), pp. 104–21 (pp. 114–18). On Livy's Sophoniba: J. Fabre-Serris, 'Identities and Ethnicities in the Punic Wars: Livy's Portrait of the Carthaginian Sophonisba', in *Identities, Ethnicities and Gender in Antiquity*, ed. J. Fabre-Serris, A. Keith and F. Klein (Berlin and Boston, MA, 2021), pp. 93–111 (seeing her as an intentional pre-echo of Cleopatra).

8 ZAMA AND PEACE

1 Peace talks and terms in 203: Livy 30.16.1–15; App., *Lib.* 31.129–32.137 (who implausibly makes the Carthaginians contact the Senate in Rome first; it then refers the matter to Scipio). Appian also sets Carthage's land boundaries at the 'Phoenician trenches' (32.135, see 54.236), but this at best is a mistaken memory of the border later drawn by Scipio Aemilianus after the destruction of Carthage in 146, between *provincia Africa* – the Carthaginian territory annexed by Rome – and the kingdom of Numidia ruled by Masinissa's sons: this was called the 'royal trench' (J. Kolendo, in *Dictionnaire de la civilisation phénicienne et punique*, ed. E. Lipiński et al. (Tournai, 1992), p. 177, *s.v.* 'Fossa Regia'; D. Hoyos, *Hannibal's Dynasty: Power and Politics in the Western Mediterranean, 247–183* BC (London, 2003), p. 180). See also note 16 below.

2 Senate at Rome rejected Scipio's peace terms in 203: Livy 30.21.11–23.8; an extraordinary, hard to explain and unacceptable fiction (Hoyos, *Hannibal's Dynasty*, pp. 167–70, 272–3 nn. 5–6). J. Seibert, *Hannibal* (Darmstadt, 1993), p. 454, uses the unreliable Appian (*Lib.* 32.134–6) to view the rejection as only temporary, being overturned once a commission of senators visited Africa and seconded Scipio. – Terms accepted at Rome: Pol. 15.8.7–9; *P. Rylands*, vol. III, no. 491.

3 The tattered papyrus fragment (in the John Rylands Library, Manchester) *P. Rylands*, vol. III, no. 491, likewise affirms that the terms were ratified at Rome (F. W. Walbank, *A Historical Commentary on Polybius*, vol. II: *Commentary on Books* VII–XVIII (Oxford, 1967), pp. 441–2; D. Hoyos, 'Polybius and the Papyrus: The Persuasiveness of "P. Rylands" III 491', *Zeitschrift für Papyrologie und Epigraphik*, CXXXIV (2001), pp. 71–9; see M. Sommer, *Schwarze Tage: Roms Kriege gegen Karthago* (Munich, 2021), p. 206. The fragment should not be seen as contradicting Polybius' and Livy's accounts: Hoyos, 'Polybius and the Papyrus'. See Special Note G.

4 Zama's eclipse of the Sun: Zon. 9.14.6; G. De Sanctis, *Storia dei Romani*, vol. III, part 2 (Florence, 1968), p. 583; Walbank, *Commentary*, vol. II, p. 446. Roman calendar in 202: P. Marchetti, 'La marche du calendrier romain de 203 à 190 (années Varr. 551–564)', *L'Antiquité classique*, XLII/2 (1973), pp. 478–86; P. Derow, 'The Roman Calendar, 218–191 BC', *Phoenix*, XXX (1976), pp. 265–81 (pp. 266 n. 6, 272 (calculating that '1 December' was actually 9 November that year)). See Special Note H.

5 Plutarch has an improbable tale of Scipio admonishing the Carthaginians for recalling Hannibal and adding that therefore, if they wanted the armistice renewed, they must pay 5,000 more talents (*Moralia* 196 C–D).

This cannot be tied to any known context and, at best, is some writer's misunderstanding of something in one of the peace talks.

6 For Appian's way of filling the time see note 8.

7 That the renewed hostilities prompted alarm at Rome (Livy 30.38.6) is of course at odds with Livy's own notion (see note 2) that the Senate had rejected Scipio's peace with Carthage and ordered war to continue – but by 30.38 Livy is too busy with other matters to notice the inconsistency.

8 Appian (*Lib.* 33.139–42) credits Hannibal with successful warfare in Masinissa's kingdom, acquiring some Numidian allies including Vermina – this during 203 and before Carthage's initial peace with Scipio. So for Appian Hannibal has returned from Italy between the Great Plains battle and the ensuing peace talks. Then in 202 Hannibal skirmishes with the Romans near Zama, makes an armistice sponsored by Masinissa, but afterwards brings on the decisive battle at a town Appian calls Cilla, otherwise totally unknown (*Lib.* 39.151–41.177). Some modern reconstructions of the lead-up to Zama try to incorporate some of these items, but Appian's material belongs almost to a different universe.

9 Varied sites for the battle of Zama: Special Note H. Marchetti, 'La marche', pp. 481–6, puts the battle only some ten days before Vermina's defeat on (Roman) 17 December (note 14), which in turn he dates to 1 November real time because of the solar eclipse of 19 October.

10 E. Groag, *Hannibal als Politiker* (Vienna, 1929), p. 99 n. 2, and J. Seibert, *Forschungen zu Hannibal* (Darmstadt, 1993), p. 315, and *Hannibal* (Darmstadt, 1993), pp. 465–6, see the meeting as fiction, partly on the ground that both men knew Greek and so needed no interpreter. This is not a strong argument.

11 Battle strengths estimated: e.g. Walbank, *Commentary*, vol. II, pp. 449–50; P. A. Brunt, *Italian Manpower, 225 BC–AD 14* (Oxford, 1971), pp. 673–4; J. F. Lazenby, *Hannibal's War: A Military History* (Warminster, 1978), pp. 220–21; P. Connolly, *Greece and Rome at War* (London, 1981), pp. 203–5 (reducing Hannibal's veterans to under 5,000); Seibert, *Hannibal*, p. 467 n. 30; A. Goldsworthy, *The Punic Wars* (London, 2000), pp. 302–3.

12 How Zama and other Second Punic War battles were fought: P. Sabin, 'The Mechanics of Battle in the Second Punic War', in *The Second Punic War: A Reappraisal*, ed. T. Cornell, B. Rankov and P. Sabin (London, 1996), pp. 59–80; S. Koon, 'Phalanx and Legion: The "Face" of Punic War Battle', in *A Companion to the Punic Wars*, ed. D. Hoyos (Chichester, 2011), pp. 77–94. The infantry's war-cries: Pol. 15.12.8; Livy 30.34.1; Goldsworthy, *Punic Wars*, p. 305; see C. Whately, 'The War Cry: Ritualized Behaviour and Roman Identity in Ancient Warfare, 200 BCE–400 CE', in *Imperial*

Identities in the Roman World, ed. W. Vanacker and A. Zuiderhoek (London, 2016), pp. 61–77.

13 App., *Lib.* 46.194–56.245. He also has Masinissa and Hannibal fight hand-to-hand (twice); for him Mago is still alive and is now sent to invade Italy; and Hannibal later encamps with a new 6,000-man army at a non-existent town, Marthama.

14 Vermina's defeat: Livy 30.36.7–8. But he was recognized later on by Rome as king in part of his father's territory (31.11.13–18, 31.19.4–6). When this was finally taken over by Masinissa we do not know.

15 Scipio's criticism of Nero and Lentulus: Livy 30.44.3.

16 Treaty of 201: Pol. 15.18.1–8; Livy 30.37.1–6; App., *Lib.* 54.234–8; De Sanctis, vol. III/2, pp. 541–2, 599–605; Walbank, *Commentary*, vol. II, pp. 465–71; H. H. Scullard, *Scipio Africanus: Soldier and Politician* (London, 1970), pp. 156–9; B. Scardigli, *I Trattati Romano-Cartaginesi* (Pisa, 1991), pp. 297–326; Seibert, *Hannibal*, pp. 473–5. Appian has some details at odds with Polybius and Livy: e.g. Hannibal's Italian troops to be handed over to Scipio, Mago to leave Liguria (in fact he had done so and was dead), 250 talents to be paid each year for fifty years. They should not be judged preferable. – Appian's phrase 'Phoenician trenches' (*Φοινίκιδες τάφροι*, *Phoinikides taphroi*) is a term found only at *Lib.* 32.137 and here (*Lib.* 54.236): see note 1 above; Scardigli, *Trattati*, p. 340 nn. 324, 329. But 'Phoenician trenches' in Greek would properly be *Phoinikikoi taphroi*. By contrast, Appian's *phoinikides*, in the singular *phoinikis*, means 'blood-red' or 'purple'. Appian may have misread one of his sources.

17 No consuls in office on 15 March 201: Livy 30.39.5. Then Cn. Lentulus held up ratifying peace until early or mid-April at least (30.40.7–43.10). No doubt Scipio at Tunes was flexible about the deadline.

18 *Fetiales*: Livy 30.43.9; E. Prescendi, '*Fetiales*', in *Brill's New Pauly Online* (2006). Himilco Phameas: K. Geus, *Prosopographie der literarisch bezeugten Karthager* (Leuven, 1994), pp. 171–2; D. Hoyos, *Mastering the West: Rome and Carthage at War* (Oxford, 2015), pp. 258–60, 269.

19 'It was as painful as if it were Carthage itself going up in flames': Livy 30.43.12. Deserters executed: 30.43.13.

20 Scipio's return and triumph: Pol. 16.23.1–7; Livy 30.45.1–7. His earlier claim that all Syphax's kingdom was Roman booty: Livy 30.14.8–10 (when demanding Sophoniba be handed over).

9 SCIPIO IN PEACETIME

1 Cato and Scipio: H. H. Scullard, *Roman Politics, 220–150 BC*, 2nd edn (Oxford, 1973), pp. 112–13; *Scipio Africanus: Soldier and Politician* (London, 1970), pp. 186–9; A. E. Astin, *Cato the Censor* (Oxford, 1978), pp. 12–16, 51–2, 60–64 (etc.). On Livy's, our main source's, treatment of Roman politics after 201: J. Briscoe, 'Livy and Senatorial Politics, 200–167 BC: The Evidence of the Fourth and Fifth Decades', in *Aufstieg und Niedergang der römischen Welt*, Part II, vol. XXX/2, ed. H. Temporini (Berlin and New York, 1982), pp. 1075–121.

2 'Fulvian' group: Scullard, *Roman Politics*, pp. 135–6, 165–7, 177–89; J. Briscoe, *A Commentary on Livy, Books XXXI–XXXIII* (Oxford, 1973), pp. 30–35; Briscoe, 'Livy and Senatorial Politics, 200–167 BC', pp. 1078–9 etc.

3 Galba an opponent of Scipio: Briscoe, *Commentary on Livy XXXI–XXXIII*, pp. 45–6. Scipio supported war with Macedon, like Galba: so W. V. Harris, *War and Imperialism in Republican Rome, 327–70 BC* (Oxford, 1979), pp. 217–18; A. M. Eckstein, *Rome Enters the Greek East: From Anarchy to Hierarchy in the Hellenistic Mediterranean, 230–170 BC* (Malden, MA, and Oxford, 2012), pp. 258–9. Scipio not in favour of the war: Scullard, *Roman Politics*, pp. 86–8, 91. Why Rome went to war is much debated: for example, see Harris, *War and Imperialism*, pp. 212–18; E. S. Gruen, *The Hellenistic World and the Coming of Rome*, 2 vols (Berkeley, Los Angeles, CA, and London, 1984), vol. II, pp. 382–98; V. M. Warrior, *The Initiation of the Second Macedonian War: An Explication of Livy Book 31* (*Historia-Einzelschriften*, 97: Stuttgart, 1996); Eckstein, *Rome Enters the Greek East*, pp. 230–70. Land commissioners unfriendly to Scipio, except Metellus: Scullard, *Roman Politics*, p. 83 (not convincing). Two others, brothers named L. and A. Hostilius Cato, Scullard later suggests were friends of his because L. Hostilius was fined along with L. Scipio in a sensational case in 187 (p. 294 n. 1; below, Chapter Eleven).

4 Scipio's and Paetus' censorship: Livy 32.7.1–3; T.R.S. Broughton, *The Magistrates of the Roman Republic*, 2 vols (Chico, CA, 1951), vol. I, p. 327. Position of *princeps senatus*: E. Badian, in *Oxford Classical Dictionary* (online, 2016), *s.v.*

5 On these machinations: E. Badian, *Titus Quinctius Flamininus: Philhellenism and Realpolitik* (Norman, OK, 1973), pp. 310–18; Scullard, *Roman Politics*, pp. 102–5; R. Pfeilschifter, *Titus Quinctius Flamininus: Untersuchungen zur Römischen Griechenlandpolitik* (Göttingen, 2005), pp. 327–35.

6 The valiant Digitius had been an Italian *socius* in 209, but clearly had

become a Roman citizen later, no doubt under Scipio's patronage (the same may have been true, at some date, for Laelius). Digitius was still active in 172 as an envoy: Livy 42.27.8.

7 Scipio against punitive embassy to Carthage: Livy 33.47.4–6. Its outcome: 33.47.7–49.4; S. Lancel, *Hannibal* (Paris, 1995), pp. 306–8; D. Hoyos, *Hannibal's Dynasty: Power and Politics in the Western Mediterranean, 247–183* BC (London, 2003), pp. 197–9.

8 Cicero, *De haruspicum responsis* 24; Asconius 69–70 C, on Cicero's lost speech for C. Cornelius and citing Valerius Antias (= Antias, frg 41 Cornell); R. G. Lewis, *Asconius: Commentaries on Speeches of Cicero* (Oxford, 2006), p. 277; T. J. Cornell, ed., *The Fragments of the Roman Historians*, 3 vols (Oxford, 2013), vol. III, p. 579. On Scipio's second consulship in Livy: A. Haimson Lushkov, 'Narrative and Notice in Livy's Fourth Decade: The Case of Scipio Africanus', *Classical Antiquity*, XXXIII/1 (2014), pp. 102–29.

9 Livy 34.43.3–9; J. D. Grainger, *The Roman War of Antiochos the Great* (Leiden and Boston, MA, 2002), pp. 129–32.

10 Roman colonies in 194: Livy 32.29.3–4 (legislated in 198), 34.45.1–2 (founded). E. T. Salmon, *Roman Colonization under the Republic* (London, 1969), p. 97, and Scullard, *Roman Politics*, p. 117, credit them directly to Scipio. They were not just small but very out of the way; finding people to live in them was difficult and they were soon forgotten by the Roman authorities themselves. It came as a surprise to the Senate some years later that colonists had decamped from several (Salmon, *Roman Colonization*, pp. 98–9). Their original purpose in 198 could have been as lookouts against possible, even though highly unlikely, raids by the powerful Macedonian fleet. Harris, *War and Imperialism*, p. 221 n. 6, thinks they were for keeping watch on land confiscated from locals in the Hannibalic war.

11 Pol. 23.14.5–6 (Scipio defied by a quaestor); Livy 38.55.13 (by quaestors); Val. Max. 3.7.2 (quaestors, and Scipio a private citizen); Plut., *Moralia* 196 F (Senate votes Scipio funds, quaestors refuse on the day); F. W. Walbank, *A Historical Commentary on Polybius*, vol. III (Oxford, 1979), pp. 244–5; J. Briscoe, *A Commentary on Livy, Books* XXXVIII–XL (Oxford, 2007), p. 196.

12 Livy 34.58.1–3; Scullard, *Roman Politics*, pp. 284–5 n. 161, disbelieves that Flamininus made the hint. Discussed by Grainger, *Roman War of Antiochos*, pp. 126–40.

13 Envoys to Antiochus: Livy 34.59.8, 35.13.6–17.2. Scipio an envoy: 35.14.5–12; Plut., *Flam.* 21.3, *Pyrrh.* 8.2; App., *Syr.* 9–10; Scullard, *Roman Politics*, pp. 198, 285–6 n. 163; J. Briscoe, *A Commentary on Livy, Books* XXXIV–XXXVII (Oxford, 1981), p. 166; Grainger, *Roman War of Antiochos*, p. 156; Hoyos,

Hannibal's Dynasty, p. 280 n. 1; Haimson Lushkov, 'Narrative and Notice', pp. 106–8. Visit to Delos and gold crown gifted, date uncertain: *SIG*[4], nos 587, 588 (lengthy lists of donors); H. Etcheto, *Les Scipions: famille et pouvoir à Rome à l'époque républicaine* (Bordeaux, 2012), pp. 30, 164. – Acilius: Cornell, *Fragments of Roman Historians*, vol. III, pp. 224–6.

14 Embassy to Carthage in 193: Livy 34.62.16–18. Senate in 172 declared the boundaries set in 201 were not to be changed: 42.24.5–10; Gruen, *Hellenistic World*, vol. I, p. 130 n. 170; J. Briscoe, *A Commentary on Livy, Books XLI–XLV* (Oxford, 2012), pp. 230, 233; D. Hoyos, *Mastering the West: Rome and Carthage at War* (Oxford, 2015), p. 244.

15 Livy 35.10.1–10 (elections for 192), 24.4–5 (for 191).

10 SCIPIO'S LAST WAR

1 Antiochus an 'ally and friend of the Roman People' (*socius et amicus populi Romani*): Livy 32.8.13 and 16; S. Dmitriev, 'Antiochus III: A Friend and Ally of the Roman People', *Klio: Beiträge zur Alten Geschichte*, XCIII/1 (2011), pp. 104–30. Background to war: e.g. E. S. Gruen, *The Hellenistic World and the Coming of Rome*, 2 vols (Berkeley, Los Angeles, CA, and London, 1984), vol. II, pp. 611–36; J. D. Grainger, *The Roman War of Antiochos the Great* (Leiden and Boston, MA, 2002), pp. 5–191; N. Rosenstein, *Rome and the Mediterranean, 290 to 146 BC: The Imperial Republic* (Edinburgh, 2012), pp. 190–95. Antiochus in Greece: Grainger, *Roman War of Antiochos*, pp. 192–246.

2 Livy 37.1.7–10; see Cicero, *Pro Murena* 12 Philippic 11.17. J. Briscoe, *A Commentary on Livy, Books XXXIV–XXXVII* (Oxford, 1981), p. 291, and R. Develin, *The Practice of Politics at Rome, 366–167 BC* (Brussels, 1985), pp. 206–7, argue that L. Scipio did win the lot and was abler than people believed.

3 Mottones (Livy calls him Muttines) was from the Phoenician colony Hippacra, now Bizerte in Tunisia; he had been granted Roman citizenship in 210 (Livy 27.5.6–7). He and his four sons were *proxenoi* (official guests) at Delphi in 190/189 (*SIG*[4], no. 585, lines 86–8); and with his officer son he fought Thracians attacking Manlius Vulso's army in 188 (Livy 38.41.12–14).

4 Scipio's son a captive: Pol. 21.15.2–5; Livy 37.34.4–7 (guest friendship between family and Antiochus, ibid. 7); 37.37.6–8 (son released); App., *Syr.* 29.146 (imagining the son was Scipio Aemilianus); Justin, *Historiae Philippicae* 31.7.4–7.

5 Scipio's arch: Livy 37.3.7; Briscoe, *Commentary on Livy XXXIV–XXXVII*, pp. 294–5; H. Etcheto, *Les Scipions: famille et pouvoir à Rome à l'époque républicaine* (Bordeaux, 2012), pp. 80, 320 n. 82; A. Haimson Lushkov,

'Narrative and Notice in Livy's Fourth Decade: The Case of Scipio Africanus', *Classical Antiquity*, XXXIII (2014), pp. 121–6; R. T. Ridley, 'The Arch of Scipio Africanus', *Classical Philology*, CIX/1 (2014), pp. 11–25.

6 Military preparations and forces: Livy 37.2.2–3; Grainger, *Roman War of Antiochos*, pp. 274–5, 320–21, 359–61. Grainger gives Glabrio, in Greece in 191, 35,400 infantry and 2,100 cavalry; L. Scipio in 190 brings levies of 8,000 foot and 300 horse, plus 5,000 volunteers from Africanus' veterans. With these at the battle of Magnesia were allied troops from Achaea, Pergamum and (supposedly) Macedonian and even Thracian volunteers (Grainger, *Roman War of Antiochos*, p. 309).

7 Roman army ordered to assemble at Brundisium on the Ides (15th) of Quinctilis: Livy 37.4.2. (Quinctilis later became July in honour of Julius Caesar.) The Ides of Quinctilis in 190 = real-time 18 March: P. S. Derow, 'The Roman Calendar, 190–168 BC', *Phoenix*, XXVII (1973), pp. 345–56 (p. 349); Grainger, *Roman War of Antiochos*, p. 278. This is calculated from the solar eclipse on 14 March 190 (real time), which was 11 Quinctilis (Livy 37.4.4) in the badly maintained Roman calendar: Derow, 'Roman Calendar', pp. 345–6; Briscoe, *Commentary on Livy XXXIV–XXXVII*, pp. 17–18.

8 Scipios in Aetolia and six-month truce: Pol.21.4.1–5.13; Livy 37.6.1–7.7; F. W. Walbank, *A Historical Commentary on Polybius*, vol. III (Oxford, 1979), pp. 93–5; Grainger, *Roman War of Antiochos*, pp. 276–8.

9 Ti. Gracchus: Livy 37.7.11–14 ('by far the most dynamic (*strenuissimus*) young man of his time'). A few years later Gracchus claimed to be a personal enemy of Africanus (38.52.9; Cicero, *De provinciis consularibus* 18; Val. Max. 4.1.8, 4.2.3; Gellius, *NA* 6.19.6), but the cause of the hostility is never stated. Scipio's letter to Philip V: Pol. 10.9.3; F. W. Walbank, *A Historical Commentary on Polybius*, vol. II (Oxford, 1967), p. 204. Sick or injured troops left in guarded forts: Livy 37.33.3.

10 Scipio brothers' letter to Prusias: Pol. 21.11.3–12; Livy 37.25.8–14; T. J. Luce, *The Composition of Livy's 'History'* (Princeton, NJ, 1977), p. 211; Walbank, *Commentary*, vol. III, pp. 102–4; Briscoe, *Commentary on Livy XXXIV–XXXVII*, pp. 327–9.

11 Scipio's halt as a *Salius*: Pol. 21.13.10–14; Livy 37.33.6–7; Briscoe, *Commentary on Livy XXXIV–XXXVII*, pp. 337–8; see Chapter Two, n. 4. Grainger (*Roman War of Antiochos*, p. 310) thinks the delay was chiefly 'for continued military preparations'. Actual date of Salian rites in 190: Briscoe, *Commentary on Livy XXXIV–XXXVII*, p. 29, relying on Derow, 'Roman Calendar'.

12 Heracleides' mission: Pol. 13.1–15.13; Livy 37.34.1–36.9; Diodorus 29.7.1–8.2; App., *Syr.* 29.143–9. Livy has Antiochus, through him, offer Scipio an actual share in ruling the Seleucid kingdom, 'excepting only the title of king' (37.36.1–8); this must be a later invention, stemming perhaps from Scipio's detractors at Rome a few years later.

13 Memnon of Heracleia (F. Jacoby, *Fragmenta Graecorum Historicorum*, no. 434), 18.6–8.

14 Livy 37.37.6–8; App., *Syr.* 31.151. Polybius' account does not survive.

15 Battle of Magnesia: Livy 37.37.9–44.3; App., *Syr.* 30.150–35.183 (making Domitius Ahenobarbus the commander, ignoring L. Scipio).

16 Peace terms: Pol. 21.43.1–27; Livy 38.38.2–18; App., *Syr.* 39.201–2; M. Austin, *The Hellenistic World from Alexander to the Roman Conquest*, 2nd edn (Cambridge, 2006), pp. 365–7 no. 205. The treaty was formally ratified in 188 by L. Scipio's successor Manlius Vulso at Apameia in Phrygia.

17 Scipios' letter to Heracleia-by-Latmus: R. K. Sherk, *Roman Documents from the Greek East: 'Senatus Consulta' and 'Epistulae' to the Age of Augustus* (Baltimore, MD, 1969), pp. 217–18 no. 35; R. K. Sherk, ed. and trans., *Translated Documents of Greece and Rome*, vol. IV: *Rome and the Greek East to the Death of Augustus* (Cambridge, 1984), pp. 13–14 no. 14; Austin, *Hellenistic World*, p. 362 no. 202; J. Ma, *Antiochos III and the Cities of Western Asia Minor* (Oxford, 1999), pp. 366–7 no. 45. To Colophon: Sherk, *Roman Documents*, pp. 219–20 no. 36; J. Ma, pp. 368–9 no. 46. Aptera's decree: *L'Année épigraphique*, 131 (1931).

11 SCIPIO UNDER SIEGE

1 Livy 37.59.2–6. Date of the triumph ('in the intercalary month, on the day before the Kalends of March', 39.59.2): P. S. Derow, 'The Roman Calendar, 190–168 BC', *Phoenix*, XXVII (1973), pp. 347–8. 'Asiagenus': 37.58.6. Livy writes 'Asiaticus', but this form of the name was not used until long after (J. Briscoe, *A Commentary on Livy, Books XXXIV–XXXVII* (Oxford, 1981), p. 392; H. Etcheto, *Les Scipions: famille et pouvoir à Rome à l'époque républicaine* (Bordeaux, 2012), p. 167). Livy himself calls Lucius 'Asiagenus' later: 39.44.1. Of the captured Seleucid grandees, it is known that Antiochus' prime counsellor Thoas of Aetolia not only was pardoned but turned into a fervent pro-Roman (F. W. Walbank, *A Historical Commentary on Polybius*, vol. III (Oxford, 1979), p. 110). It seems unlikely that many of the others suffered death and perhaps none did.

2 Glabrio's triumph was held before the consular elections for 189 but after the Senate learned of the naval victory at Myonnesus (Livy 37.46.1–2, 47.3, 47.6–8). That battle had been fought in September 190, real time (Briscoe,

Commentary, p. 29); the news would take at least two weeks to reach Rome. The new consuls for 189, Fulvius and Manlius, took office on the Ides of March 189, which was 8 November 190 real time (Derow, 'Roman Calendar', p. 348). So Glabrio triumphed most likely during the previous month. Controversy over his censorship candidacy: Livy 37.57.9–58.2.

3 Pol. 23.14.1–12; Livy 38.50.4–55.7, 58.1–60.10. Other ancient authors apart from Aulus Gellius (note 5) add little; for a list, H. H. Scullard, *Roman Politics, 220–150 BC* (Oxford, 1973), p. 290 n. 1. Recent discussions of the 'Trials of the Scipios' (a topic 'intimidatingly vast and alarmingly discordant': E. S. Gruen, 'The "Fall" of the Scipios', in *Leaders and Masses in the Roman World: Essays in Honour of Zvi Yavetz*, ed. L. Malkin and Z. W. Rubinsohn (Leiden, 1995), pp. 59–90 (p. 59)) include H. H. Scullard, *Scipio Africanus: Soldier and Politician* (London, 1970), pp. 216–20, 222–3, 288–90 nn. 174–8; and *Roman Politics*, pp. 133–52, 290–303; T. J. Luce, *The Composition of Livy's 'History'* (Princeton, NJ, 1977), pp. 92–104; A. E. Astin, *Cato the Censor* (Oxford, 1978), pp. 60–64, 68–73; R. Develin, *The Practice of Politics at Rome, 366–167 BC* (Brussels, 1985), pp. 243–9; Gruen, 'The "Fall" of the Scipios', pp. 59–90; M. Jaeger, *Livy's Written Rome* (Ann Arbor, MI, 1997), pp. 132–76; J. Briscoe, *A Commentary on Livy, Books XXXVIII–XL* (Oxford, 2007), pp. 170–79; J. Rich writing in T. J. Cornell, ed., *The Fragments of the Roman Historians*, 3 vols (Oxford, 2013), vol. III, pp. 352–8, on Valerius Antias' version as relayed through Livy.

4 Livy cites Antias: 38.50.5, 55.8. Later he notes that P. Africanus in reality died some years after Antias said he did: 39.52.1–6 (arguing, though, against 183 as the year). Variants known to Livy: 38.55.13–56.13. Choosing Antias as best of a perplexing lot: Luce, *Livy's 'History'*, pp. 102–4.

5 Gellius, *NA* 4.18.1–12 (Africanus), 6.19.1–8 (Ti. Gracchus). That Gellius was drawing on Cicero's contemporary Cornelius Nepos' book of moral tales, *Exempla* (Scullard, *Roman Politics*, p. 290 n. 1; Gruen, 'The "Fall" of the Scipios', p. 76), should not be assumed: see Briscoe, *Commentary*, p. 170. Though Gellius calls his own items *exempla* too, his section headings at both *NA* 4.18 and 6.19 cite *annales*, and so do his comments at 6.19.5 and 8 (stressing 'auctoritates veterum annalium', the weighty opinions of old annals).

6 Minucius Augurinus is not known otherwise. His *gens*' supposedly long association with Cornelii: Scullard, *Roman Politics*, p. 46 n. 2. To replace him, as accusing tribune, with Culleo as investigating praetor required Antias (or Antias' source, whoever that was) to envisage an entirely different procedure: that is, a law put successfully to the People by the Petillii, then a resulting commission of inquiry (*quaestio*) and a praetor (Culleo)

appointed to run it. By putting a Scipionic friend in charge of it, ultimately to find L. Scipio guilty, an imaginative writer would confer even more drama on the story than Augurinus' role did – not a recommendation.

7 On the *inimicitia*, see Develin, *Practice of Politics*, pp. 247–9. J. Briscoe ('Livy and Senatorial Politics, 200–167 BC: The Evidence of the Fourth and Fifth Decades', in *Aufstieg und Niedergang der römischen Welt*, Part II, vol. XXX/2, ed. H. Temporini (Berlin and New York, 1982), p. 1102) thinks Cato himself prompted Gracchus to save Lucius from extra humiliation. Another variant story was that Africanus – at the Senate's urging – on that same day betrothed Gracchus to Cornelia (Livy 38.57.5–7; Gellius, *NA* 12.8.1–4; so too other ancient writers). Not to be believed against Polybius' statement cited by Plutarch (*Ti. Gr.* 4.4) that it happened after Africanus died: Walbank, *Commentary*, vol. III, pp. 506–8; Briscoe, *Commentary*, p. 202.

8 Growing concern in the early second century about aristocrats' eagerness for triumphs and booty: E. S. Gruen, 'Philosophy, Rhetoric, and Roman Anxieties', in *Studies in Greek Culture and Roman Policy* (Leiden, 1994), pp. 158–92.

9 The Vulso controversy: Livy 38.44.9–50.3, 39.6.3–17; Luce, *Livy's 'History'*, pp. 90–91; Gruen, 'The "Fall" of the Scipios', pp. 64–5, 74–5. Vulso's booty contributing to moral decay: Livy 39.6.6–9; Luce, pp. 270–75; Briscoe, *Commentary*, p. 225.

10 Scipio and Laelius on the seashore: Val. Max. 8.8.1. The Liternum estate: Seneca, *ad Lucilium* 13.86.1–12. 'Never less leisured': Cicero, *De officiis* 3.1, and *De re publica* 1.27; Plut., *Moralia* 196. B. Scipio and the pirate chiefs: Val. Max. 2.10.2.

11 Romans' deepening responsiveness to Greek culture after the Second Punic War: e.g. E. Rawson, 'Roman Tradition and the Greek world', in *Cambridge Ancient History*, vol. VIII: *Rome and the Mediterranean to 133 BC*, ed. A. E. Astin et al. (Cambridge, 1989), pp. 422–76; Gruen, *Studies*, pp. 158–92; note R. MacMullen, 'Hellenizing the Romans (2nd Century BC)', *Historia: Zeitschrift für Alte Geschichte*, XL/4 (1991), pp. 419–38, for caveats. Cato teased Polybius: Pol. 35.6.1–4 (= Plut., *Cato* 9.3).

12 Quoted by Lactantius, *Divine Institutes* 1.18 ('si fas endo plagas caelestum ascendere cuiquam est/ mi soli caeli maxuma porta patet'), and Cicero, *Tusculan Disputations* 5.49 ('a sole exoriente supra Maeotis paludes/ nemo est qui factis aequiperare queat').

13 Cicero thought P. Scipio the son gifted, and judged a historical work of his in Greek 'very delightfully' written (*Brutus* 77, 'dulcissime'); if Cicero can be believed, Cato thought so too (*De senectute* 35). Polybius on

Aemilia: 31.26.1–5. Her tolerance of Scipio's affair: Val. Max. 6.7.1; Scullard comments primly that it 'reflects more credit perhaps on his wife than on Scipio' (*Soldier and Politician*, p. 292 n. 182).

14 L. Scipio expelled from *equester ordo*: Livy 39.44.1; Plut., *Cato* 18.1; 'Victor', *de Viris Illustribus* 53. Veturius: Cato, *Orations*, ed. H. Malcovati, *Oratorum Romanorum fragmenta* [1930], 4th edn (Turin, 1976), frgs 72–82, speech *in L. Veturium*; Plut., *Cato* 9.3; Gellius, NA 6.22; A. E. Astin, *Cato the Censor* (Oxford, 1978), pp. 81–2; Develin, *Practice of Politics*, p. 250.

15 M. Naevius *trib. pleb.* 184: T.R.S. Broughton, *The Magistrates of the Roman Republic*, 2 vols (Chico, CA, 1951), vol. I, p. 376. Gruen, 'The "Fall" of the Scipios', pp. 59–90, rejects him as accuser and 184 as the date. Not so: e.g. Briscoe, *Commentary*, pp. 175–9; J. Rich in Cornell, *Fragments*, vol. III, pp. 355–6.

16 Naevius accuses, and is rebuffed by, Scipio: Gellius, *NA* 4.18.1–6. The curt account in Pol. 23.14.1–4 is a clumsy excerptor's résumé: Scipio, faced with bitter accusations, simply responds that 'it was not fitting for the Roman people to listen to anyone accusing Publius Cornelius Scipio, thanks to whom accusers had the very power to speak,' and at this the entire gathering disperses apart from the unnamed accuser. Disbelief that it happened on Zama's anniversary: Scullard, *Scipio Africanus*, pp. 298–9; Walbank, *Commentary*, vol. III, p. 244. Scipio was 'posturing': Gruen, 'The "Fall"', p. 87.

17 Polybius recorded Scipio dying in the same year as both Hannibal and the Achaean leader Philopoemen (Livy 39.52.1–6); surviving Polybian excerpts show that the Olympiad year was 183/182 (Walbank, *Commentary*, vol. III, pp. 235–9; Briscoe, *Commentary*, pp. 395–7; see Etcheto, *Les Scipions*, p. 165). Cicero's offer of a precise-looking date (*De senec.* 19) was either erratic or a later copyist mangled it: his Cato dates the death to the 'thirty-third year' before 150 BC, and to the year before Cato himself was censor, and to nine years after Cato's consulship – thus to 182 (in Roman inclusive reckoning), 185 *and* 186 (or perhaps again 185).

18 Scipio's death and will: Pol. 31.27.1–4 (daughters' dowries); Livy 38.53.8; 56.3–4 (death, tomb at Liternum).

19 Africanus' son expelled from Senate by censors, along with two other praetors: Livy 41.27.2 (no details). Val. Max. 4.5.3, 3.5.1 (wrongly naming him 'Gnaeus') calls this son morally and physically degenerate, claims he needed Cicereius' backing and adds that when elected he was prevented by his kinsmen from taking up his duties or even wearing his father's ring. Val. Max. names no source and does not indicate how this L. Scipio could be blocked from his duties by relatives, nor mention the expulsion. The

claims look like fictions from later critics of the family. Epitaph of Asiagenus' son: ILS, no. 5; Etcheto, *Les Scipions*, pp. 249–51.

20 Etcheto, *Les Scipions*, pp. 181–2, 241–7, suggests that a P. Scipio, known only from his brief epitaph in the Tomb of the Scipios, was a son of Africanus' son Publius. The epitaph shows that he became *flamen Dialis* (special priest of Jupiter), but (Etcheto thinks) he died young and this loss led his father to adopt one of his uncle Aemilius Paullus' sons who thus took the same name plus 'Aemilianus' and was to be the destroyer of Carthage.

21 On Scipio Aemilianus: A. E. Astin, *Scipio Aemilianus* (Oxford, 1967); Etcheto, *Les Scipions*, pp. 176–9. Paullus and Africanus Fabius Maximus: R. Syme, *The Augustan Aristocracy* (Oxford, 1984), pp. 75, 403–20 and Table XXVII.

12 EVALUATING SCIPIO

1 38.53.9–11 (trans. J. C. Yardley, *Livy: The Dawn of the Roman Empire. Books Thirty-One to Forty* (Oxford, 2000); slightly adapted by D. Hoyos).

2 Polybius lauding Scipio: 10.2.1–5.10 (character sketch); 11.24a.4 (charm); 15.4.6–12 (magnanimity); 23.14.1–12 (popularity and dignity, see F. W. Walbank, *A Historical Commentary on Polybius*, vol. III (Oxford, 1979), pp. 242–7). Cato portrayed as respecting Scipio: Cicero, *De senectute* 19, 29, 35 (Scipio's *magnitudo animi*), 61, 82 – and Cato is even made to claim (*De senec.* 77) great friendship with both Scipio's son Publius and with Laelius. Cato's relations with Aemilianus: A. E. Astin, *Scipio Aemilianus* (Oxford, 1967), pp. 36, 63, 280–81; see M. Raimondi, 'Tra Spagna e Africa: Scipione Emiliano nel 151/150 a. C.', *Mediterraneo antico: Economie, società, culture*, XX/1–2 (2017), pp. 368–73. Cicero at least trying to be factually correct: A. E. Astin, *Cato the Censor* (Oxford, 1978), pp. 297–9.

3 Scipio Africanus figures in an odd item of Greek anti-Roman polemic relayed by Phlegon of Tralles, a cultured freedman of the emperor Hadrian, in a compilation of 'wondrous events'. It tells of supposed omens and wonders during the expedition against Antiochus. The general 'Publius' goes mad, declaims prophetic verses denouncing Rome – and is devoured by a wolf, though this does not stop his head from continuing to prophesy doom: Phlegon, *Mirabilia* 3.8–11, ed. A. Stramaglia (Leipzig, 2011); J. Doroszewska, *The Monstrous World: Corporeal Discourses in Phlegon of Tralles' 'Mirabilia'* (Frankfurt am Main, 2016), pp. 68–79.

4 On the phenomenon of Republican Rome's imperialism, see A. M. Stone et al. in *A Companion to Roman Imperialism*, ed. D. Hoyos (Leiden and Boston, MA, 2013), Part I, pp. 23–193; W. V. Harris, *Roman Power: A Thousand Years of Empire* (Cambridge, 2016), pp. 1–98.

BIBLIOGRAPHY

Astin, A. E., *Scipio Aemilianus* (Oxford, 1967)

—, *Cato the Censor* (Oxford, 1978)

Austin, M., *The Hellenistic World from Alexander to the Roman Conquest*, 2nd edn (Cambridge, 2006)

Badian, E., *Titus Quinctius Flamininus: Philhellenism and Realpolitik* (Norman, OK, 1973)

Barceló, P., *Hannibal: Stratege und Staatsmann* (Stuttgart, 2004)

Baronowski, D., *Polybius and Roman Imperialism* (London, 2011)

Beck, H., 'The Causes of the War', in *A Companion to the Punic Wars*, ed. D. Hoyos (Chichester, 2011), pp. 225–41

Bellón, J. P., et al., 'An Archaeological Analysis of a Battlefield of the Second Punic War: The Camps of the Battle of Baecula', *Journal of Roman Archaeology*, XXIX (2016), pp. 73–104

Bellón Ruiz, J. P., et al., *La Segunda Guerra Púnica en la península ibérica: Baecula, arqueología de una batalla* (Jaén, 2015)

Bourgeon, C., 'Le Récit de Tite-Live sur la bataille de Zama', *L'Antiquité classique*, LXXXVII (2018), pp. 137–53

Brill's New Pauly Online, ed. H. Cancik and H. Schneider, with English trans. by C. F. Salazar (1996–) (English edn of *Der Neue Pauly*: online access via Sydney University Library)

Briscoe, J., *A Commentary on Livy*, 4 vols: *Books XXXI–XXXIII*, *Books XXXIV–XXXVII*, *Books XXXVIII–XL*, *Books XLI–XLV* (Oxford, 1973, 1981, 2007, 2012)

—, 'Livy and Roman Politics, 200–167 BC: The Evidence of the Fourth and Fifth Decades', in *Aufstieg und Niedergang der römischen Welt*, ed. H. Temporini, vol. XXX, part 2 (Berlin and Boston, MA, 1982), pp. 1075–121

—, and S. Hornblower, eds, *Livy: Ab Vrbe Condita, Book XXII*, Cambridge Greek and Latin Classics (Cambridge, 2020)

Broughton, T.R.S., *The Magistrates of the Roman Republic*, 3 vols (Chico, CA, and Atlanta, GA, 1951–81)

Brunt, P. A., *Italian Manpower, 225 BC–AD 14* (Oxford, 1971)

Cambridge Ancient History, 2nd edn, vol. VII, part 2: *The Rise of Rome to 220 BC*, ed. F. W. Walbank et al. (Cambridge, 1989)

Cambridge Ancient History, 2nd edn, vol. VIII: *Rome and the Mediterranean to 133 BC*, ed. A. E. Astin et al. (Cambridge, 1989)

Campbell, D. B., and L. A. Tritle, eds, *The Oxford Handbook of Warfare in the Classical World* (Oxford and New York, 2013)

Caven, B., *The Punic Wars* (London, 1980)

Champion, C. B., *Cultural Politics in Polybius' 'Histories'* (Berkeley, CA, and London, 2004)

—, 'Polybius and the Punic Wars', in *A Companion to the Punic Wars*, ed. D. Hoyos (Chichester, 2011), pp. 95–110

Cimolino, E., 'Scipion l'Africain chez Tite-Live: Remarques sur le portrait d'un jeune général exceptionnel', *Vita Latina*, CLXXXIX–CXC (2014), pp. 104–21

Connolly, P., *Greece and Rome at War* (London, 1981)

Cornell, T. J., ed., *The Fragments of the Roman Historians*, 3 vols (Oxford, 2013)

Corzo Sánchez, R., 'La segunda guerra púnica en la Bética', *Habis*, VI (1975), pp. 213–40

De Sanctis, G., *Storia dei Romani*, 2nd edn, vol. III, parts 1–2: *L'età delle guerre puniche* [1907, 1916] (Florence, 1967–8)

Derow, P. S., 'The Roman Calendar, 190–168 BC', *Phoenix*, XXVII/4 (1973), pp. 343–56

—, 'The Roman Calendar, 218–191 BC', *Phoenix*, XXX/3 (1976), pp. 265–81

Dessau, H., ed., *Inscriptiones Latinae Selectae*, 3 vols in 5 (Berlin, 1892–1916)

Develin, R., *The Practice of Politics at Rome, 366–167 BC* (Brussels, 1985)

Dictionnaire de la civilisation phénicienne et punique, ed. C. Bonnet et al. (Tournai, 1992)

Dmitriev, S., 'Antiochus III: A Friend and Ally of the Roman People', *Klio: Beiträge zur Alten Geschichte*, XCIII/1 (2011), pp. 104–30

Dobson, M., *The Army of the Roman Republic: The Second Century BC, Polybius and the Camps at Numantia, Spain* (London, 2008)

Doroszewska, J., *The Monstrous World: Corporeal Discourses in Phlegon of Tralles' 'Mirabilia'* (Frankfurt, 2016)

Drogula, F. K., *Commanders and Command in the Roman Republic and Early Empire* (Chapel Hill, NC, 2015)

Eckstein, A. M., *Mediterranean Anarchy, Interstate War, and the Rise of Rome* (Berkeley and Los Angeles, CA, and London, 2006)

—, *Rome Enters the Greek East: From Anarchy to Hierarchy in the Hellenistic Mediterranean, 230–170 BC* (Malden, MA, and Oxford, 2012)

Edwell, P., 'War Abroad: Spain, Sicily, Macedon, Africa', in *A Companion to the Punic Wars*, ed. D. Hoyos (Chichester, 2011), pp. 320–38

Etcheto, H., *Les Scipions: famille et pouvoir à Rome à l'époque républicaine* (Bordeaux, 2012)

Geus, K., *Prosopographie der literarisch bezeugten Karthager*, Studia Phoenicia, XIII (Leuven, 1994)

Gibson, B., and T. Harrison, eds, *Polybius and His World: Essays in Memory of F. W. Walbank* (Oxford, 2013)

Goldsworthy, A., *The Punic Wars* (London, 2000)

Grainger, J. D., *The Roman War of Antiochos the Great* (Leiden and Boston, MA, 2002)

Groag, E., *Hannibal als Politiker* [1929] (Rome, 1967)

Gruen, E. S., *The Hellenistic World and the Coming of Rome*, 2 vols (Berkeley and Los Angeles, CA, and London, 1984)

—, 'Philosophy, Rhetoric, and Roman Anxieties', in *Studies in Greek Culture and Roman Policy* (Leiden, 1994), pp. 158–92

—, 'The "Fall" of the Scipios', in *Leaders and Masses in the Roman World: Studies in Honour of Zvi Yavetz*, ed. L. Malkin and Z. W. Rubinsohn (Leiden, 1995), pp. 59–90

Guirguis, M., et al., 'Contribuzione alla localizzazione del campo della battaglia di Zama tra storia, epigrafia ed archeologia', *Hormos: richerche di storia antica*, VIII (2016), pp. 102–39

Haimson Lushkov, A., 'Narrative and Notice in Livy's Fourth Decade: The Case of Scipio Africanus', *Classical Antiquity*, XXXIII/1 (2014), pp. 102–29

Harris, W. V., *War and Imperialism in Republican Rome, 327–70 BC* (Oxford, 1979)

—, *Roman Power: A Thousand Years of Empire* (Cambridge, 2016)

Hoyos, B. D., *Unplanned Wars: The Origins of the First and Second Punic Wars* (Leiden and Boston, MA, 1998)

Hoyos, D., 'Generals and Annalists: Geographic and Chronological Obscurities in the Scipios' Campaigns in Spain, 218–211 BC', *Klio: Beiträge zur Alten Geschichte*, LXXXIII/1 (2001), pp. 68–92

—, 'Polybius and the Papyrus: The Persuasiveness of "P. Rylands" III 491', *Zeitschrift für Papyrologie und Epigraphik*, CXXXIV (2001), pp. 71–9

—, 'The Battle-Site of Ilipa', *Klio: Beiträge zur Alten Geschichte*, LXXXIV/1 (2002), pp. 101–13

—, *Hannibal's Dynasty: Power and Politics in the Western Mediterranean, 247–183 BC* (London, 2003)

—, 'Carthage in Africa and Spain, 241–218', in *A Companion to the Punic Wars*, ed. D. Hoyos (Chichester, 2011), pp. 204–22

—, *Mastering the West: Rome and Carthage at War* (Oxford, 2015)

—, *Rome Victorious: The Irresistible Rise of the Roman Empire* (London, 2019)
—, ed., *A Companion to the Punic Wars* (Chichester, 2011)
—, ed., *History of Warfare*, vol. LXXXI: *A Companion to Roman Imperialism* (Leiden and Boston, MA, 2013)
Huss, W., *Geschichte der Karthager* (Munich, 1985)
Jaeger, M., *Livy's Written Rome* (Ann Arbor, MI, 1997)
Keppie, L., *The Making of the Roman Army: From Republic to Empire* (London, 1984)
Koon, S., 'Phalanx and Legion: The "Face" of Punic War Battle', in *A Companion to the Punic Wars*, ed. D. Hoyos (Chichester, 2011), pp. 77–94
Kromayer, J., *Schlachten-Atlas zur antiken Kriegsgeschichte: 2. Lieferung, Römische Abteilung 2: Von Cannae bis Numantia* (Leipzig, 1922)
—, *Antike Schlachtfelder: Bausteine zu einer antiken Kriegsgeschichte*, vol. IV: *Schlachtfelder … bis Augustus* (Berlin, 1931)
—, and G. Veith, *Antike Schlachtfelder: Bausteine zu einer antiken Kriegs-geschichte*, vol. III, part 2: *Schlachtfelder in Italien und Afrika* (Berlin, 1912)
Lancel, S., *Hannibal* (Paris, 1995); English trans. A. Nevill (Oxford, 1998)
Lazenby, J. F., *Hannibal's War: A Military History* (Warminster, 1978)
Le Bohec, Y., *Histoire militaire des guerres puniques, 264–146 av. J.-C.* (Paris, 1996)
—, ed., *The Encyclopedia of the Roman Army*, 3 vols (Malden, MA, and Oxford, 2015)
Lintott, A., *The Constitution of the Roman Republic* (Oxford, 1999)
Lomas, K., 'Rome, Latins, and Italians in the Second Punic War', in *A Companion to the Punic Wars*, ed. D. Hoyos (Chichester, 2011), pp. 339–56
Lowe, B. J., 'Polybius 10.10.12 and the Existence of Salt-Flats at Carthago Nova', *Phoenix*, LIV/1–2 (2000), pp. 39–52
Luce, T. J., *The Composition of Livy's 'History'* (Princeton, NJ, 1977)
Ma, J., *Antiochos III and the Cities of Western Asia Minor* (Oxford, 1999)
MacDonald, E., *Hannibal: A Hellenistic Life* (New Haven, CT, and London, 2015)
McGing, B., *Polybius' 'Histories'* (Oxford, 2010)
MacMullen, R., 'Hellenizing the Romans (2nd Century BC)', *Historia*, XL (1991), pp. 419–38
Malcovati, H., ed., *Oratorum Romanorum Fragmenta* [1930], 4th edn (Turin, 1976)
Marchetti, P., 'La Marche du calendrier romain de 203 à 190 (années Varr. 551–564)', *L'Antiquité classique*, XLII (1973), pp. 473–96
Mineo, B., ed., *A Companion to Livy* (Chichester, 2015)
Nicholson, E., 'Polybius', in *Oxford Classical Dictionary* (online edn, 2016)
Oxford Classical Dictionary, ed. T. Whitmarsh et al. (online edn, 2015–)
Pfeilschifter, R., *Titus Quinctius Flamininus: Untersuchungen zur Römischen Griechenlandpolitik* (Göttingen, 2005)

Picard, G.-C., *Hannibal* (Paris, 1967)

Polito, E., 'Emblèmes macédoniens: une hypothèse sur une série de boucliers de Macédoine en Numidie', *Antiquités africaines*, XXXV (1999), pp. 39–70

Prescendi, F., '*Fetiales*', in *Brill's New Pauly Online*

Raimondi, M., 'Tra Spagna e Africa: Scipione Emiliano nel 151/150 a. C.', *Mediterraneo antico: economie, società, culture*, XX/1–2 (2017), pp. 341–74

Rawson, E., 'Roman Tradition and the Greek World', in *Cambridge Ancient History*, vol. VIII: *Rome and the Mediterranean to 133 BC*, ed. A. E. Astin et al. (Cambridge, 1989), pp. 422–76

Richardson, J. S., *Hispaniae: Spain and the Development of Roman Imperialism, 218–82 BC* (Cambridge, 1986)

Ridley, R. T., 'Was Scipio Africanus at Cannae?', *Latomus*, XXXIV/1 (1975), pp. 161–5

—, 'The Arch of Scipio Africanus', *Classical Philology*, CIX/1 (2014), pp. 11–25

Rosenstein, N., *Rome and the Mediterranean, 290 to 146 BC: The Imperial Republic* (Edinburgh, 2012)

—, and R. Morstein-Marx, eds, *A Companion to the Roman Republic* (Malden, MA, and Oxford, 2006)

Sabin, P., 'The Mechanics of Battle in the Second Punic War', in *The Second Punic War: A Reappraisal*, ed. T. Cornell, B. Rankov and P. Sabin (London, 1996), pp. 59–80

Sage, M., 'The Rise of Rome', in *The Oxford Handbook of Warfare in the Classical World*, ed. D. B. Campbell and L. A. Tritle (Oxford and New York, 2013), pp. 216–35

Salmon, E. T., *Roman Colonization under the Republic* (London, 1969)

Scardigli, B., *I trattati romano-cartaginesi* (Pisa, 1991)

Scullard, H. H., *Scipio Africanus in the Second Punic War* (Cambridge, 1930)

—, *Scipio Africanus: Soldier and Politician* (London, 1970)

—, *Roman Politics, 220–150 BC* [1951], 2nd edn (Oxford, 1973)

—, *Festivals and Ceremonies of the Roman Republic* (London, 1981)

Seibert, J., *Forschungen zu Hannibal* (Darmstadt, 1993)

—, *Hannibal* (Darmstadt, 1993)

Sherk, R. K., *Roman Documents from the Greek East:* Senatus Consulta *and* Epistulae *to the Age of Augustus* (Baltimore, MD, 1969)

—, ed. and trans., *Translated Documents of Greece and Rome*, vol. IV: *Rome and the Greek East to the Death of Augustus* (Cambridge, 1984)

Smith, C., and L. M. Yarrow, eds, *Imperialism, Cultural Politics, and Polybius* (Oxford, 2012)

Sommer, M., *Schwarze Tage: Roms Kriege gegen Karthago* (Munich, 2021)

Sylloge Inscriptionum Graecarum, ed. W. Dittenberger, vol. II, 4th edn (Hildesheim, 1960)

Talbert, R.J.A., ed., *Barrington Atlas of the Greek and Roman World* (Princeton, NJ, 2000)

Taylor, M. J., 'Reconstructing the Battle of Zama', *Classical Journal*, CXIV/3 (2019), pp. 310–29

Van Sickle, J., 'The Elogia of the Cornelii Scipiones and the Origin of Epigram at Rome', *American Journal of Philology*, CVIII/1 (1987), pp. 41–55

Vervaet, F. J., and T. Ñaco del Hoyo, 'War in Outer Space: Nature and Impact of the Roman War Effort in Spain, 218/217–197 BCE', in *Impact of the Roman Army (200 BC–AD 476)*, vol. VI: *Economic, Social, Political, Religious, and Cultural Aspects*, ed. L. De Blois et al. (Leiden, 2007), pp. 21–46

Walbank, F. W., *A Historical Commentary on Polybius*, 3 vols (Oxford, 1957, 1967, 1979)

—, *Polybius* (Berkeley and Los Angeles, CA, and London, 1972)

Walsh, P. G., *Livy: His Historical Aims and Methods* (Cambridge, 1963)

Warrior, Valerie M., *The Initiation of the Second Macedonian War: An Explication of Livy Book 31* (Stuttgart, 1996)

Whately, C., 'The War Cry: Ritualized Behaviour and Roman Identity in Ancient Warfare, 200 BCE–400 CE', in *Imperial Identities in the Roman World*, ed. W. Vanacker and A. Zuiderhoek (London, 2016), pp. 61–77

Whitby, M., and H. Sidebottom, eds, *The Encyclopedia of Ancient Battles*, 3 vols (Malden, MA, and Oxford, 2017)

Yardley, J. C., trans., *Livy: The Dawn of the Roman Empire. Books Thirty-One to Forty*, introduction and notes by W. Heckel (Oxford and New York, 2000)

ACKNOWLEDGEMENTS

It is a pleasure for me to thank the University of Sydney and the University Library for their continuing support of my academic work. The Library's resources, especially its databases, access to online books and journals, and ready help from its staff with document finding and transfers, have made research possible. The university has been my academic home for over half a century, and since 2008 has conferred my affiliation as Honorary Associate Professor in the Department of Classics and Ancient History, one of Australia's most distinguished centres of ancient studies.

I have the pleasure also of thanking the editors and staff of Reaktion Books for their encouragement and patience as I came to grips with Scipio Africanus: especially David Watkins, who commissioned this book, Michael Leaman, the publisher, and Alex Ciobanu, whose advice and aid have been crucial. I am happy too to thank Sebastian Ballard for his fine maps.

My family (who never read my writings) are the mainstay of my life and effort, and make both worthwhile. I dedicate this book to them.

PHOTO ACKNOWLEDGEMENTS

The author and publishers wish to express their thanks to the following source for illustrative material and/or permission to reproduce it: Ny Carlsberg Glyptotek, Copenhagen, photo Carole Raddato/Flickr, CC BY-SA 2.0: p. 8.

INDEX

Frequently recurring names – for example, Scipio Africanus, Carthage, Hannibal, Livy and Polybius – are not indexed. Romans are listed under their family (second) name, for example, Cornelius, Licinius, Valerius.